The European Social Model

The European Social Model

Modernisation or Evolution?

Nick Adnett

Division of Economics, Faculty of Business and Law, Staffordshire University, UK

and

Stephen Hardy

School of Law, University of Manchester, UK

Edward Elgar

Cheltenham, UK • Northampton, MA, USA

Published by
Edward Elgar Publishing Limited
Glensanda House
Montpellier Parade
Cheltenham
Glos GL50 1UA
UK

Edward Elgar Publishing, Inc.
136 West Street
Suite 202
Northampton
Massachusetts 01060
USA

A catalogue record for this book
is available from the British Library

ISBN 1 84376 125 4

Printed and bound in Great Britain by MPG Books Ltd, Bodmin, Cornwall

Contents

Glossary of terms

ARD	Acquired Rights Directive
CEEP	Conseil Européene Employeurs Publique (EU Public Sector Organisation)
CIFE	Conseil des Fédérations Industrielles d'Europe
CRD	Collective Redundancies Directive
DG V/DG Empl	EU Commission's department managing social affairs and employment relations
EC	European Community
ECHR	European Convention on Human Rights
ECJ	European Court of Justice
ECS	European Company Statute
ECSA	European Community Shipowners' Association
ECSC	European Coal and Steel Community
EDWS	economically dependent workers
EEA	European Economic Area
EEC	European Economic Community
EES	European Employment Strategy
EFREP/FERPA	European Federation of Retired and Elderly Persons
EFTA	European Free Trade Association
EMU	European monetary union
EP	European Parliament
ESF	European Social Fund
ESM	European Social Model
ETO	economic, technological and organisational
ETUC	European Trade Union Confederation
ETUI	European Trade Union Institute
EU	European Union
EWC	European Works Council
FSA	Financial Services Authority
FST	Federation of Transport Workers' Unions
GDP	Gross Domestic Product
ILO	International Labour Organisation
ITUCs	Interregional Trade Union Councils
NAPs	National Employment Action Plans
NIC	National Information and Consultation

OMC	Open Method of Co-ordination
SAPs	Social Action Programmes
SE	Societas Europea
SMEs	Small and medium-sized enterprises
SPA	Agreement on Social Policy
TEU	Treaty on European Union
UN	United Nations
UEAPME	Union Européenne de l'Artisant et des Petits et Moyennes Entreprises (EU Association of Small Businesses)
UNICE	Union industria employeurs Européenne (EU Employers' Organisation)
WTD	Working Time Directive
WTO	World Trade Organization

Table of cases

Adoui and Cornuaille v. *Belgian State* (Joined Cases 115 and 116/81) [1982] ECR 1665
Albany International BV v. *Stichting Bedrijfspensioenfonds Textielindustrie* (Case C-67/96), judgment of 21 September 1999
Arcaro, Criminal Proceedings against (C-168/95) [1996] ECR I-4705
Barber v. *Guardian Royal Exchange* (Case C-268/88) [1990] ECR I-1889
Bettray v. *Staatssecretaris van Justitie* (Case 344/87) [1989] ECR 1621
Bilka-Kaufhaus v. *Weber von Hartz* (Case 170/84) [1986] ECR 1607
Bork International v. *Foreningen af Arbejdsledere I Danmark* (Case C-101/87) [1988] ECR 3057
Botzen v. *Rotterdamse Drbogdok Maatschappij* (Case C-186/83) [1985] ECR 519
Boyle v. *Equal Opportunities Commission* (Case C-411/96) [1998] ECR I-6401
Brasserie du Pêcheur v. *Bundesrepublik Deutschland* and *R* v. *Secretary of State for Transport, ex parte* and *Factortame* (No. 3) (Joined Cases C-46/93 and C-48/93) [1996] ECR I-1029
Brown v. *Secretary of State for Scotland* (Case 197/86) [1986] ECR 3205
Centre Public d'Aide Sociale de Courcelles v. *Lebon* (C-316/85) [1987] ECR I-2811
CILFIT and Lanificio di Gavardo SpA v. *Ministry of Health* (Case 283/81) [1982] ECR 3415
Commission v. *Denmark* (Case 143/83) [1985] ECR 427
Commission v. *UK* (Case C-383/92) [1994] ECR I-2479
D'Urso v. *Ercole Marelli Elettromeccanica Generale* (Case C-362/89) [1991] ECR I-4105
Da Costa en Schaake NV, Jacob Meijer NV, & Hoechst-Holland NV v. *Nederlandse Belastingadministratie* (C-28-30/62) [1963] ECR 31
Danskmetalarbejderforbund v. *Nielsen* (C-284/83) [1985] ECR I-553
Defrenne (no.1) v. *Belgian State* (Case 80/70) [1971] ECR 445
Defrenne v. *SABENA (No. 2)* (Case 43/75) [1976] ECR 455
Dekker v. *Stichting Vormingscentrum voor Junge Volwassen Plus* (Case C-177/88) [1990] ECR I-3941
Diatta v. *Land Berlin* (Case 267/83) [1985] ECR 567
Dietrich v. Westdeutscher Rundfunk (C-11/99) [2000] ECR I-5589

Dillenkofer and Others v. *Bundesrepublik Deutschland* (Joined Cases C-178, C-179, C-188, C-189 and C-190/94) [1996] ECR I-4845
Federal Republic of Germany v. *European Parliament and Council of the European Union* (C-233/94) [1997] ECR I-2405
Foreningen af Arbejdsledere i Danmark v. *Daddy's Dance Hall A/s* (Case 324/86) [1988] ECR 739
Francovich (No. 1) and Bonifaci v. *Italian Republic* (Joined Cases C-6 and Case C-9/90) [1991] ECR I-5357
Grant v. *South West Trains* (Case C-249/96) [1998] ECR I-621
Groener v. *Minister for Education* (Case 379/87) [1989] ECR 3967
Gül v. *Regierungspräsident Düsseldorf* (Case 131/85) [1986] ECR 1573
Henke (Annette) v. *Gemeinde Schierke and Verwaltungsgemeinschaft* (Case C-298/94) [1996] ECR I-4989
Hill (Kathleen) and Anne Stapleton v. *Revenue Commissioners* (Case C-243/95) [1998] ECR I-3739
Hoeckstra v. *Bedrijfsvereniging Detailhandel* (Case 75/63) [1964] ECR 347
Internationale Handelsgesellschaft mbH v. *Einfuhr- und Vorratsstelle für Getreide und Futtermittel* (Case 11/70) [1970] ECR 1125
Jiminez Melgar v. *Ayuntamiento de Los Barrios* (Case C-438/99)
Johnston v. *Chief Constable of the RUC* (C-222/84) [1986] ECR 1651
Kalanke v. *Freie und Hansestadt Bremen* (Case C-450/93) [1995] ECR I-3051
Kempf v. *Staatssecretaris van Justitie* (Case 139/85) [1986] ECR 1741
Kolpinghuis Nijmegen BV, Criminal Proceedings against (Case 80/86) [1987] ECR 3969
Kortner v. *Council of the European Communities* (C-175/73) [1974] ECR 917
Kremzow v *Austrian Republic* (Case C-299/95) [1997] ECR I-2629
Lair v. *Universität Hannover* (Case 39/86) [1988] ECR 3161
Landeshauptstadt Kiel v. *Jaeger* (C-151/02) [2003] ECR I-8389
Levin v. *Staatssecretaris van Justitie* (Case 53/81) [1982] ECR 1035
Marleasing SA v. *La Comercial Internacional de Alimentacion* (Case C-106/89) [1990] ECR I-4135
Marschall v. *Land Nordhrhein-Westfalen* (Case C-409/95) [1997] ECR I-6363
Marshall v. *Southampton and South West Hampshire Area Health Authority (Teaching)* (No. 2) (C-271/91) [1993] ECR I-4367
Maurissen and European Public Service Union v. *Court of Auditors* (Joined Cases C-193/87 and C-194/87) [1990] ECR I-95
Merckx v. *Ford Motors Company and Neuhuys* (Joined Cases C-171 and C-172/94) [1996] ECR I-1253
Nold KG v. *Commission* (Case 4/73) [1974] ECR 491
Oy Liikenne Ab v. *Liskojärvi and Juntunen* (C-172/99) [2001] ECR I-745
P v. *S and Cornwall County Council* (Case C-13/94) [1996] ECR I-2143

R v. *Bouchereau* (Case 30/77) [1977] ECR 1999

R v. *Immigration Appeal Tribunal (Antonissen)* (C-292/89) [1991] ECR I-745

R v. *Immigration Appeal Tribunal and Surinder Singh, ex parte Secretary of State for the Home Department* (Case C-370/90) [1992] ECR I-4265

R v. *Secretary of State for Employment ex parte Seymour-Smith and Perez* (Case C-167/97) [1999] ECR I-623

Rask and Christensen v. *ISS Kantineservice* (Case C-209/91) [1992] ECR I-5755

Redmond (Dr Sophie) Stichting v. *Bartol* (Case C-29/91) [1992] ECR I-3189

Reed (Case 59/85) [1986] ECR 1283

Rewe-Zentralfinanz eG v. *Landwirtschaftskammer für das Saarland* (Case 33/76) [1976] ECR 1989

Rockfon A/S v. *Specialarbejderforbundet I Danmark, acting for Neilson* (Case C-449/93) [1995] ECR I-4291

Rush Portuguesa Ltda v. *Office Nationale d'Immigration* (Case C-113/89) [1990] ECR 1417

Rutilli v. *Ministre de l'intérieur* (Case 36/75) [1975] ECR 1219

Rygaard v. Stroe Moelle Akustik A/S (C-48/94) [1995] IRLR 51 ECJ/[1995] ECR I-2745

Schmidt v. *Spar und Leihkasse* (Case C-392/92) [1994] ECR I-1311

Sindicato de Medicos de Asistencia Publica (SIMAP) v. *Consellaria de Sanidad y Consumo de la Generalidad Valencia* (Case 303/98), Opinion of 16 December 1999

Spijkers v. *Benedik* (Case C-24/85) [1986] ECR 1119

Steymann v. *Staatssecretaris van Justitie* (Case 196/87) [1988] ECR 6159

Suzen (Ayse) v. *Zehnacker Gebäudereinigung GmbH Krankenhausservice* (Case C-13/95) [1997] ECR I-1259

Union royale belge des sociétés de football association and others v. *Bosman and others* (C-415/93) [1995] I-4921

United Kingdom v. *Council* (Working Time Case) (Case C-84/94) [1996] ECR I-5755

Van Duyn v. *Home Office* (Case 41/74) [1975] ECR-1337

Van Gend en Loos v. *Nederlandse Administratie der Belastingen* (Case 26/62) [1963] ECR 1

Von Colson and Kamann v. *Land Nordrhein-Westfalen* (Case 14/83) [1984] ECR 1891

Table of legislation

European Convention on Human Rights, 1950
European Coal and Steel Community Treaty, 1951
Treaty of Paris, 1952
Treaty of Rome, 1957
European Social Charter, 1961 (additional protocol guaranteed a series of fundamental rights, 1988)
Paris Declaration of the Council (COM(91) 511), 1972
Social Action Programme, 1974
Commission Recommendation on the promotion of positive action for women, 1984
Single European Act, 1987
Community Charter of Fundamental Social Rights of Workers, 1989
Treaty of Maastricht (Treaty on European Union/EC Treaty), 1992
Concordat of the Social Partners (COM(93) 600), 1993
Protocol to the European Social Charter providing for a system of collective complaints, 1995
Treaty of Amsterdam, 1998
Council (Social Affairs – Employment Guidelines), 1999
Commission Code of Practice on sexual harassment, 1999
EU Charter of Fundamental Rights, 2000
Treaty of Nice, 2002
EU Constitutional Treaty (EU Constitution), 2004

Table of EU Regulations

Regulation 1612/68 on the free movement of workers, amended by Regulation 312/76/EEC and Regulation 2434/92/EEC
Regulation 1251/70 on the right to remain in the host Member State
Regulation 1408/71 Social Security Regulation
EC Merger Regulations, 1986
Regulation 2157/2001 Regulation for a European Company Statute

Table of Council Directives

Table of national laws

Age Discrimination in Employment Act 1967 (US)
Fair Labor Standards Act 1994 (US)
Irish Trades Union Act 1941 (Ireland)
Irish Trades Union Act 1975 (Ireland)
Industrial Relations Act 1990 (Ireland)
Joint Regulation of Working Life Act 1976 (Sweden)
New Works Constitution Act 2001 (Germany)
Trade Union Law 1982 (France)
Trade Union Recognition Act 2000 (Ireland)

Preface

A distinguishing feature of economic integration in Europe has been a concern for social, as well as economic development. The creation and consolidation of a European Social Model has been the manifestation of this concern. This model features a relatively high level of social protection, both in terms of social welfare provision and in the creation of workers' rights and employment regulation. The impact of this model on the economic and social development of Europe has been much debated, but since the 2000 Lisbon Council the Member States have agreed that this model is in need of modernisation.

The objective set at Lisbon was of creating in Europe the most competitive and dynamic knowledge-based economy in the world. This was felt by many EU Member States to require fundamental reforms of social policy and the explicit coordination of European social, employment and macroeconomic policies. In the following chapters we explore the current status of European social policy, examine its economic rationale, identify the main factors promoting reform and assess the priorities for reform in the enlarged EU. Our underlying concern is to question whether the successful modernisation of employment regulations and social policies requires a new priority of EU objectives in which economic and employment objectives supersede social ones.

In seeking to answer this question we initially examine the history of European social policy and employment regulation and examine the evolution of legal and decision-making processes in the EU. In particular we report the shift towards 'soft law' measures and the increasing use of derogation and more flexible means of transposing European law into that of the individual Member States. We assess the extent to which these shifts are a reflection of the diversity of labour market behaviour in the EU or a response to a perceived need to promote more flexible regulations. Our approach throughout is to examine the economic rationale for regulations and to analyse the extent to which individual Directives and regulations are consistent with both the EU's economic and social objectives. We conclude that in some areas, soft law approaches provide a more effective mechanism, legally, politically and economically, for promoting social development in an EU of 25 Member States (EU25). The current Treaty base for social protection has served the EU well in terms of developing principles, rights and freedoms. However this hard law approach has not prevented continuing large variations in effective workplace rights across Member States. The emerging importance of social dialogue proffers a more effective vehicle for resolving conflicts between the economic and social objectives of the Union.

Our broad conclusion is that well-designed and clearly targeted employment regulations, when framed with sensitivity towards the diversity of labour market behaviour in an enlarged Europe, can promote both economic and social development. We argue that the decline of Social Europe is not inevitable: indeed the continuing widespread popularity of these policies remains a crucial element in maintaining the social consensus essential for continued European economic integration.

This book arises due to the timely events of enlargement, incorporating the extension of Social Europe, and as a result of a fruitful collaboration of nearly 12 years between the authors, culminating in several contributions to the economic-legal analysis of the EU social policy, as this book's bibliography will attest. As ever the authors wish to both warmly thank spouses and families for their support in the writing of this book, as well as apologise for the mental and physical absences caused by this publishing project. Thanks are also expressed to Mark Butler for research assistance, Laura Short for efficient secretarial service, and to our publisher for patience and kind assistance in relation to its publication. The normal disclaimers apply, and the law is stated as at 1 July 2004.

NJA and STH
Stoke-on-Trent and Manchester

1. The development of the European Social Model

1.1 INTRODUCTION

This book investigates the interaction between the social and economic foundations of the European Union (EU) and traces the development of the European Social Model (ESM). Since its advent the European Economic Community (EEC), progressing as the Treaty of Rome 1957 expounded, sought to further both the social and economic interests of the peoples of Europe. To that end the ESM emerged. In the three decades since the first Social Action programme of 1974, the EU's creation of 'Social Europe' has been both a controversial and a turbulent process. Some argue that this is inevitable given conflicting economic, social and political interests. Others question whether this reflects the lack of coherent analytical and philosophical foundations for social policy. This book considers these two perspectives, whilst assessing the future of the ESM within an EU of 25 (EU25) and possibly more Member States. This process of development has been affected by the dynamic role of the European Court of Justice (ECJ) which has manifestly sought to uphold the competing social and economic aims. Now with an enlarged Social Europe, the development of EU social and employment policy has hit a crossroads. In this book we chart the possible pitfalls and challenges, and offer pathways forward for the ESM.

In assessing whether the ESM can be sustained in an expanded Union, we initially examine, in Chapter 2, the development over the last three decades, 1974–2004, of the EU's legal decision-making methods, both old and new. Chapter 3 critically reviews the theory of labour market regulation and examines the rationale for the high level of government intervention that characterises the ESM. These initial chapters seek to set out the EU's agenda for the establishment of the free movement of workers, as well as the 'floor of minimum rights' approach. Chapter 4 examines the current issues facing the labour market of the enlarged EU, particularly in terms of the changing nature of employment and the extent and consequences of the diversity of custom, practices and performance across EU Member States.

EU social policy covers a range of areas; the importance of these individual areas has differed over time and between countries. The emphasis in this book is on policies instigated at the EU level, which affect conditions of employment and the framework within which industrial relations are conducted. Hence our concern is with the establishment of workers' rights regarding conditions of employment, working time and occupational health and industrial safety (Chapter 5). In Chapter 6 we concentrate upon a further dimension of EU social policy: equal opportunities and anti-discriminatory policies. In the following chapter we discuss EU Regulations and Directives concerned with the rights of workers facing dismissal, redundancy or transfer. Chapter 8 contains our analysis of EU policies concerned with workers' participation, information and consultation. In Chapter 9 we draw conclusions and suggest new pathways for the future development of the ESM.

Before we look forward and examine the prospects for the future development of EU social policy, in this opening chapter we chart its history and development to date. To that end, this chapter records and analyses the emerging legal basis of the Social EU, from Rome to the current enlargements (sections 1.2 and 1.3). Emphasis is laid on the development of the Social Policy Agenda and the emergence of the ESM. In order to further contextualise this development, we set out in section 1.4 the roles of the various social actors – the Commission, the European Court of Justice (ECJ) and the social partners. In section 1.5 we consider the policy drivers and the role of derogation as a means of reconciling conflicts regarding the details of employment regulation between EU Member States. Assessing the impact of these processes, we examine the free movement of workers (section 1.6), initially considered to be the overarching facilitator of workers' rights in the EU. In section 1.7 we examine the diversity of social policy systems amongst the EU Member States: here we describe the philosophical, historical, political and economic origins of this diversity. In the following section, we consider how the recent expansion of the EU has further increased this diversity. These latter two sections identify problematical transnational issues relating to the varying legal traditions, economic bases and underlying ideology in relation to regulation. We conclude this chapter by setting out the issues and themes to be examined in the following chapters.

Throughout this work we largely ignore policy related to education, training and health care or the provision of social security benefits, since these particular areas remain in the competence of individual Member States. However even application of the principle of subsidiarity cannot prevent large spillovers between policy areas and European and national competencies, for example our discussion of EU-level policies to promote the free movement of workers clearly relates to these other policy areas.

At the Nice Summit (2000) the Presidency Conclusions recorded that 'the European Social Model, characterised in particular by systems that offer a high level of social protection, by the importance of social dialogue and by services of general interest covering activities vital for social cohesion, is today based, beyond the diversity of the Member States' social systems, on a common core of values' (p. 4). These core values include democracy, individual rights, free collective bargaining, equality of opportunity and social welfare, and solidarity. The latter three objectives reflect a willingness to countenance using regulations, subsidies, taxes and benefits to interfere with market outcomes in the search for higher social welfare. These core values were not created by the EU but reflect the dominance of a particular approach to social welfare policies amongst the original Member States (see section 1.7 below). However as Vaughan-Whitehead (2003) argues, the establishment of the EU and the willingness of Member States to co-ordinate policies and construct common social policy rules has sustained and strengthened the commitment to these core values.

Social policies have been viewed, especially by the European Commission, as being important for the maintenance of economic and social cohesion in the Community and hence for continuing political support for European economic integration and improving economic performance. The direct economic benefits of these policies has also been recognised; indeed a 2003 Commission study suggested that the annual cost of not having a social policy was between 1 and 2 billion euro. These costs include a lack of access to the labour market of particular groups (for example women, older workers and those with disabilities) and the effects on society as a whole (for example crime and a lack of social cohesiveness). However there have been significant changes in the relative importance of, and priority attached to, social objectives over the last 30 years and our discussion below tracks this rise and fall.

1.2 EUROPEAN SOCIAL POLICY: FROM ROME TO THE ENLARGED EU CONSTITUTION

The European Economic Community (EEC) was formed as a result of the Spaak Report (1956) and established under the Treaty of Rome in 1957. This foundational Treaty of the EU sought to provide a vehicle for economic integration. As the Treaty noted, its aim was to 'lay the foundations of an ever closer union among the peoples of Europe' (Preamble). The Treaty of Rome reflected the Monnet and Schumann view that economic integration would spill over into political and social union. Whilst the Treaty of Rome did not initially expound much social integration, it did have a Title on Social Policy, contained originally in Article 117 (now the heavily amended Article 136). Article 117 sought to 'promote improved working conditions and standards of living of workers'. The Spaak Report relied for direction on social policy upon the Ohlin Report of International Labour Organisation (ILO) experts of 1956 which argued for transnational harmonisation, rejecting a general EEC role for harmonisation and favouring economic flexibility above social protection. But Spaak remained concerned about market distortions, which social policy should act to eliminate.

From 1957 to 1993 the European Union, as it became known, steadily accumulated new powers formalised in the Treaty on European Union (TEU), more commonly known as the Maastricht Treaty 1992. The Maastricht Summit had two main aims: to sustain the pace of change captured by previous changes to voting, and to create the European Union. This continued the process towards full economic integration (under the EEC) and political union (under the EC, the European Community) and with a new emphasis on Social Europe (under the auspices of the EU). In other words, the Maastricht Treaty was seeking to set out the framework for a Social Europe, to the exclusion of the UK which had opted out of such plans. Consequently the newly formed EU under the Treaty on European Union increased the Community's powers in the social sphere. The Community was supposed not only to work towards raising living standards but also to ensure a high level of social protection. For example the Social Fund's remit was widened to include education and vocational training. The involvement of the European Parliament (EP) in the legislative process was again increased, by extending the co-operation procedure further and by the introduction of co-decision procedures. The TEU overall broadened the aims of the EU to include monetary union and social and environmental protection.

In an EU social policy context, the adoption of the Treaty meant that two sets of rules applied in the social area: the EC Treaty covering all 15 Member States and the Agreement set out in the Protocol (No. 14) on social policy from which the UK opted out. The Agreement set out in Protocol No. 14, which was annexed to the TEU, contained two significant innovations: a major boost for the role of management and labour (that is, extending bargaining rights to workplace level); and extension of qualified majority voting in the Council in the following areas: improvements in the working environment to protect employees, working conditions, information and consultation of workers, equal opportunities for men and women on the labour market and equal treatment at work, and the integration of people excluded from the labour market. On the basis of the Agreement, the 14 Member States adopted four Directives: Council Directive 94/45 on the introduction of European works councils, Council Directive 96/34 on the Framework Agreement on parental leave (a proposal on parental leave had been blocked in the Council for several years), Council Directive 97/80 on the burden of proof in cases of discrimination based on sex and Council Directive 97/81 concerning the

Framework Agreement on part-time work. Whilst the momentum for a social Europe gathered some pace, due to the Maastricht Treaty, it was not until 1998 at Amsterdam that this was fully formally recognised. At the Maastricht Summit, one of the most contentious elements of the then draft Treaty was the changes proposed to Articles 117–22, which sought to expand the EU's social competence. In order to secure the UK's agreement to the Maastricht Treaty as a whole, the Agreement on Social Policy was integrated in the Treaty with the following amendments. Firstly, matters which before came under the co-operation procedure were now subject to the co-decision procedure and qualified majority in the Council. Secondly, a new paragraph was inserted enabling the Council, with qualified majority and co-decision with the European Parliament, to adopt measures to encourage the exchange of information and best practice in tackling social exclusion.

The original 1989 Charter of Fundamental Social Rights of Workers was a result of a Working Party of the Commission on Social Rights. All Member States, except the UK, approved the Charter. Consequently, as already noted, the UK opt-out until 1997 ensured that the Charter could not be integrated into the Treaty and therefore its legal status was that of a political declaration, a status confirmed in its Preamble and later by the European Court of Justice in the *Albany* case (C-67/96, para. 137, per A.-G. Jacobs). The Charter provided for a core set of social rights:

- free movement (Articles 1–3)
- remuneration (Articles 4–6)
- improved living and working conditions (Articles 7–9)
- social protection (Article 10)
- freedom of association (Articles 11–14)
- vocational training (Article 15)
- equal treatment between men and women (Article 16)
- information, consultation and participation (Articles 17–18)
- health and safety (Articles 19)
- protection of children and adolescents (Articles 20–23)
- elderly persons (Articles 24–5)
- disabled persons (Article 26)
- Member States' action (implementation) (Articles 27–30)

Its focus was on 'workers' rather than citizens. The 1989 Charter was similar in intent to that of the 1972 Paris Declaration of the Council (COM(91) 511). The overall impact of the Charter was that it formed a legislative agenda that proved useful in refocusing of labour law issues across the EU. The Charter led to the adoption of Directives on: information (91/533), collective redundancies (92/56), pregnant women (92/85), working time (93/104), young people (94/33) and posted workers (96/71). The Charter endorsed individual employment rights as well as endorsing collective rights. In any event the Charter proved to be the impetus required for the development of social rights in the context of the social dimension, not the internal market. Above all, labour and workers' rights were given special relevance under this Charter. Historically the Agreement on Social Policy (SPA) was enacted in order to enable the UK Government's opt-out from the processes that formalised the role of the social partners in decision-making at Community level. In 1997 the newly elected UK Government ended its opt-out under the Agreement on Social Policy. Overall, the SPA allowed the Member States to utilise the EU institutions in an innovative way to establish a clearly defined legal basis for Community labour law. It also provided for the beginning of the development of the role of the social partners in creating an EU-wide collective agreement on social affairs and employment strategy.

The Treaty of Amsterdam (1998) was essentially a consolidating Treaty. Its main purpose was to improve law-making, decision-making and policy-formulating processes. Consequently, greater openness in decision-making was brought about. The Amsterdam Treaty (1998) further strengthened the provisions formerly contained in Article 118B (now Articles 138–9) by providing an obligation on the part of the Commission to consult the social partners before making any labour law proposals (COM(96) 488). Article 136 (former Article 117) was also altered to include references to the European Social Charter of Turin and the Community Charter of the Fundamental Social Rights of Workers. The Amsterdam Treaty also provided that the Council act by unanimity, as before, but now in co-decision with the European Parliament on matters concerning decisions relating to the European Social Fund. Provisions also facilitated the exercise of citizens' right to move and reside freely within the territory of the Member States and extend social security entitlements for Community migrant workers. In particular, new additions to the Treaty included a non-discrimination provision, which provided the authority to create legislation covering gender, race, ethnic origin, religion or belief, disability, age and sexual orientation. The usage of the co-decision procedure was expanded so as to allow the wider applicability of majority voting, as well as putting an end to the EU institutions, namely the Parliament and Council, stifling decision-making on each other's policy initiatives. However it was not until the Nice Treaty that co-decision making was affirmed as the most effective way for the future of the EU to be determined.

Romano Prodi, then President of the EU, described the aim of the Nice Summit as 'the reunification of Europe'. The outcome of the December 2000 Summit was the Nice Treaty that was eventually ratified in December 2002. This Treaty facilitates the enlargement of the EU. It anticipated that ten or more new Member States would join the EU and that fundamental institutional changes were required. Decisions taken included increasing the number of Commissioners to 26 (though larger Member States lost their second Commissioner in 2005); extending qualified majority voting within the Council (a decline in unanimity being expected); and a reweighting of votes in the Council in favour of the larger Member States. Following on from the Giscard-Estaing Report (2003) on the Convention of Europe, at the Intergovernmental Conference in 2003, the enlargement of the EU to 25 Member States (EU25) was accepted in principle. Eventually on 18 June 2004, the amended draft European Union Constitutional Treaty was finally agreed, founding the extended Union on the values of 'respect for human dignity, liberty, democracy, the rule of law and respect for human rights'. Significant changes in the social sphere include the enhancement of co-operation and the desire to promote greater economic, social and territorial cohesion with the intention of 'reducing disparities between the levels of development'.

Such a reinforced agenda places social and economic cohesion high on the new EU's priorities list, and the new voting method requires a greater level of agreement than previously. The new Constitution ensures that the EU's new Charter of Fundamental Rights is viewed as a political document and therefore not necessarily legally binding in each EU Member State. This was in keeping with the 1989 Charter.

Prior to the new Constitution, the 1994 Essen Council confirmed the EU's commitment to the promotion of employment objectives. This followed on from the contradictory proposals of the Commission's Green (COM(93) 551) and White (COM(94) 333) Papers on the future of European social policy which set out conflicting arguments for and against the development of the European Social Model. Following on from Essen, five emerging themes were identified (Goetschy, 1999): promoting employment; reorganising work; combating social exclusion; mainstreaming gender equality; and consolidation, compliance and enforcement of social legislation. These co-ordinated priorities became known as the European Employment Strategy (EES). Whilst these priorities were in the first instance without Treaty powers and were therefore a non-binding legal instrument, they were later formalised in Title VIII (Articles 125–30) of the Amsterdam Treaty (Ball, 2001). This Title was fast-tracked following an initiative by the Commission in 1997 (COM(97) 497). This Title, as Velluti notes (2004) later reformulated as the European Employment Strategy (EES), sought to converge both labour market policy and employment levels within the EU. Member States were requested to draw up National Employment Action Plans (NAPs) by June 1998. The EES sought to promote the practices that NAPs be focused around employability, entrepreneurship, adaptability and equal opportunities (the 'four pillars' of the Luxembourg Jobs Summit, 1997 (COM(99) 442)).

1.3 EXTENDING SOCIAL EUROPE TO EU25

The term 'enlargement' is used to describe the widening of membership of the EU. The six founding nations (Belgium, France, Germany, Italy, Luxembourg and the Netherlands) established the EEC under the Treaty of Rome in 1957. The UK, Ireland and Denmark joined in 1973. Greece joined in 1981. Portugal and Spain acceded in 1986 and Austria, Finland and Sweden in 1995. In 2004, Cyprus, Malta, as well as the former Eastern Bloc countries of Croatia, the Czech Republic, Estonia, Hungary, Poland, Romania, Slovenia and Slovakia acceded, following the ratification of the Treaty of Nice in December 2003.

The history and development of the ESM, outlined above, provides ample evidence of the problems to be faced in extending Social Europe. However there now exists a demonstrable set of underlying principles, as evidenced by free movement, non-discrimination and a 'level playing field' approach to labour law which has been applied across the EU25. In this section, a discussion of these key principles and processes is undertaken. Since the first social action programme, EU legislators initially sought to harmonise existing policies and practices amongst Member States. Positive harmonisation (that is, the establishment of minimum standards) being recognised in all Social Action Programmes (SAPs) since the beginning in 1974.

The originally predominant underlying principle in EU social policy-making was the need for a broad equivalence in labour standards. Such an aspiration emerges under the EU's banner of promoting a need for a 'level playing field' of competition. It should be noted that the ECJ in 1988 (C-324/86 *Foreningen af Arbejdsledere I Danmark* v. *Daddy's Dance Hall A/s*) defined 'harmonisation' as 'not intending to establish a uniform level of protection throughout the Community, but by extending the protection guaranteed to workers independently by the laws of the individual Member States'. Essentially 'harmonisation' seeks to identify a common problem in Europe, though as we shall argue below, it is the variance in EU Member States' employment relations and systems of labour law that prevents full harmonisation. Institutional change has further developed social policy-making in the EU. For instance since the Treaty of Amsterdam's amendment to Article 138, the European Parliament, the EU Member States and the EU Commission have had divergent views on its interpretation. An example being in 1994, when the UK instituted proceedings against the Council in the European Court of Justice (Case C-84/94) claiming that Article 138 did not provide a legal basis for adopting rules on working time. The Court ruled that Article 138 should not be interpreted restrictively, thus supporting the European Parliament's broad interpretation of this article.

The enactment of the Treaty on European Union and the desire to combat unemployment and maintain high levels of social protection stimulated additional activities under the new Article 3. This marked a crucial stage in the evolution of EC social policy. Both the EU Commission's Green (1993) and White (1994) papers on social policy attempted to clarify the EU's social competencies. The EU's desire to combat social dumping further encouraged the development of EU labour law and social policy, as a preamble to enlargement. The controversial 'Hoover Affair' (1990), involving the decision by Hoover to switch production from Dijon in France to Glasgow, culminating in 600 job losses and the recruitment of some 400 fixed-term contract employees, clearly defined the potential for large-scale social dumping. In the Hoover case, the motive was clear: cheaper Scottish labour, partly reflecting the UK's deregulated employment regulations, generated social dumping. Social dumping in effect describes behaviour designed to give a competitive advantage to companies based on low labour standards rather than high productivity. Due to the prospect of increased social dumping as economic integration proceeds, the EU sought, according to Bercusson (1993), to commit itself to 'legislating for higher labour standards and employee rights across the EU in the social field', in order to ensure that social dumping was avoided.

In order to combat social dumping, the EU's Social Policy Agenda sought to work towards core European objectives and increased co-ordination of social policies (COM(2000) 379). As noted above, the Treaty of Amsterdam moved social policy to the centre of EU policy. The strategic objectives for 2000–05 (Shaping the New Europe, COM(2000) 154) include promotion of: new forms of European governance (meaning co-decision making and the promotion of open methods of policy co-ordination); a new economic and social agenda, and a better quality of life. In conjunction with such a strategy the social policy agenda also seeks to assist policies aimed at building a competitive and inclusive knowledge-based economy promoting social cohesion and full employment. Subsequently, the European Employment Strategy (EES) has emerged as the new social policy agenda-setter.

1.4 THE EU'S SOCIAL AFFAIRS PROTAGONISTS

From modest beginnings and encouraged by the principles and processes identified above, the ESM emerged. The institutions underpinning contemporary EU social policy can be separated into three: the ECJ as the law enforcer, the Commission (DG V) as the policy-maker, and the social partners themselves as the bargaining units.

1.4.1 Enforcing the ESM

The European Court of Justice (ECJ) is composed of a judge from each EU Member State. Overall, as Article 234 provides, its role is to give preliminary rulings on the interpretation of the Treaty and the validity of secondary legislation. The purpose of a preliminary ruling is to ensure the uniform application and interpretation of Community law by national courts. Whilst the ECJ does not bind itself, it having no rule of precedent, it is supposed to ensure its own consistency (see C-28-30/62, *Da Costa*). The referring national court is bound by the ECJ's ruling. Above all, the preliminary ruling procedures provide an important linkage between the national courts and the ECJ. The availability of such procedures also allows EU Member States' courts to familiarise themselves with EU law.

Article 234 provides that any court or tribunal of a Member State may request a reference. A national court will only make a reference where it considers that its decision rests upon a point of Community law. Notably it is the court that decides to make the reference, not the parties to the case under scrutiny. Whilst the right to refer is discretionary, it becomes an obligation where there is no remedy in national law. Though, following the *CILFIT* (C-283/81) ruling, it is not necessary to refer the case to the ECJ where: the question of EC law is irrelevant to the case being heard by the national court; the question of EC law has already been interpreted by the ECJ in a previous ruling; the correct interpretation is so obvious as to leave no scope for doubt (*acte clair*). The actual referral procedure requires the national court to formulate a question or questions to be addressed by the ECJ.

In *Rewe-Zentralfinanz* (C-33/76) the European Court of Justice was careful to ensure that appropriate remedies (that is, compensation) be available with regard to breaches of Community laws and rules. Yet the ECJ ruled that it relied upon the national courts to ensure that remedies available for similar breaches of national law should also be available for breaches of EC law. The remedy should therefore be an effective remedy. Such was defined in *Von Colson* (C-14/83) where the ECJ explained that Article 10 of the Treaty (ex Article 5) provided that EU Member States' national courts should have remedies which act as a deterrent and be adequate to remedy the damage sustained.

The ECJ later developed this principle based on proportionality in *Johnston* v. *Chief Constable of the RUC* (C-222/84), highlighting the need for effective judicial protection for those who have sustained losses as a result of a breach of EU law. It was eventually their ruling on *Marshall* v. *Southampton and SW AHA* (No. 2) (C-271/91) which declared that not only did the remedy have to be comparable with that available for a similar national breach, but where such an effective remedy was not available, EU Member States should devise a new suitable remedy.

The above seek to promote uniformity amongst the Community remedies. However there is one exception to the rule: *Francovich* claims (see C-6 and 9/90, *Francovich*). Where a Member State has failed to correctly implement the aims of a Directive, compensation should be available from the State due to its breach that caused the ensuing losses of those concerned. This right ensures that Member States do not benefit from their own breaches of Community law. As a result of *Brasserie du Pêcheur* (C-46/93) (see also *Factortame* (No. 3), C-49/93) only serious breaches are included. Serious breaches are considered to be those breaches which were intended (see *Dillenkofer*, C-178, 179, 188–90/94). Following *Brasserie du Pêcheur*, a threefold test applies:

- the law infringed must be intended to confer rights on individuals
- the breach must be sufficiently serious
- there must be a causal link established between the breach and the individual's damage being claimed.

Consequently these guidelines ensure that the ECJ holds the overall responsibility to enforce Community law and plays a pivotal role in the development of the ESM in enforcement terms.

As explained above, much of the EU's social policy is contained in Directives that have to be implemented by the individual EU Member States. Directives provide vertical and horizontal direct and indirect effects. The EU's Doctrine of vertical direct effect was established by the European Court of Justice to provide rights and obligations to individuals, enforceable in national courts. This right was established in *Van Gend en Loos* (C-26/62). This case involved Dutch importers challenging the imposition of a duty, having imported chemicals from Germany. The ECJ affirming its 'new legal order' observed that EU law conferred rights and obligations on individuals, as well as Member States, without the need for implementing legislation. Consequently EU law was given direct effect, which means that both EU Member States and individuals are granted rights and obligations and these rights and obligations are enforceable by individuals through their national courts. Due to the European Court of Justice's refusal to initially permit the direct applicability of laws to all citizens (horizontal direct effect) by way of Directives, the principle of indirect effect has emerged. Indirect effect is also known as the 'interpretive obligation'. It was the *Von Colson* ruling (C-14/83) that was instrumental in creating the principle of indirect effect. Clearly whilst Directives do not have direct effect, EU Member States have a duty to implement Directives. Yet post-*Colson* Member States' courts also hold a duty to interpret national legislation in the light of Community Directives, subject to three limitations: (1) where to interpret national legislation in light of a

Directive would conflict with other general principles of EU law (see *Kolpinghuis Nijmegen*, C-80/86); (2) only measures enacted prior to the Directive may be interpreted in this manner (see *Marleasing*, C-106/89); (3) not where criminal proceedings could result (see *Arcaro*, C-168/95). Certain EC law provisions place obligations on both EU Member States and individuals. The concept of horizontal direct effect permits individuals to enforce such rights against another individual, although the success of such horizontal direct effect claims is conditional on the *Van Gend* criteria applying. That is, the direct effect under Van Gend applies where the provision to comply must be clear and sufficiently precise, the right relied upon must be unconditional, and the right is not subject to any other implementing measure at either Community or national level; for example, the case of *Dekker* (C-177/88), where the horizontal direct effect was applied against a private employer. Overall Article 249 provides 'that a directive shall be binding, as to the result to be achieved, upon each Member State to which it is addressed'. Directives are therefore not directly applicable; they require implementation before taking effect. Within the EU such implementation is undertaken by the EU Member States.

Since Community law forms part of each EU Member State's domestic legal system, rights and obligations under EU social policy are normally enforced before the national courts. It has been left to the EU Member States' discretion to designate which national courts will hear actions founded on Community law, as well as the procedures to be adopted.

1.4.2 The EU Commission's Role

The EU Commission is the EU's civil service body. DG V, or 'DG Empl' as it is termed, is the Commission's department managing social affairs and employment relations. Articles 211–13 of the EC Treaty, as amended by the new Constitutional Treaty 2004, confirm the various roles of the Commission. Essentially the Commission is the EU's administrative and enforcement body, comprising of Commissioners (representatives from each Member State) and Directorate-Generals (DGs), each given a policy area to co-ordinate. The Commission's role is to represent the interests of the Community as a whole. Article 211 provides that the Commission ensures 'the proper functioning and development of the EU'. As a result the Commission has gained the title 'Guardian of the Treaties'. Its functions are therefore legislative, administrative, executive and quasi-judicial. In terms of its legislative role, the Commission initially drafts legislation and will thereafter consult both the Council and the Parliament. The Commission will therefore amend legislative proposals, as directed. In addition, at pre-draft stage the Commission will be involved in research and producing reports and Green and White papers. Once enacted, the Commission's task is to implement the policy in a supervisory manner, ensuring EU Member States comply. Its executive role requires the Commission to manage the EU's annual budget, including the Social Fund. The Commission is also the EU's international negotiating body with international organisations, such as the United Nations (UN), World Trade Organisation (WTO) and International Labour Organisation (ILO). The Commission's quasi-judicial role consists of the power to investigate (Article 226) where it considers breach of EU law has occurred and maintaining fair competition (Articles 81–2 and Regulation 17) through formal decisions and fines.

1.4.3 The Role of the Social Partners

The implementation of EU law through collective agreements was first put to the European Court of Justice in 1985 in *Commission* v. *Denmark* (C-143/83), when the Danish Government sought to implement the 1975 Equal Pay Directive through collective agreements. It is a common practice in Denmark for labour law to be enforced through collective agreements. The Court ruled that 'Member States may leave the implementation of [laws] to representatives of management and labour'. Yet the Court went on to affirm that the obligation to implement the law remains fully with the EU Member State. More recently the 1992 Collective Redundancies Directive was implemented in Belgium by a collective agreement that was binding in national law. The principle of subsidiarity (to be discussed in Chapter 2) encourages such a method of implementation (see COM(89) 471, para. 27). This reliance on collective bargaining encourages a move away from a centralised approach towards a decentralised method of implementation of EU law. Article 137(4) of the Treaty now permits such decentralised implementation. Furthermore social dialogue now also provides an opportunity for such collective agreements at both EU and national levels.

The Val Duchesse social dialogue was initiated in 1985. This process aimed to involve the social partners – European Trade Union Confederation (ETUC), Union of Industrial and Employers' Confederations of Europe (UNICE) and the European Centre of Enterprises with Public Participation (CEEP) – in the internal market process. With the introduction of Article 118B in the Single European Act, the promotion of the social dialogue process became one of the Commission's official tasks. In October 1991, UNICE, ETUC and CEEP adopted a joint agreement that called for mandatory consultation with the social partners on Commission proposals in the area of social affairs, and an option for negotiations between the social partners to lead to framework agreements. This agreement became enshrined in the Agreement on Social Policy annexed to the Treaty on European Union (this agreement later became the ratified Concordat of the Social Partners of 1993 (COM(93) 600)). In

October 1992 the ETUC, CEEP and UNICE formed a new Social Dialogue Committee which is consulted on social, macroeconomic, employment, vocational training and other policies of interest to the social partners. In recent years a number of other organisations have requested participation in this process, and the Commission therefore calls upon the social partners to 'reinforce the social dialogue by ensuring the adequate representation of all appropriate interests'.

Originally, Article 118B of the Treaty of Rome recognised 'relations based on agreement'. Now Article 138 promotes such consultation between 'management and labour'. Subsequently the EU Commission is obliged under Articles 136–45 to involve the social partners in a two-stage consultation process, pre-legislative, and request their opinion before concluding its proposal. However this social dialogue amongst the recognised social partners was challenged in 1996 by UEAPME (Union Européenne de l'Artisant et des Petits et Moyennes Entreprises), a group representing small and medium-sized businesses, arguing about the representativeness of the self-selected, designated social partners. UEAPME agued that their exclusion from consultation and negotiation created an unfair, unrepresentative closed shop. The Court ruled that UEAPME did not have a general right to be consulted. Consequently the Council and the Commission must verify the representativeness of labour and management of the signatories to any agreement affecting labour and management. Since this ruling UEAPME has become an umbrella organisation of UNICE. Clearly the social partners now have a fundamental role to play in the development of social policy and labour law in the EU. In fact, the Parental Leave Directive (96/34) was an outcome of this process formulated in the new Article 139(2). This Directive was designed, formulated and agreed between the social partners, under the social dialogue process (to be discussed further in Chapter 7). January 2004 saw a further step in the development of the social dialogue process with the EU-level social partners establishing a sectoral social dialogue committee for local and regional government.

Such examples of social dialogue at work have been enhanced by the advent of the Open Method of Co-ordination (OMC), to be further discussed in Chapter 2. The OMC was implemented post-Lisbon Summit to further the 'coherent and systematic approaches' to policy and law-making achieved at the Luxembourg, Cardiff and Cologne Council meetings. The OMC is designed to assist Member States in developing their own policies. Part of the OMC model is to instigate a high-level forum bringing together the EU institutions, the social partners and other bodies to consider progress of policies to date. The OMC provides for: the fixing of timetables for achieving prescribed and agreed EU policy goals, short, medium and long term; the establishment of benchmarking against global indicators, as a means of comparing best practice; the translation of EU guidelines into national and regional policies, accepting differences; the monitoring and evaluation of such policy development, by way of peer review. The OMC supports the principle of subsidiarity insofar as it encourages activities at regional and local levels, as well as at national and social partner levels. The OMC creates a horizontal method of EU governance. The Treaty of Nice presented an opportunity for the OMC to expand its remit. In fact at the Stockholm Council in 2001, the OMC was extended to education and pensions. The OMC represents a 'soft' law approach to EU social policy and labour law. This will be discussed in later chapters and its future as a strategy evaluated in Chapter 9.

1.4.4 The Individual Social Partners

The European Trade Union Confederation (ETUC) was established in 1973 to provide a trade union counterbalance to the economic forces of European integration. Following the changes in Central and Eastern Europe, a large number of new trade unions have joined. At present, the ETUC has in its membership 78 National Trade Union Confederations from a total of 34 European countries, as well as 11 European industry federations, representing a total of 60 million members. Other trade union structures such as Eurocadres (the Council of European Professional and Managerial Staff) and EFREP/FERPA (European Federation of Retired and Elderly Persons) operate under the auspices of the ETUC. In addition, the ETUC coordinates the activities of the 39 ITUCs (Interregional Trade Union Councils), which organise trade union cooperation at a cross-border level. The ETUC is recognised by the European Union, by the Council of Europe and by EFTA as the only representative cross-sectoral trade union organisation at European level. Since 1991, the EU has recognised it as a leading social partner. The Union of Industrial and Employers' Confederations of Europe (UNICE) arose from a 1949 initiative that created the Conseil des Fédérations Industrielles d'Europe (CIFE), and, within this organisational framework, the Union des Industries des Pays de la Communauté Européenne. It was a natural evolution for this body to become the Union des Industries de la Communauté Européenne (UNICE) in March 1958, to track the political consequences of the community created by the Treaty of Rome. The six countries of this first European Community were all represented by the eight founder-member federations of UNICE, the BDI and BDA (Germany), the CNPF (France), Confindustria (Italy), the FEDIL (Luxembourg), the FIB (Belgium), the VNO and FKPCWV (the Netherlands). The Federation of Greek Industries was accepted as an associate member. CEEP (European Centre of Enterprises with Public Participation) is an employer-focused social partner organisation which was recognised in 1985 under the 'Val Duchesse' social dialogue. CEEP was established in 1961, originally as an international association consisting of enterprises and organisations with public participation or carrying out activities of general interest, whatever their legal or ownership statute. This employer association is located in Brussels and is recognised as a social partner by the European Commission in accordance with the Treaty on European Union. CEEP, whose statutes are very open, does not impose any exclusive clauses on recruitment. Thus members that operate at every level – European, national, regional or local – may also be affiliated to various other national professional federations, and thus indirectly be members of other associations. Moreover CEEP's territorial area is not limited; thus while its full members belong to European Union countries, enterprises from non-EU countries can join as associated members.

1.5 CUSTOMISING THE EUROPEAN SOCIAL MODEL

In this section we address the mechanisms that allow for customising or opting-out of the ESM: derogations and subsidiarity. These two methods allow Member States to subscribe to those social measures they accept and to determine at the national level provision for the preferred targeting of Directives. To that end, a derogation is a special provision in a Directive that allows it to be applied to particular groups of people or organisations in different ways. A derogation is not an exemption, it just permits greater flexibility in the application of the law to take into account special circumstances. For example although security workers are given a derogation in the Working Time Directive, an employer must still provide for compensatory time off to comply with the general working time limitations. Article 5 of the EC Treaty (formerly Article 3b) provides for the principle of subsidiarity. Subsidiarity as a principle has existed since 1951, when under Article 5 of the European Coal and Steel Community (ECSC) Treaty it stipulated that the Community should exert direct influence on production only when circumstances so required. Although it was not expressly so defined, a subsidiarity criterion was also included in Article 130 on the environment, by the Single European Act in 1987. However prior to the EC Treaty the ECJ ruled ([1995] ECR II-289 at 331), that the subsidiarity principle was not a general principle of law, against which the legality of Community action should be tested.

The principle of subsidiarity pursues two opposing aims. On the one hand, it allows the Community to act if a problem cannot be adequately settled by the Member States acting on their own; on the other, it seeks to uphold the authority of the Member States in those areas that cannot be dealt with more effectively by Community action. The purpose of including this principle in the European Treaties is to bring decision-making within the Community as close to the citizen as possible. In defining this important principle, the general aim is to guarantee a degree of independence for a lower authority in relation to a higher body, or for a local authority in respect of a central authority. It therefore involves the sharing of powers between several levels of authority, a principle which forms the institutional basis for federal states. When applied in a Community context, the principle means that the Member States remain responsible for areas which they are capable of managing more effectively themselves, while the Community is given those powers which the Member States cannot discharge satisfactorily. Under Article 5(2) there are three preconditions for Community action in accordance with the principle of subsidiarity:

- the area concerned must not fall within the Community's exclusive competence;
- the objectives of the proposed action cannot be sufficiently achieved by the Member States;
- the action can therefore, by reason of its scale or effects, be implemented more successfully by the Community.

Consequently the scope of the principle of subsidiarity may be seen from two points of view. In areas in which the Treaty gives responsibility to the Community – shared with the Member States – the principle is a yardstick for measuring that responsibility (limiting the exercise of powers). In areas in which the Treaty does not give the Community responsibility, the principle does not create additional competence (no allocation of powers).

The principle of subsidiarity applies only to areas shared between the Community and the Member States. It therefore does not apply to areas which fall within the exclusive competence of the Community or those which fall within exclusively national competence. This dividing line is blurred however because Article 308 may extend the Community's areas of competence if for instance action by the Community proves necessary to attain Treaty objectives. The demarcation of the areas of exclusive Community competence continues to be a problem, particularly because it is laid down in the Treaties not by reference to specific fields but by means of a functional description. In a number of decisions stemming from the Treaties for example, the ECJ has defined and recognised certain competences (which are not explicitly regulated in the Treaties) as exclusive, but it has not laid down a definitive list of such competences. The lack of any clear dividing line for applying the principle of subsidiarity will continue to result in different interpretations of this principle. At the same time however the EU clearly has the aim of limiting European action to the objectives of the Treaty and ensuring that decisions on new actions are taken as closely as possible to the citizen. In its judgments in cases C-84/94 (*United Kingdom* v. *Council*) and C-233/94 (*Federal Republic of Germany* v. *European Parliament and Council of the European Court*), the ECJ found that compliance with the principle of subsidiarity was one of the conditions covered by the requirement to state the reasons for Community acts, under Article 253 (190) EC Treaty. This requirement is met even if the principle is not expressly mentioned in the Act's recitals but it is clear from reading the recitals as a whole that the principle has been complied with. Without changing the wording of the subsidiarity criterion, Article 5(2) of the Treaty of Amsterdam incorporated the doctrine of proportionality. The overall approach to the application of the subsidiarity principle agreed in Edinburgh in 1992 thus became to a large extent subject to judicial review via the Protocol on subsidiarity. The aim of these changes is to use procedures for implementing the principle of subsidiarity to regulate the details of the powers conferred on the Community institutions by the Treaties, so that the objectives laid down in the Treaties can be attained. It therefore follows that in exercising its right of initiative, the Commission will take into account the principle of subsidiarity and show that it has been observed. The same applies to Parliament and the Council, in accordance with the powers conferred on them by Articles 192 (138b) and 208 (152), respectively.

1.6 FREE MOVEMENT OF WORKERS

One of the cornerstones of both economic and social policy in the EU is the free movement of workers. Without such movement, the tenets of a common market and the ESM would be inoperative. The freedom to go from one State to another to work is also a concrete realisation of European integration, although in reality locational mobility within the EU remains low with just 2 per cent of employees currently working in a Member State other than that where they are a national. In Chapter 4 we examine the nature and determinants of geographical mobility in Europe in more detail. To ensure free movement, a legislative framework has been created based on Articles 39 to 42 of the EC Treaty. Regulation 1612/68, the Directive 68/630 and a certain number of case laws complete this framework.

Free movement of workers implies that certain rights have been granted to European workers. They are entitled to work in the territory of another Member State and be protected by the abolition of all discrimination based on nationality regarding their working conditions. They have the right to enter another Member State and also to stay in another Member State. This right has also been granted to their family. Article 43 deals with the pursuit of an economic activity through a fixed establishment in another Member State for an indefinite period. Two rights are expressed in the Article: 'the right to take up and pursue activities as a self-employed person and the right to set up and manage undertakings, in particular companies and firms within the meaning of Article 48 under the conditions laid down for the nationals by the law of the country'. These rights, which concern therefore both legal and natural persons, have been recognised as directly effective by the Court. The Article prohibits discrimination based on nationality, and it should be noted that this has to be respected by the Member State and also national professional bodies. This non-discrimination principle applies to conditions of access to the profession, but also to any other benefit or opportunity which facilitates the pursuit of the profession.

Another fundamental principle of the TEU of 1998 is expressed by Articles 49 and 50. These directly effective articles prohibit any restrictions on the freedom to provide services. Services are defined as those normally provided for remuneration and generally include 'activities of an industrial character, of a commercial character, activities of craftsmen'. It should be pointed out that the ECJ has recognised the right for a person who travels to receive services in Case 286/82. Free movement of workers is guaranteed under the Treaty by Articles 39–42 which establish a principle that workers should enjoy the right to free movement including the abolition of any discrimination based on nationality, as regards employment remuneration and any other conditions of work or employment. However, central to all the rights guaranteed is the key term 'worker', which is not defined by either the Treaty or any other European legislation. Consequently, the European Court of Justice has interpreted this salient term: *Hoekstra* (75/63) defined the term 'worker' to also include job-seekers; *Levin* (53/81) and *Kempf* (139/85) accepted part-time workers; *Steymann* (196/87) noted that workers need not necessarily receive formal wages; and *Bettray* (344/87) determined limits to the term 'worker' by requiring workers to be engaged in 'economic activities' or employment of a 'genuine nature'. Notwithstanding these cases, the ECJ accepted that the term 'worker' generally refers to an employed person. The rights given under the Treaty and Directives 68/360 and 64/221, as well as Regulation 1612/68 include the:

- right to exit, enter and reside. C-292/89, *Antonissen*, allows job-seekers a reasonable length of residence in order to job search, though C-41/74, *Van Duyn*, disallows entry on public policy or national security grounds. But such restrictions must be proportionate (see C-36/75 *Rutilli*; C-115 and 116/81 *Adoui and Cornuaille*; and C-30/77 *Bouchereau*);
- right to equal treatment (both Articles 12 and 39 of the Treaty and Regulation 1612/68, in terms of housing, social and tax advantages, access to training and trade union membership (see C-39/86 *Lair* and C-197/86 *Brown* (education – tuition fees); C-316/85 *Lebon* (social

advantages); C-379/87 *Groener* (linguistic knowledge); right to remain (Regulation 1251/70); rights relating to workers' families (Regulation 1612/68, including spouses, children – see C-267/83 *Diatta*, C-131/85 *Gül*, C-59/85 *Reed* and C-370/90 *Singh*).

Articles 43–55 provide similar rights and protections for self-employed persons under the right to establishment. The mobility of workers in the EU labour market raised concerns about transnational protections. Directive (96/71/EC) aims at the promotion of the transnational provision of services which requires a 'climate of fair competition and measures guaranteeing respect for the rights of workers' (Preamble, par. 5). Based on Articles 57(2) and 66 of the EC Treaty, it aimed at co-ordinating the legislation of Member States and creating a core of rules that must be respected by undertakings assigning their employees to work in another Member State. The key element is the employment relationship existing between the service-providing undertaking and the posted worker. 'Posted workers' means workers as defined by the law of the host State who for a limited period carry out their work in the territory of a Member State other than the State in which they normally work (Articles 2(1) and (2)). According to Article 3, the undertakings must guarantee posted workers the host state's terms and conditions of employment regarding the maximum work and minimum rest periods, minimum paid holidays, minimum rates of pay, health, safety and hygiene at work, protective measures regarding the terms and conditions of employment of pregnant women or women who have recently given birth, and equality of treatment between men and women.

The posting of workers can take three forms:

1. Undertakings posting workers in a host Member State on their account and under their direction under a contract concluded between the undertaking and the party for whom the services are intended.
2. Undertakings posting workers to an establishment or to an undertaking owned by the group in the territory of a Member State.
3. Uundertakings which are temporary employment or placement agencies hiring out workers to a user undertaking established or carrying out services in the territory of another Member State.

In all three cases, a key feature is that an employment relationship exists between the service-providing undertaking and the posted worker. Due to the Treaty rules on the provision of services and continuing economic integration, transnational contracting is increasing. As a result companies established in one Member State have sometimes to relocate their employees to another Member State in order to supply particular services to comply with the contract they have signed. This leads to fears of social dumping as the service provider may be considered as taking advantage of cheaper labour standards in their own State to win contracts in the host State. Therefore a certain degree of protection has been considered as necessary for these posted workers.

Regulation 1612/68 facilitates the free movement of workers and their families. Article 10(1) allows a worker's spouse, descendants and dependants to enter and reside with the worker and be employed or seek employment. The term 'spouse' has been conventionally construed (see *Reed*, C-59/85) as married, though cohabiting has been subsequently included, as have separated couples (see *Diatta*, C-267/83). The ECJ in *Lebon* (C-316/85) made it clear that dependency was determined by the facts of each case. This is a central text when dealing with the question of free movement of workers but also their families. The text deals with employment conditions. Its title II provides specific example of the application of the principle of non-discrimination on the ground of nationality. Directive 86/613 concerns the application of the principle of equal treatment between men and women engaged in an activity including self-employed capacity, and on the protection of self-employed women during pregnancy and motherhood. Self-employed workers are all persons pursuing a gainful activity for their own account, under the conditions laid down by national law, including farmers and members of liberal professions (Article 3). Member States have to take all measures necessary to ensure the elimination of all provisions which are contrary to the principle of equal treatment and which may affect self-employed workers (Article 4). Where self-employed workers face problems of discrimination, the national legal systems should be adapted in order that these workers are able to pursue their claims (Article 9). The Council was supposed to have reviewed this Directive by 1993 but no actions have been taken to date.

According to Article 39(3) of the EC Treaty, derogations can be accepted from the principle of free movement of workers. Three reasons can be given for limiting the free movement: public policy, public security and public health. In the *Van Duyn* case (41/74), the European Court of Justice underlined that such derogations have to be interpreted strictly so that their scope cannot be determined unilaterally by each Member State without being subject to the control of the Community institutions. At the same time, they must be read within the general principles of law, including fundamental human rights. Yet Member States do retain a certain amount of discretion to determine what constitutes public policy according to their national needs.

1.7 THE EUROPEAN SOCIAL MODEL(S)

Our discussion above has concentrated on the development of EU social policy and in this section we examine the nature and origins of the diversity of national systems of social policy of EU25. Within post-war Western Europe, comparative social policy theorists have identified a variety of social policy regimes; we initially present a fourfold classification. The traditional-rudimentary model was where the state did little to regulate labour market behaviour or redistribute income and wealth. Religion and local loyalties dictated prevailing social and political customs and restrained the operation of market forces. Agricultural production dominated and the extended family internalised childcare and provisions for the elderly. Greece, Portugal, Southern Italy and Spain up until the 1960s and 1970s are often cited as exhibiting behaviour approximating to this model. Even today less than 10 per cent of the unemployed receive benefits in Greece and Italy, and less than 30 per cent in Portugal and Spain.

The liberal-individualist or Anglo-Irish, what Esping-Andersen (1990) called the 'residual' approach, is where market forces dominate labour market behaviour, with *laissez-faire* policies resolving social welfare problems for all but the non-participants. Safety nets are provided for such groups but these are means-tested and provide minimum support so as to avoid affecting the competitiveness of enterprises or providing disincentives to work. In exchange for this assistance the beneficiary has the duty to engage in work. Thus although nearly 60 per cent of the unemployed in the UK are covered by benefits, the Job Seekers Allowance is means-tested and requires active search and co-operation with the placing agency. The predominance of economic liberalism saw the adoption of this model of social policy in Anglo-American countries, with its latest manifestation extolling the virtues of the deregulated, flexible labour market.

The adoption of this approach to social policy reflected the dominance of the common law tradition in England since the twelfth century (Botero et al., 2003). This tradition is characterised by the importance of decision-making by juries, independent judges, the supremacy of freedom of contract and an emphasis upon judicial discretion rather than codes. From England this common law tradition was exported to its former colonies such as Ireland and the US.

The alternative Romano-Germanic legal tradition, based upon civil law, evolved from Roman law and was incorporated into civil codes in France and the German States in the nineteenth century and spread throughout Western Europe via the Napoleonic Wars. This tradition favoured less-independent judges and more reliance on both substantive and procedural codes as opposed to judicial discretion, whilst viewing juries as relatively unimportant. This civil law tradition also favoured regulation rather than markets and contracts. The conservative-corporatist model of social policy emerged from this tradition. This approach is much more willing to constrain market forces by establishing legal rights for workers and citizens. Such rights are designed to prevent class conflicts and establish limited political influence for workers. The development of social insurance is favoured as a means of providing a safety net without requiring a significant redistribution of income and wealth. In contrast with the two previous systems, coverage rates are much higher with the proportion of the unemployed who receive benefits over 81 per cent in Belgium and 70 per cent in Germany. This model is associated with Catholic social thought as well as with the development of modern Germany and the Roman-Germanic labour law system discussed above. The dominance of this model amongst the founding Member States explains the evolution of Social Europe outlined in section 1.2 above.

Finally, in the social democratic model the state becomes the vehicle for breaking the constraints which market forces impose upon workers' social, economic and political behaviour. In general, regulations protecting workers are in these systems introduced by socialist and social-democratic governments to benefit their political constituencies. In this model social insurance is typically universal and contains elements of redistribution. Denmark and Sweden are usually considered to be closest to this universalistic regime. Here funding of the relatively generous support provided for the disadvantaged typically relies upon the attainment of full employment. In turn, this requirement leads to tripartite decision-making in the labour market where bargaining becomes centralised and active manpower policies are pursued to encourage the social partners to internalise inflation and employment externalities into the wage-fixing process. The corporatist policies pursued by the Nordic countries in the 1970s and 1980s are the usual example given of this variant.

Underlying the attempts to classify the different European traditions of social policy are competing theories of institutional choice. Botero et al. (2003) identify three major theories of institutional choice: the efficiency theory, the political power theory and the legal theory. The efficiency theory views institutions as adjusting to ensure that the needs of society are efficiently met. Each society chooses a system and level of social protection, labour market regulation, and taxes and benefits which is socially optimal. External changes such as globalisation eventually result in institutional change to ensure adjustment to the changed economic environment. We examine this approach in more detail in Chapter 4, where we consider the different philosophies underlying approaches to employment regulation in North America and Europe.

According to the political power theory, institutions emerge and are modified to suit the preferences of those with political power and their supporters. Voting and the actions of special interest groups result in institutional change motivated by a desire of the winners to redistribute power and wealth in their favour. Finally, the legal theory holds that a country's legal tradition determines its approach to social policy and regulation. Countries with a common law tradition favour *laissez-faire* with market failures being largely addressed by freedom of contract and private litigation. In contrast, those countries with a civil code tradition are more likely to countenance direct regulation and subversion of markets.

As noted above, at Lisbon in March 2000 the European Council agreed the need to modernise social policy, the resulting European Social Agenda being ratified at their Nice meeting in December 2000. This renewed emphasis upon social and employment policies within the EU coincided with a swing of political power to centre-left parties in the Member States. In particular, the election victories of Blair and Schröder have been interpreted as a break with 'old' social democratic policy-making, which was perceived to have failed to deliver its core economic objectives (Glynn, 1998), and the emergence of a 'Third Way' response to neo-liberalism. A key element of the philosophy of 'modernising' social democrats is a rejection of the anti-market bias of the 'old' state intervention, and the acceptance of the need to redesign welfare systems and labour market regulations in the face of the needs of the 'New Economy' (to be examined in Chapter 4). The full nature and extent of these developments, and their consequences for the ESM, remain unclear. It is evident however that the economic and social objectives of labour market regulation within the EU are now more directly juxtaposed than previously, a tendency that Giddens (2000) suggests is inevitable in the new economic and social environment.

The economic history of the European social model has been reinterpreted by Eichengreen and Iversen (1999) reflecting a new orthodoxy. Strong European economic growth after the Second World War was, in their view, based upon Fordist technology supported by solidaristic wage bargaining. Whilst centralised wage bargaining compressed the distribution of wages and was associated with the growth of welfare programmes and labour market regulation, these were sustainable given the prevailing production technologies. This can be termed Stage 1 of Social Europe's evolution (see Figure 1.1). With the emergence of flexible specialisation and the growth of holistic firms, labour market institutions and employment regulations no longer sustained the EU's competitiveness in the fast-growing sectors of the global market (Gual, 1998). The perceived overexpansion of welfare and regulation was now identified as a cause of chronic unemployment amongst the unskilled, falling male participation rates (through early retirement and permanent disability), and slow employment growth in the high-tech and service sectors. In the UK this emergence of euro-sclerosis coincided with the political ascendancy of neo-liberalism. As a response the Thatcher government invoked a programme of deregulation, privatisation and reform of employment and trade union legislation with the objective of creating

STAGE I

Challenge	FORDISM
Prevailing Philosophy	CONSERVATIVE-CORPORATIST AND SOCIAL DEMOCRATIC
Policy Response	EUROPEAN SOCIAL MODEL

↓

STAGE II

Challenge	EURO-SCLEROSIS
Prevailing Philosophy	NEO-LIBERALISM
Policy Response	DE-REGULATION AND FLEXIBLE LABOUR MARKETS

↓

STAGE III

Challenge	NEW ECONOMY AND GLOBALISATION
Prevailing Philosophy	THIRD WAY(S)
Policy Response	REGULATION FOR COMPETITIVENESS

Figure 1.1 The evolution of the European social policy

more-flexible labour markets and reducing the power of core workers ('insider-power'). This we have classed as Stage II in our Anglo-Saxon variant of the evolution of Social Europe (Figure 1.1), though the associated policies of privatisation and competitive tendering in the shrunken public sector were widely adopted throughout the EU.

The establishment of European Monetary Union (EMU) has intensified the concern that an EU social policy based upon levelling-up may be inconsistent with increased economic integration and continuing international competitiveness. As Otmar Issing (2000) argued, a then member of the Executive Board of the European Central Bank, what orthodox economics indicates is required instead is greater labour cost variability between and within EU labour markets, though perversely, integration itself tends to promote both greater wage interdependence and wage convergence (Andersen et al., 2000). Finally, globalisation has been identified as a further reason why Social Europe is no longer sustainable. The growth of trade and capital mobility increases the resistant of demand for labour to labour costs, and rigidities in wage adjustments increase the employment consequences of regulating labour market behaviour. In extending this argument, Saint-Paul (1997) argues that Europe's rigid labour markets encourage a concentration on producing a small range of relatively secure goods and services at a late stage of their product life cycle, a specialisation associated with low market growth, low innovation, low learning externalities and therefore a low potential for European economic growth. As international trade and capital mobility increase, an international product cycle becomes established with specialisation in new goods and services in those economies with decentralised wages and 'employment-at-will'. Hence these countries over time will experience a faster growth in living standard.

We noted earlier the consensus that 'old' social democracy's economic policies had failed to produce their desired objectives of both full employment and a more egalitarian distribution of income and wealth. When this view is combined with recognition of the above economic trends and assorted insights from sociological and political research, then Giddens's 'Third Way' emerges. From this perspective traditional social democracy elevated rights above responsibilities, and modernising social democrats recognise that the modern, globalised knowledge economy requires a different steer:

> Flexible markets are essential to respond effectively to technological change. Companies should not be inhibited by the existence of too many rules and regulations. (Giddens, 2000, p. 7)

or:

> The essential function of markets must be complemented and improved by political action, not hampered by it. (Blair and Schröder, 1999)

Hence the championing of regulation for competitiveness: social regulations need to be assessed in terms of their impact on overall economic performance. This can be represented as Stage III in our evolution of Social Europe (Figure 1.1) with the emphasis now being placed on the modernisation of social policies to support the competitiveness of European producers. Since, as we noted, in Europe neo-liberalism only inspired significant and sustained policy reform in Britain, in some ways the 'Third Way' is Anglocentric. It rests upon an implicit assumption that social solidarity is insufficient to sustain Swedish- or even Dutch-style corporatist policies, these two countries having shown that it was possible to combine social solidarity and a dynamic economy; though as we note in Chapter 4, doubts remain as to the sustainability of these systems.

1.8 THE ENLARGED SOCIAL EUROPE

Our fourfold classification of social policy regimes in the EU is no longer appropriate given the recent accession of ten additional Member States

(EU25). The majority of these new members experienced a significant period under a socialist regime that effectively suppressed both labour markets and unemployment. Transition to market economies therefore required not only deep structural changes but also the creation of free labour markets and the extension of the social protection system to the unemployed. The 2004 accession was the fifth enlargement since the creation of the European Community in 1951, though this latest was the largest in terms of population (105 million), and the majority of new members have much lower levels of economic and social development than was the case in previous enlargements. The basic conditions for accession for the then 12 candidate countries were set down in the 'Copenhagen Criteria'. These include: the establishment of democratic principles and structures; the development of a functioning market economy and acceptance and transposition into national law of the whole EU legal *acquis communautaire*, including social and employment regulations.

Two common features of the labour markets of the new Member States of Central and Eastern Europe are their relatively low levels of employment and productivity. Thus enlargement caused the EU employment rate to fall from 64 per cent to 62.5 per cent and average GDP per head to fall by 13 per cent. In part, as we explain in Chapter 4 below, the low level of productivity in these countries reflects an over-reliance on employment in agriculture and the traditional industrial sectors. It is anticipated that full membership of the EU will provide a further stimulus to employment growth in these transition economies, and assist their slow convergence on the employment performance of the EU15 (Fertig, 2002). In part this stimulus reflects the reduction of institutional uncertainty resulting from compliance with the *acquis* (Belke et al., 2004). However income gaps between countries and regions will increase significantly in the EU of 25 Member States and these differences are likely to persist for decades.

The Commission initiated in 1999 a co-operation process on employment with the candidate countries, with the objective of ensuring a progressive adjustment of their institutions and policies to enable full implementation of the 'Employment' Title of the Amsterdam Treaty and the Community *acquis* in general. In addition the Commission has also tried to extend the other instruments for the development of the European social model discussed above: the Open Method of Co-ordination (OMC) and the social dialogue. However as Vaughan-Whitehead (2003) points out, most of the new Member States of Central and Eastern Europe have adopted the liberal-individualist approach to social and welfare policies. Moreover in general during the transition process these countries have paid much more attention to economic restructuring than in developing appropriate social policies for their new market economies. Indeed their adoption of deregulation and means-tested benefits, and their overall low levels of social protection together with the absence of widespread social dialogue and worker participation, has been represented as posing a significant challenge to the continuation of the European Social Model. Iankova and Turner (2004) argue that EU accession has pushed domestic actors in these new market economies towards greater social dialogue, though in some ways their current policies represent a more radical form of the regulation for competitiveness approach examined in the previous section. To what extent in combination these approaches threaten prevailing European policies is a question that is addressed in the following chapters.

1.9 CONCLUSIONS

Social policy has been an important, but rarely central, element of EU policy. Nevertheless the main structures of the ESM have proved to be resilient, not least because of the strong popular support they attract. We have outlined above its changing importance in policy debates from the early 1970s to date. It can be argued that the underlying proposition behind the Maastricht Treaty was that economic progress would result in social progress and that, as a consequence, over time national social policies would be levelled upwards in the EU. However over the last few years a number of internal and external pressures have threatened this benign view of the future development of Social Europe. The recent emphasis upon global competitiveness and on restraining government deficits in Euroland, together with the challenges posed by enlargement, persisting high unemployment and an ageing population have in combination refocused attention on the 'modernisation' of social policies in Europe. This 'modernisation' has been seen from some viewpoints as threatening effective convergence on the liberal-individualist model (Chapon and Euzéby, 2002). In this work we examine the likelihood of this outcome, concentrating initially in Chapter 4 on the nature of the challenges to Social Europe and in the following chapters providing a detailed examination of the sustainability of current mandatory benefits and employment regulation.

A further development examined above has been the adoption of a target-based or management-by-objectives approach to policy-making, the Open Method of Co-ordination adopted in the European Employment Strategy being the most prominent example. We examine these developments in more detail in our review of European labour market developments in Chapter 4.

A common theme of our later chapters, which examine individual aspects of employment regulation, is how different national traditions of employment regulation affect the transposition and implementation of European Directives and prevent a single standardised European model. Since Regulations are absolutely binding and directly applicable to all EU Member States, they are inflexible and EU social policies have largely relied upon Directives. Directives are able to pay more regard to the prevailing national differences in legal practices and institutions through both their transposition and the implementation. As Keller (2002) explains, since according to the principle of subsidiarity Member States can freely choose all means and instruments, then there are considerable differences in the process and variations in the outcomes of transposition. Hence the impact of any Directive differs across Member States dependent upon prevailing systems of labour law and industrial relations. In the following chapter we explore the EU legal and decision-making context in more detail.

We have outlined above the evolution of social policies from an initial concern predominantly with redistribution and equity to the present emphasis upon competitiveness, equal opportunities and social inclusion. Although the quality of employment is now emphasised as well as the quantity in the modernisation of policy, post-Lisbon social policy appears subservient to the economic objectives. With the recent EU enlargement of 2004, the explicit objective is now to create minimum, rather than identical, social standards. Our later discussion assesses the implications of this shift for the future development of the ESM. However before such discussion we need to identify the nature of the EU legal and decision-making processes and address the economic rationale for regulating labour markets and providing social insurance. These are the subjects of the following two chapters.

2. The EU legal and decision-making context

2.1 INTRODUCTION

In the first chapter we examined the development of the European Social Model (ESM) and suggested that soft law was seeking to usurp hard law as a method of co-ordination, post-enlargement. In this chapter we examine the legal basis for European social and employment policies. We also assess the impact of the successive Treaties on the decision-making processes relating to economic and social rights at work in an extended Europe. This assessment re-examines the role of the EU Commission in the decision-making process. In section 2.2 we establish the legal base supporting EU social policy, following this in section 2.3 with an explanation of the central role played by the EU Member States in the implementation of EU social policy. Section 2.4 explains the importance of the transposition of EU Directives in the EU legislative process. In section 2.5 we evaluate an alternative legislative method introduced in the previous chapter: social dialogue. Social dialogue is consistent both with the development of the Open Method of Co-ordination and with soft *acquis* prevailing over hard law. Section 2.6 introduces some of the problems generated by the previous reliance upon hard law, whereas in section 2.7 we re-examine the role of the European Court of Justice (ECJ) in determining social policy. Globalisation together with increased economic integration have renewed fears of social dumping, which are introduced and analysed in section 2.8. The principle of subsidiarity as a basis for dividing responsibilities for social policy legislation is critically examined in section 2.9. Finally, we build on the opening chapter's tracing of the historical development of the ESM in providing a reassessment of the appropriateness of the overarching legal framework.

As recorded in Chapter 1, the EU Commission has periodically sought to expand the extent of the EU's social activities under its social action programmes. For instance the Commission's Social Action Plan of 1989 marked pivotal progress towards developing 'Social Europe'. It was built upon a belief that providing a common European standard in economic, social and monetary activities would bring about closer integration, an aim set in the Preamble of the Treaty of Rome. We note that it was not until 1992, when the

Maastricht Treaty was concluded, that the social aspect re-emerged, and this was later strengthened at Amsterdam in 1998 and the Nice Summit in 2000. To this end, we examine the Treaty's legal base, explain how EU labour law is made and comment on the ECJ's growing legal activism. In addition we evaluate the impact of social dialogue and the new post-Amsterdam decision-making process. Overall, this chapter assesses whether there currently exists a competent legal basis for the ESM.

In legal terms, EU membership, through being a signatory to the Treaty of Rome and its succeeding Treaties (Maastricht, Amsterdam and Nice), has had a profound affect on the constitutional frameworks of all Member States. Of most importance is the fact that, as a consequence of EU membership, European law prevails over domestic law when incompatibilities arise. To that end, EU Member States must comply; otherwise they will be held accountable before the ECJ. As Watson (1997) argues, this provides 'a new Community "Social legal order" ... resulting in "substantive social rights"'. The Member States are therefore fundamentally bound by the Treaties and the rulings of the ECJ, which provides a flexible platform for the development of EU social policy.

2.2 THE EC TREATY: ITS FOUNDATIONAL LEGAL BASE

As previously noted in Chapter 1, the Treaty forms the primary legal basis of the EU. The EU as a legal entity has only specific competencies or enumerated powers given to it by its Member States in the Treaties. As Barnard (2000) explains, 'This means that until the Community acts in these fields the Member States may act, providing they do so within the limits set by the Treaty relating to, for example free movement of goods and persons, discrimination on the grounds of nationality under Article 12' (p. 67). Therefore the supremacy of the wishes of the EU is concurrence by agreed normative standards. Thus, in terms of EU labour law, the EU Member States have agreed not to legislate directly in respect of the right to strike or the right to impose lockouts, given the variant national levels of politicisation of these issues. Prior to the Social Policy Agreement being incorporated into the EU Treaty, the only legal basis for social policy was Article 118a(1) of the Treaty of Rome. This Article provided that 'Member States shall pay particular attention to encouraging improvements, especially in the working environment, as regards health and safety of workers'. The legal basis of such a provision not only confers on the Community the power to act, but it also sets out the legislative procedure by which the measure must be adopted. This could be through simple consultation with the European Parliament and the achievement of unanimity, the co-operation procedure under Article 252 (ex Article 189c) (abolished by the Amsterdam treaty with the exception of the Title on EMU) or the co-decision procedure under Article 256 (new Article 189b). Which procedure applies to a particular measure has been disputed. For example the UK challenged the Working Time Directive 93/104/EC on the basis that the organisation of working time envisaged by the Directive was intended to achieve both job creation and social policy objectives. Hence they argued recourse should have been had to Article 100 EC (new Article 94) or Article 235 (new Article 308), both requiring unanimity in Council. The ECJ rejected these arguments, holding that since Article 118a appeared in the section dealing with social provisions it related only to measures concerning the health and safety of workers. The Court reasoned that it therefore constituted a more specific rule that Article 100 and 100a, an interpretation confirmed by the fact that the provisions of Article 100a was to apply 'save where otherwise provided in this Treaty'. The UK then argued that the link between health and safety and working time was too tenuous. The outcome of the case was unsurprising, with the UK's legal argument being rejected by the ECJ. This served to reinforce Article 118a as an autonomous legal basis for social policy measures. As previously discussed in Chapter 1, the Social Policy Agreement substantially amended Article 118a in respect of the then 11 EU Member States, and extended the areas to which qualified majority voting (the co-operation procedure) applied. More significantly, after the Amsterdam Treaty this legal basis was further revised. Accordingly Articles 137(1) and (2) now enable the Community to adopt measures, by Article 251, through a co-decision procedure. The co-decision procedure is, as Heriter (2001) notes: 'a method of co-operation that has been developed to avoid the classical forming of legislation through deadlock due to institutionalization'. Article 137(2) also gives the Council the power to 'adopt measures designed to encourage cooperation between Member States through initiatives aimed at improving knowledge, development exchanges of information and best practices, promoting innovative approaches and evaluating experiences in order to combat social exclusion'. According to Article 137(3), the Council also has the power to adopt minimum standards directives by unanimous vote, after consulting the European Parliament, the Economic and Social Committee and the Committee of the Regions, concerning:

- social security and social protection of workers;
- protection of workers where their employment contract is terminated;
- representation and collective defence of the interests of workers and employers, including co-determination, subject to paragraph 6 (which provides that the provisions of this Article shall not apply to pay, the right of association, the right to strike and the right to impose lock-out);

- conditions of employment for third country nationals legally residing in Community territory;
- financial contributions for promotion of employment and job creation without prejudice to the provisions relating to the Social Fund.

When the Council adopts a measure setting minimum requirements under Article 137(2) or (3), Member States remain free to maintain or introduce more stringent protective measures compatible with the Treaty. The principle of subsidiarity states, as discussed in the last chapter, that decisions should be taken as close as possible to those affected, and it now pervades the nature and form of all action by the EU (this will be discussed further in section 2.9). In the legislative context the principle of subsidiarity is specifically defined by Article 5(2) (ex Article 3b(2)). It requires that Community action should be taken 'only if and insofar as the objectives of the proposed action cannot be sufficiently achieved by the Member States and can therefore, by reason of the scale and effects of the proposed action, be better achieved by the Community'.

2.3 TRANSPOSING EU LEGISLATION

Though Treaties set out the broad aims of the EU's social agenda, it is the EU Commission that proposes the specific directives which seek to achieve the Treaties' aims. To that end, EU Member States must co-operate with, and act in accordance with, the will of the EU legislators. However the differing traditions in Member States of legal regulation of employment, identified in Chapter 1, lead to problems when directives are transposed into national law. For example some EU Member States pursue economic goals more predominantly, whilst others see further social protection as a priority. Such a blend of variant policy agendas often collides and causes a social and economic debate to emerge at the centre of the transposition of Directives.

For reasons that we identify in Chapter 3, the EU Commission has consistently held the view that the increased competition generated by European economic integration might by itself fail to produce both efficiency and equity. Consistent with the prevailing social philosophies in Member States, the Commission has historically favoured regulation rather than a reliance on *laissez-faire* policies. We will critically examine the rationale for this dominant view in the following chapter. The EU, since its advent under the Treaty of Rome 1957, has sought to regulate economic activities amongst the EU Member States. Alongside its economic union, the EU both politically and socially desires to regulate citizens' behaviour, both in and outside the workplace. The intervention is in terms of minimum standards, basic rights and promotion of social cohesion. EU policy therefore reflects the underlying Romano-Germanic regulatory orthodoxy. Applying Ogus's (1998) strands of categorised social and economic regulation, EU labour law emerges as a mixture of both social and economic desires. In an EU context, regulation has brought with it provisions to avoid an abuse of that power entrenched by informational advantages: advantages which may be used to exploit employees. By comparison, as Adnett (2001) observes, the UK Government's consistent view on regulation, for example, is that if there were no EU law obligations to undertake, then lower labour costs and higher employment levels may ensue. The initial aim of European social policy was to establish a 'level playing field', eradicating distortions by removing 'unfair' competition. EU social policy was also concerned with redressing unequal distribution of benefits and the costs of EU economic integration and was therefore viewed as a way of spreading the net benefits of economic integration more evenly by creating rights and transferring resources.

Primarily, as already discussed in Chapter 1, the Charter of Fundamental Social Rights of 1989 (amended at Nice) was concerned to rectify the lack of social policy. The subsequently initiated Social Action Programmes sought to incrementally create basic, minimum standards of social protection. The Social Protocol annexed to the Maastricht Treaty committed itself, in Article 1, to building 'Social Europe', whilst it also refers to: 'the need to maintain the competitiveness of the Community economy', thus preserving the EU's economic objectives. Within the EU since 1975 there has been a dominant trend towards establishing social rights. In particular the Delors legacy has maintained a consistent commitment to the Romano-Germanic approach of regulation. This Romano-Germanic approach requires the setting of standards by Member States' governments, so as to allow them to compensate for the excesses of the markets.

The EU's underlying rationale for its intervention through social and employment policies is that society as a whole should decide how to allocate resources between competing demands. Control and supervision of economic activities by government therefore maintains efficiency, fairness and safety (this will be discussed further in the next chapter). The EU since the Marshall Plan and the European Coal and Steel Community (ECSC) Treaty in the early 1950s, has made such regulatory practices commonplace. For example the Customs Union, under Article 12 of the Treaty of Rome 1957, exists in order to ensure fairness and reciprocity across Europe in terms of the removal of any hindrances to trade. With the diversity in the systems of employment relations across the EU, different national approaches to the regulations of labour standards have forced the Community to consider its own approach to legislating. Consequently it focused on flexibility before the term itself became in vogue. Even this practice of adopting minimum standards-based directives, endorsed by the Council Resolution on Certain Aspects for a European Union Social Policy, has not prevented some EU Member States from seeking to obstruct social progress. The 'floor of minimum rights' approach aims to ensure that each EU Member State conforms to a basic level of implementation. Post-Lisbon, the EU's Council has agreed that a comprehensive legislative programme is not necessary. Rather it believes in agreement on specific fields of action in order to build up core minimum social standards gradually in a pragmatic and flexible manner. Reducing the diversity of the national systems by means of rigorous approximation of laws has therefore been rejected.

2.4 THE EU LEGISLATIVE PROCESS

The Commission retains the initiative for submitting proposals for legislation. Before doing so it must now consult the social partners on the possible direction of Community action. Article 138(1) (ex Article 3(1) SPA) provides that the Commission has the task of promoting consultation between management and labour at Community level. The Treaty offers no guidance on which organisations should be consulted, though in Chapter 1 we explained the current process. Consultation for the purposes of legislation occurs in two stages. First, before submitting proposals in the social policy field, the Commission should consult management and labour about the possible direction of Community action. If after such consultation, due to last no longer than six weeks, the Commission considers that Community action is advisable, the second stage of consultation is triggered. The Commission must then consult management and labour on the content of the envisaged proposal.

2.4.1 The Legislative Route

If management and labour do not inform the Commission of their wish to negotiate collectively, the measure follows the legislative route. If the measure concerns one of the items listed in Article 137(1) (ex Article 2(1) SPA), the Council will adopt a minimum requirement Directive. If the measure concerns one of the matters listed in Article 137(3) then the Council must act unanimously after consulting the European Parliament, the Economic and Social Committee and the Committee of the Regions. Once Directives are adopted, Article 137(4) provides for the possibility of Member States entrusting the social partners, at their joint request, with the implementation. Member States do however retain the ultimate responsibility for ensuring that, by the date which the Directive must be transposed, management and labour have introduced the necessary measures by agreement.

2.4.2 The Collective Route to Legislation

The social partners at Community level may negotiate agreements that are then extended to all workers by Council 'decision'. The collective route is triggered when, at the second stage of the consultation process, the social partners inform the Commission that they would like to negotiate Community-level agreements. As noted already in the previous chapter, EU social policy now accepts that the social partners play a vital role in the legislative process. The greater usage of the open method of co-ordination in the future will enhance this role further.

2.5 SOCIAL DIALOGUE

In Chapter 1 we introduced the concept of social dialogue. Bercusson (1996) has long referred to the non-Commission legislative power as 'bargaining in the shadow of the law'. If the social partners inform the Commission of their wish to negotiate they have nine months, or longer with the agreement of the Commission, to enter into a dialogue at Community level which may lead to contractual relations, including agreements. The EU Commission must assess the validity of an agreement in the light of its content, which requires an assessment of whether those affected by an agreement have been represented. To date, in the interests of efficient bargaining, negotiation over agreements which apply generally to all employment relationships has been conducted only by the established general cross-industry organisations (ETUC, UNICE and CEEP, discussed previously), 'based on principles of autonomy and mutual recognition of the negotiation parties'.

The Open Method of Co-ordination (OMC) seeks to empower EU Member States to undertake legislative activity themselves. Whilst an attractive idea to many EU Member States, it is based on a segregation of ways and means. That is, hard law prevails when this soft law approach implemented by the Member States actually fails. The recent experience of reliance on social dialogue as a vehicle for extending and refining social policy is examined in Chapter 8.

2.6 IMPLEMENTING EU LABOUR LAW AND SOCIAL POLICY

Article 139 provides two methods of implementation of social policy. First, an agreement can be implemented 'in accordance with procedures and practices specific to management and labour and the Member States'. These provisions attach the social dialogue to the existing structures of collective bargaining and labour law in the Member States. The alternative method for implementation envisaged by Article 137(2) is for management and labour jointly to request the Commission to propose that the Council adopt a 'decision' to implement the agreement in respect of matters covered by Article 137.

In the case of the Parental Leave Collective Agreement the Commission held that the content of the Agreement and its framework nature suggested that a Directive was the most appropriate legal form, based on Article 2(1) SPA (new Article 137(1)) (equal opportunity for men and women on the labour market). The European Parliament has no formal role in this collectively negotiated legislation. A similar model has been followed in the case of legislation covering part-time work and fixed-term work. It was also followed in the sectoral agreement on the organisation of working time by seafarers which was negotiated under the collective route by the European Community Shipowners' Association (ECSA) and the Federation of Transport Workers' Unions (FST) and extended by Directive 99/63/EC to all seafarers on board every commercial seagoing ship registered in the territory of a Member State. This led UEAPME, representing small and medium-sized employers, to bring judicial review proceedings seeking annulment of the agreement and/or Directive 96/34 on parental leave, with respect to its application to small and medium-sized undertakings. The Court went on to find that notwithstanding the legislative character of Directive 96/34, it might nevertheless be of direct and individual concern to UEAPME. The Court noted that such individual concern would be present where a measure affected an applicant in a special way 'by reason of certain attributes peculiar to them or by reasons of circumstances which differentiate them from all other persons'. The ECJ dismissed UEAPME's claim. A consequence of this ruling is that social dialogue at EU level is restricted to the large and powerful groups, not necessarily to the most representative or those individuals most affected by the outcome. Bernard (2000) describes this process as legitimising the social dialogue method on a large scale, that is, empowering the majority to the detriment of the minority. Since the Parental Leave Agreement applied to all employment relationships, the signatories, in order to satisfy the requirements of sufficient collective representativity, had to be qualified to represent all categories of undertakings and workers at Community level. Since the signatories (ETUC, UNICE and CEEP) were general cross-industry organisations with a general mandate, as distinct from cross-industry organisations representing certain categories of workers and undertakings with a specific mandate, they were deemed sufficiently representative. Bercusson (1996) argues that they are representative of the interests of their members, rather than the actual number of those members, from whom they have a mandate to negotiate. In summary, whilst social dialogue is not a perfect system, given that it largely does not represent all the interests of business and the workforce, it does offer a voice – and now a strong voice – which can legislate on matters of mutual concern. In any event, social dialogue offers an opportunity for a more transnational dialogue than that offered solely by EU Member States. Further, social dialogue offers a discussion that transcends from the bottom upwards, rather than descends from the top downwards.

EU social policy decision-making and the role of the ECJ previously noted in Chapter 1, the Treaty of Amsterdam introduced a new decision-making procedure to implement the Employment Title. According to Article 125, the key provision of the new Title was that 'Member States and the Community shall, in accordance with the Title, work towards developing a coordinated strategy for employment and particularly for promoting a skilled, trained and adapted workforce and labour markets'. Article 126 makes clear that the principal actors are the Member States. In an important recognition of the diversity of social policy, the States must have regard when policy-making to 'national practices related to the responsibilities of management and labour'. Article 128 contains more provisions governing the process, since the newly-created Employment Committee, with which the Council must consult, consists of two nominees from each Member State and two from the Commission. It has an advisory status, to promote co-ordination between Member States on employment and labour market policies. Its tasks are to monitor employment policies both within the Member States and the Commission, and to formulate opinions at the request of the Commission or the Council or on its own initiative. The Employment Committee must also consult with the social partners. This procedure is the main innovation in the new Title. If the employment guidelines are not being observed by a Member State, a recommendation can be issued which is in effect a warning against failure to comply. Given the national diversity in employment relations systems and the differing economic situations, often the EU social agenda finds itself in conflict with the labour market conditions in each EU Member State. Such new legislative competences also enhance the power of the ECJ. As Sciarra (2001) notes, it makes the Court become a 'pre-Federal device', insofar as it means that the ECJ by interpreting the law effectively designs Social Europe, albeit in a piecemeal fashion. Relying upon major legislative would have been much slower and rather unlikely. Harnay and Vigoroux (2002) further argue that such legal developments have transformed Social Europe. Moreover as they observe: 'Repeated decisions by the ECJ in the direction of the constitutionalization of the initial set of European Treaties, the so-called "judicial activism" of the judges, and the growing importance of the European Jurisprudence have gradually affected not only the content of domestic law of member states but also the legal enforcement process by their nationals.' In other words, the ECJ's 'judicial activism' requires both national courts and the ECJ to work co-operatively in order to create a stronger Social Europe. As Shaw (2003) contends, 'a strong Europe is a Social Europe', since each EU Member State is relying upon the others to conduct themselves in a manner consistent with EU regulation, particularly in terms of a level playing field in the labour market. Yet as Sciarra (2001) observes, the success so far of an integrated Europe has largely been a result of judicial strategies rather than political ones. Hence the ECJ takes its rightful position at the centre of the creation and continuing enforcement of EU social policy. Throughout the remainder of this book, several case law examples will be provided in support of the notion that judicial strategies very much underpin the EU's social progress, whilst at the same time such strategies can promote economic flexibility. In the next section, an example of such judicial intervention emerges.

2.7 EU REGULATION AND FEARS OF SOCIAL DUMPING

Social dumping involves capital, and hence jobs, moving from high social protection economies to those countries with lower levels of protection for their workers. In other words, high-protection Member States are concerned that if minimum standards are not set, then some other Member States will be able to offer 'cheap labour' rates which will undercut their own producers and hence threaten their domestic employment. A celebrated example of social dumping is the closure of Hoover's plant at Dijon and its consequential relocation to Scotland (see Whiteford, 1993; and Dehousse, 1992), such movement being facilitated under the auspices of free movement and establishment of workers, principles contained in the Treaty, as discussed in Chapter 1.

Much of the EU's social agenda has been born out of a desire to combat, or more probably a fear of, social dumping, the nature and extent of which we examine more fully in Chapter 3. Consequently, using the Treaty's foundations, the EU Commission has sought to develop and enact through Directives, social policies that counteract such tendencies in the labour market. In part, social dumping can be addressed by encouraging a convergence of social security systems across the EU. Though as we show in Chapter 4, different labour market institutions and welfare systems have slowed convergence in practice, Articles 117–20 (now 136–43) of the EU Treaty facilitate this European-wide harmonisation. It is these provisions therefore which impose basic employment rights at an EU level, limiting social dumping by establishing minimum standards and creating a level playing field. In addition, as noted earlier, in order to alleviate these social dumping problems the EU Commission enacted the Posted Workers Directive in 1996 which sought to ensure that companies would apply local rates of pay and social provisions to other EU workers.

2.8 EU LABOUR REGULATION: A QUESTION OF SUBSIDIARITY?

Within the 'intervention versus *laissez-faire*' debate, to be examined in Chapter 3, there exists another critical question relating to EU labour law-making: at what level should employment be regulated? As explained above, the answer within the EU lies within the remit of the principle of subsidiarity. Many commentators (Gonzalez, 1995; Shaw, 2000; Szyszczak, 2000; Kenner, 2003) have expressed concern about the lack of clarity in this central principle. Begg et al. (1995) describe the term 'subsidiarity' as 'the most contentious abstract noun to have entered European politics' (pp. 101–2). Despite this term's sixteenth-century Calvinistic origins, its use in a contemporary context remains controversial. Economic analyses have in general demonstrated that greater efficiency is linked to greater accountability. Consequently Article 5 (ex 3b) of the Maastricht Treaty, the 'subsidiarity' principle, epitomises EU policy to enhance regulatory efficiency. This Article provides that:

> The Community shall act within the limits of the powers conferred upon it by this Treaty and of the objectives assigned to it therein. In areas which do not fall within its exclusive competence, the Community shall take action, in accordance with the principle of subsidiarity, only if and in so far as the objectives of the proposed action cannot be sufficiently achieved by the Member States and can therefore, by reason of the scale or effects of the proposed action, be better achieved by the Community. Any action by the Community shall not go beyond what is necessary to achieve the objectives of this Treaty.

Subsidiarity concerns the institutional balance of power between the EU and individual EU Member States. Subsidiarity is a provision that enables competitiveness, by means of facilitating efficient performance of tasks at the most appropriate level. In view of the deregulation–regulation debate, we now explore the benefits of each approach to reducing regulation. An example of how the EU legislation has operated under the principle of subsidiarity is its merger regulation policy. Merger policies are often instrumental in managing business restructuring in response to changing economic circumstances. However national differences in the regulation of mergers may distort the consolidation process across Member States. As a consequence the EU has enacted Merger Regulations (1986), though the Treaty of Rome contained no explicit provision for mergers. The demarcation between EU and domestic law makes this provision possible under the principle of subsidiarity.

The rationale for centralisation is that it leads to greater efficiency, since it gives visible transparency, as EU Member States' citizens and governments alike can see the legal provisions at work. Thus central co-ordination allows for standards to be clearly set and understood. These basic characteristics clearly identify the EU's approach to social policy that seeks to establish a set of minimum rights. This economic ideal also justifies the enactment of such legislation relating to insolvency, business reorganisation and transfers and collective redundancies, since in order not to distort the market, changing workers' terms and conditions is allowed.

In contrast, decentralisation purports that efficiency is produced by removing local uncertainties and responding to local preferences, hence ensuring greater accountability. Ostensibly decentralisation allows local citizens the opportunity to voice their own preferences. Its central claim is that centralisation is less responsive and accountable. Notwithstanding the above economic analysis, Begg et al. (1995) in their study remarked that: 'both centralized and decentralized forms of government could end up implementing rather similar policies' (p. 104). Their report concluded that: 'it accepts that centralization may make some sense when there are benefits to Member States in pursuing co-operative policies, and when coordination between fully sovereign countries to achieve these benefits has little credibility ... But centralization has a cost: the risk of government failure' (p. 110). Evidently the principle of subsidiarity epitomises a compromise between decentralisation and centralisation, although the fear of 'social dumping' also provides encouragement for social protection at the EU level. Thus national sovereignty versus 'a level playing field' provides the economic context under which EU labour law is made. It also explains, as will be discussed in later chapters, the growing activism of the ECJ (Sciarra, 2001; Shaw and More, 1995) in interpreting the intentions of the EU legislators in case law, enabling guidance to be given to obstructing EU Member States to ensure compliance and eliminate evasionary tactics.

The rationale for the centralisation of some labour market policies may initially appear straightforward, since retaining sovereignty at the individual national level would tend to generate protective policies in member countries designed to distort EU trade patterns. A race to the bottom (social dumping) could result as countries each try to gain a competitive advantage by reducing their domestic levels of social protection and employment regulation (Chapon and Euzéby, 2002). National governments may be tempted to pursue such beggar-thy-neighbour policies in order, say, to export unemployment to other Member States. In general, national policy spillovers need co-ordinating in the EU and only centralised policy-making provides a credible mechanism for that co-ordination. Further, if preferences differ at national and regional levels then it is possible to develop a centralised system that contains regional variations. Finally, common rules and regulations reduce the transaction costs of operating in different national economies, and promote European economic integration. Centralisation of employment regulation may however reduce the quality of information available to policy-makers and make those policy-makers less responsive to the interests of individual citizens, especially when there is a divergence of preferences across Member States. The latter follows because the more centralised is decision-making, the less effective is the movement of taxpayers as a device for promoting efficient and responsive government and the smaller the incentive for individuals to vote, thus 'government failure' becomes more likely. This loss in the accountability of decision-makers may also make 'regulatory capture' more likely, a situation where the regulator comes to represent the interests of those they are supposed to be regulating. Finally, devolution itself creates greater institutional competition. It enables individual Member States to devise their own policies, reflecting the preferences of their own voters and the idiosyncrasies of their own labour markets. As national economies compete over time, then the more successful national institutional structures will be reflected in the performance of their economy and be imitated by other Member States, whilst less-successful ones disappear.

The centralisation–decentralisation debate really centres on the benefits of increased co-ordination against the costs of reduced accountability. However in practice any actual assessment of appropriate policy jurisdiction needs to recognise that we are always operating in the real world within second-best systems. Desirable changes may sometimes make matters worse if they interact with existing distortions. Thus for example adoption of a centralised Social Fund for the training of unemployed youths may weaken the policing of those schemes for fraud, since although Member States are required to police the schemes, they have to repay any amounts recovered to the central EU budget. It follows that national governments now have fewer financial incentives to ensure that expenditure is properly targeted. In practice therefore, trying to apply the principle of subsidiarity provides no magic rule for the division of policy responsibilities between the different layers of government, though Van den Bergh (2002) attempts to provide appropriate guidelines for such rules. The success of the EU in increasing intra-union trade and mobility of resources creates additional problems for policy-makers, since policy spillovers consequently increase between Member States. In the labour market this increase in competitiveness takes the form of increasing the wage sensitivity of the demand for labour within member countries, whilst increased mobility increases the sensitivity of labour supply. Such changes increase the attractiveness of 'beggar-thy-neighbour' unilateral policies. For example suppose one Member State introduces lower social welfare contributions for domestic employers. Since increased European economic integration has increased the sensitivity of demand for labour, such policies can significantly increase domestic employment, in part because resident firms increase their share of EU markets. The resulting displacement of foreign producers causes an export of unemployment from the country that introduced the subsidy to the other EU Member States. Such policies are likely to invoke retaliation and therefore have the potential for causing a competitive deregulation of labour markets within the EU. Hence European integration has two countervailing effects. First, the increased mobility of labour between countries presents a danger for the welfare state by eroding the basis for redistributive taxation. However it also opens up new possibilities of overcoming this general problem by implementing a common tax and welfare system. Such a policy can mitigate intergenerational problems associated with welfare policies by creating a more credible commitment device (Thum and Übelmasser, 2001).

2.9 CONCLUSIONS

As this chapter has demonstrated, EU social policy inherently concerns the issue of 'efficiency' and potential conflicts with 'equity'. The advent of the EU with its internal market and its free movement of workers places much importance on competitive efficiency. The legal and institutional framework of EU social policy permits a consideration of an 'efficiency versus rights' debate, to be evaluated in the next chapter. The EU's dominant approach in the past, the so-called 'floor of rights', involves no parity of cost, unlike the alternative 'level playing field' approach. The fact that EU directives permit EU Member States to adopt more favourable provisions does not imply a parity of costs. In effect, the ESM, as discussed in this and the preceding chapter, refers to the compromise between a floor of rights approach and a levelling up of rights to high set standards amongst all EU Member States.

At the centre of EU decision- and law-making is the question of the enforcement of social protection. As this chapter has illustrated, it is often a negotiation between social and institutional rights. In particular, threats of legal enforcement often result in collective bargaining and worker participation in resolving the issue. Essentially a so-called 'floor of rights' means that social rights will either grant prerogatives or eradicate liberties. Herein lies the current struggle in the evolution of EU labour law: rights or no rights. For example in the UK, due to deregulation, an erosion in collective rights has occurred resulting in less worker participation in decision-making processes and weaker consultation. This is of concern to trade unions since they argue that strong collective rights are integral to an efficient and equitable workplace, as well as to the survival of a pluralist industrial democracy. The response to this decline, and a similar though weaker trend elsewhere in the EU, has been to revise consultation rights and to make collective bargaining legally enforceable across the EU through national works councils (to be discussed in Chapter 8). Growing fears about global competition might explain some of the reasons for EU regulation, particularly since trade predominantly displaces the unskilled in EU labour markets.

The difficulty of gaining broad political support for policy changes has led to alternative forms of decision-making and co-operation being developed. The social partners are now involved in policy-making whilst Regulations and Directives have been avoided by greater reliance on the Open Method of Co-ordination. Finally, this chapter has shown that EU Member States' policy differences have resulted in a broader debate regarding the level at which to regulate. This debate eventually turns on the application of the principle of subsidiarity. In conclusion, EU membership has been instrumental in leading to a process of harmonisation in a large number of areas of social policy, but large differences remain.

3. The economics of employment regulation

3.1 INTRODUCTION

There are three main theories attempting to explain the nature and evolution of employment law (Botero et al., 2003). According to the legal theory, a country's approach to regulation reflects its legal tradition. Thus in countries where common law dominates, the emphasis is placed upon contracts and private litigation, whilst in most civil law countries direct supervision is relied upon to address failures in the functioning of the labour market. Under the political power theory, it is the governing party and their voters who design regulations to suit their own interests and redistribute power and wealth from their opponents. In this chapter, whilst we recognise the relevance of these two approaches to understanding the evolution of European social policy, we concentrate upon a third approach: the efficiency theory. This approach argues that institutions evolve to provide the most efficient regulation of the employment relation. Each society, it argues, chooses that combination of regulation, litigation and corrective taxes and subsidies that best suits its aspirations and economic environment.

The key economic function of the labour market is to generate a match between workers and jobs, a match that maximises the level of output for the minimum amount of working time and effort. Due to the failures in the working of market forces and equity considerations, a set of institutions are required to mediate or condition the behaviour of agents to facilitate the achievement of this function. These labour institutions include social norms, collective agreements, organisations and, as we are primarily concerned with here, employment law. As Argandoña (2001) explains, these institutions set the rules of the game in the labour market, reducing transaction costs (costs associated with matching workers and employers), promoting co-operative whilst penalising opportunistic behaviour, and reducing uncertainty. That is, collectively they solve the market failures and assist the attainment of society's preferred distributional outcomes. Given the diversity of labour market behaviour and the changing cultural, economic, social and political environment, the combination of institutions that is favoured will differ between countries and over time. Thus where market failures are limited or social norms, customs and other non-legal institutions effectively correct these failures, the role of the legal framework may be relatively small. However institutions which assist the efficient operation of labour markets at one moment in time may, as that market evolves, come to harm efficiency (North, 1990).

In this chapter we concentrate upon the economic rationale for regulating the labour market and its relevance for determining the evolving general principles of labour law in Europe. Our later chapters then utilise this framework to examine the specific features of individual laws at Member State and, more particularly, at European level. Deakin and Wilkinson (1999) identify three related features of labour law which illustrate its separation from private law. The first is that the contract of employment is subject to different norms than those applied to other contracts. Second is the emergence of labour standards. These may be substantive, procedural or promotional in nature. Substantive standards are those that directly regulate the employment relationship, such as working hours or health and safety standards. Normally these set a default 'floor of rights', such as a minimum wage, from which improvements are permitted but from which derogation is not generally possible. Procedural standards, or indirect regulations, provide the legal support for collective bargaining and/or representation of workers and employers. These include laws requiring employers to consult with their workforce on certain issues, or those providing arbitration or conciliation of industrial disputes. Promotional standards incorporate policies that enhance labour market opportunities such as job creation and training. The third feature of labour law is the creation of institutions that produce, monitor and enforce labour standards. These include specialised labour courts, regulatory bodies for health, safety and equal opportunities, and conciliation and arbitration bodies.

In this chapter we initially outline the limited role of employment law according to the simple competitive model of the labour market. We utilise this model to explain the rationale for the 'at-will' employment system found in the US. This is followed by an examination in section 3.3 of the sources of market failure, which provide the basis for developing a positive role for a more extensive regulation of the employment relationship in terms of raising labour market efficiency. Equity and paternalistic reasons for intervention are then introduced. Regulations may not only produce possible benefits but are also likely to generate costs in the form of inefficiencies and dysfunctional effects on employment and distributional outcomes. These arguments are introduced and assessed in section 3.4. The determinants of compliance with regulations, and the relative attractions of waivable and targeted rights, rather than universal mandates, are then considered in section 3.5. Our discussion next turns to current debates concerned with the relationship between regulation and competitiveness, and the emphasis upon individual rather than collective employment rights. Section 3.7 contains our conclusions and explains how this chapter's analysis is developed further in the remainder of this book.

3.2 THE SIMPLE ECONOMICS OF COMPETITIVE LABOUR MARKETS

The orthodox competitive model of the employment relationship views labour as essentially no different from commodities. Workers have different preferences regarding the terms and conditions of employment available, and firms face different costs of making offers incorporating these different terms and conditions. In competitive labour markets, well-informed employers and workers are assumed to be continually seeking to improve the quality of the job-match between these preferences and cost differences. Workers who have a preference for a particular combination of wage and job characteristics, say high job security or health benefits, will gradually gravitate towards those firms who are in a position to make such offers relatively cheaply. This process ends when the current workforce's valuation of the non-wage benefits provided by the employer corresponds to the employer's costs of funding those benefits (Summers, 1989). Since conventional economic analysis assumes rational individual utility-maximising behaviour, decision-makers know their own interests best and they consistently make optimal choices given the offers available. It follows that these decision-makers will also generate socially optimal outcomes in the absence of market failures and government induced constraints and distortions. Hence a policy of *laissez-faire* promotes efficient labour markets, ensuring an optimal allocation of labour and that the terms and conditions of employment reflect the distribution of preferences and tastes subject to the constraints of a given technology and the current stock of human capital.

Implicit in this scenario is that workers have freedom of contract so that they can exercise their preferences in choosing that job opportunity which maximises their expected utility. A supportive legal framework is also required to ensure that contracts are honoured or, in the case of default, that appropriate damages are available. The freedom of employers and employees not to renew contracts, freedom of contract, provides a market discipline on decision-makers, ensuring that remuneration reflects workers' potential earnings with alternative employers and reducing the incentives for opportunistic behaviour. This abstract model of an ideal competitive environment has generated a political philosophy which has proved influential in several Member States and more particularly in the US: economic liberalism. This philosophy holds that the task of governments is to create such an environment. In particular this requires that government should police competition and ensure that any potential market-power amongst organised employers or labour is not exercised to subvert the operation of market forces. In the absence of market-power, since workers and employers are able to sign employment contracts should they wish, there is no need to require written contracts. The existence of employment-at-will therefore reflects a mutually beneficial response to the costs of drawing up contracts. This philosophy has dominated the approach to employment law in the US since the latter half of the nineteenth century. In this system where there is no written contract and the term of employment is of indefinite duration, employees are able to quit and employers fire largely without restriction (Blau and Kahn, 2002). With this at-will rule, employers avoid costly and possibly frivolous litigation when employees are discharged, and gain a sanction which deters shirking, which may otherwise be costly to monitor. Indeed this analysis assumes that employers have no incentive to fire without good cause, since employees are costly to replace and harmful reputational consequences may result. Hence the at-will system reduces non-wage unit labour costs, providing benefits to employers and all employees apart from those marginal workers who may be protected from firing by a for-cause system. Within this framework, private companies are encouraged to operate purely on the basis of the interests of their shareholders, and employees are 'outsiders' with rights strictly delimited by contracts (Parkinson, 2003).

In essence, employment-at-will represents a system of waivable employers' rights. The legal system confers rights upon employers who are then able to sell them to their employees. This 'managerial prerogative' approach means that employers do not need to gain the consent of their workers to changes in the way in which a job is carried out. Workers only retain their right to their own labour-power, but rights regarding job security, workplace safety, working time, pensions, sickness benefits and so on, are vested in employers. Hence our previous emphasis on the employment relation in competitive markets as one of a continuous process of renegotiations ignores the employer's implicit right to avoid the need for renegotiation (Deakin and Wilkinson, 1999). The flexibility of this common law approach is its chief attraction, allowing bilateral bargaining to promote efficiency. In addition it can be combined with a system of collective bargaining that may reduce the transaction costs associated with this bargaining process.

The US-style employment-at-will is just one example of the *laissez-faire* approach to employment that views any regulation as potentially welfare-reducing. Since in competitive markets decision-makers know their own interests best, any restriction on their behaviour prevents welfare-increasing trade between employers and workers. Thus mandated benefits such as occupational pensions and prohibition of certain combinations of wage and job characteristics (for example occupational health and safety restrictions), prevent decision-makers from negotiating market-based solutions. In the former case, employers and workers are prevented from negotiating their own remuneration package consistent with their own time preferences and work–leisure trade-offs. In the latter, workers with a high tolerance of the risk of industrial accidents and disease are prevented from negotiating a high risk-premium wage with employers who find it expensive to improve health and safety.

The US has witnessed a decline of trade unions, generally at a faster rate than found in the EU; this has meant that common law has become the prime arena for resolving disputes about the nature of management–worker relations. The general rule of employment-at-will has recently been subject to several major exceptions by the US courts (Muhl, 2001; Sunstein, 2001) on a State by State basis. First, under public policy exceptions an employee is wrongly dismissed when the termination is against an explicit, established public policy of the State. Thus a worker cannot be dismissed for filing a compensation case concerning workplace safety, or refusing to behave illegally. As Muhl points out, courts have at times explicitly justified this exception by the emergence of unequal bargaining power consequential on the growth of large corporations and firm-specific skills. A second exception applies in around a dozen US States who require that a covenant of good faith and fair dealing is required in all employment relationships. Here the danger of encouraging opportunistic behaviour is seen as reason for limiting employment-at-will practices, for example preventing dismissal of a worker before a large bonus or promised promotion is due. Third, employment-at-will may be tempered by courts ruling that an implicit contract is formed between an employer and employee even in the absence of a written contract.

These exceptions to employment-at-will in the US are symptomatic of fundamental problems with reliance solely on freedom of contract for policing employment relationships. In practice all governments recognise that in reality the labour market does not approach that of the perfectly competitive model. For example in addition to policing market-power, even neo-liberal governments also favour measures that improve information flows, such as health and safety information, and protect those deemed unable to express their preferences, such as children. In reality debates about the extent of regulation address the trade-off between the benefits of regulations that target correcting market failures and promoting equity objectives, and the costs of constraining and distorting market behaviour and of creating government failure. In Europe the outcome of this debate has so far been a preference for greater regulation than that found in the American system. In addition the continental European tradition is to view companies as being partly public bodies, with responsibilities that extend beyond those to their shareholders to include their employees and local communities (Parkinson, 2003).

3.3 THE RATIONALE FOR EMPLOYMENT REGULATION

An alternative to employment-at-will with its waivable employers' rights is to create non-waivable or inalienable employees' rights. Here the law confers specific rights that cannot be bargained away. This type of regulation of the employment relationship has the potential to produce beneficial effects on aggregate welfare given the presence of market failures which prevent efficient outcomes. For example unregulated private markets are unlikely to accommodate workers' demands for insurance against labour income risk. Given the dominance of human capital (their accumulated skills and knowledge) in most workers' portfolios of wealth, then employment protection may be justified as a second-best instrument for risk-sharing in the absence of insurance or a futures market for labour (Agell, 2002).

Markets may also not resolve situations where there are potential net aggregate welfare gains but some participants would lose from a change. However even where intervention would increase net social welfare it does not follow that regulations are the optimal response. It may be that establishing, or reallocating, property rights or introducing compensating cash transfers may be more efficient responses. For instance the extension of property rights may be an alternative to mandates. Thus rather than creating health and safety regulations and an enforcement agency, establishing rights to a healthy and safe working environment combined with disability and sickness benefits could provide an alternative and possibly more effective response. Similarly cash transfers offer an alternative solution to minimum wage legislation to resolve the problem of low pay, whilst transfers in kind could resolve market failures in education and training markets.

Before we discuss these alternative mechanisms, we first need to identify the source and nature of these market failures and explore the equity and paternalism rationales for employment regulation. However we should point out that typically, labour law effectively sets procedural standards, therefore creating what Deakin and Wilkinson (1999) call a space for collective bargaining. Even where the rights established are inderogable, such as a minimum wage, other options for reducing unit labour costs, such as improved utilisation of labour, are not precluded. Regulations therefore guide or channel contractual outcomes, and only in limited areas do they predetermine those outcomes in a prescribed way.

3.3.1 Asymmetric Information

The nature of the employment relationship is such that employers and employees are each likely to possess relevant information that is not available to the other party. Employees are likely to have superior information about their potential and actual productivity and their likelihood of quitting, whilst employers will have superior knowledge about the market value of work undertaken and longer-term job security and promotion prospects. Neither party are likely voluntarily to share this information with the other, for fear of reducing the likelihood of the current contract being renewed on the current terms or because such a disclosure would not be deemed credible. Asymmetries may result not only from differences in the access to information but also from differences in the ability to process that information. Employers are repeat players and quickly accumulate expertise in formulating, interpreting and finessing contracts of employment. For example retirement packages are often very complex, and understanding, verifying and holding employers to their previous agreements may be difficult for most individual workers.

Given the existence of asymmetric information, signalling creates particular problems in the matching process and even if both parties would be better off with a specific benefit included in the contract, individual bargaining may fail to generate this benefit. Take the case of an employer considering offering a contract with sickness benefits. Her problem is in distinguishing between those applicants who have a high risk of sickness-related absences and those with a low risk. She knows that in offering this particular contract she faces an adverse selection problem, in that less-healthy workers will be disproportionately attracted by this benefit. Since those with a high risk will attempt to disguise this characteristic, the firm may offer a high-wage, no-sickness pay contract so that high-risk applicants look elsewhere. Alternatively, if the firm offers sickness benefits, its wage would now be too low to attract all but the high-risk applicants. Moreover once in operation the sickness benefit scheme reduces the costs to workers of taking sick leave, the moral hazard problem, the consequence of which is higher absenteeism and a further rise in the employers' unit labour costs. Hence in a competitive market, employers who offer a sickness benefit scheme are likely over time to be displaced by those who do not. These adverse selection problems generate the potential for mandatory benefits to raise aggregate welfare.

Similar insurance-related arguments can be extended to the provision of maternity and parental benefits, and as we now explain, to employment protection. Firms have an incentive to offer workers job security, since this encourages the take-up of firm-specific training, the returns from which would otherwise be uncertain (Hashimoto, 1990). However if only one firm offers job-security provisions then it will attract applicants who believe that they have a higher probability of being discharged from their jobs. The inability of employers to discriminate between applicants with a low and high probability of being discharged reduces their incentive to provide job security. Once again mandatory job-security measures can potentially solve the adverse selection problem and raise economic efficiency (Blau and Kahn, 1999a). Though as Addison et al. (1997) point out, the more diverse are free market contracts and the more successful they are in matching the various worker types, the less likely it is that mandates will increase overall efficiency.

A further informational problem concerns worker ignorance of their legal position. Freeman and Rogers (1999) found that many US workers falsely believed that they had protection against unfair dismissal and they were also overoptimistic about the extent of their other legal rights as employees. In part this may reflect their understanding of workplace norms rather than the law, though behavioural economics and cognitive psychologists suggest that cognitive dissonance is common (Rabin, 1998). As Sunstein (2001) speculates, people's belief about what the law is, tends to reflect their belief about what the law should be. Given such misinformation, workers cannot be relied upon to bargain efficiently with employers over the terms and conditions of employment. Widespread misinterpretation of their legal position also has implications for the desirability of regulations concerning the information rights of employees, which are discussed further in Chapter 8.

There is a final asymmetric information issue that concerns regulation. Most mandated regulations initially impose additional costs on employers. What typically happens over the long term is wages adjust to compensate and the employment effects of these regulations is minimal (Nickell and Quintini, 2002). Thus over time it is the employees who pay for the new benefits in the form of lower wages than would otherwise have prevailed. However this reality is hidden from workers, given their inability to separate out the impact of a new mandate on wages. Moreover normally both government and employers wish to claim that the costs of the new regulation are borne by profits. Hence in a democracy, employees may over-demand employment rights since they systematically underestimate the costs of these policies in the form of lower wages.

3.3.2 Incomplete Employment Contracts

The simplest competitive model treats the labour market as a spot market in which employment is a simultaneous transaction of work for pay, with the rights and responsibilities of employer and employee then at an end. In reality employment contracts exist, both explicit and implicit, in order to specify the ongoing rights and responsibilities of both parties (Malcomson, 1999). Employment contracts have three main functions. Firstly, given differences in attitude to risk-taking between employers and employees, they enable parties to allocate risk in a way different from its allocation in a spot market. Risk-averse employees may be willing to accept lower average wages in return for employers, who may be less risk-averse, insuring them against wage instability. Such behaviour is consistent with the short-run rigidity of nominal wages common in EU labour markets. Secondly, they protect the returns from investment made by one party from being captured by the other, hence increasing the efficiency of, say, training decisions. Finally, they assist employers in selecting and motivating their employees, typically by linking remuneration to performance. For example in efficiency wage models, firms pay wages above the market norm in order to raise productivity or reduce employee turnover, hence higher wages may actually be consistent with lower unit labour costs.

We discuss in more detail the relationship between employment contracts and labour market behaviour in Chapter 5; here we concentrate upon the inability of contracts to prevent market failures. The presence of asymmetric information in part explains why employment contracts are not fully self-enforcing. Employment contracts are incomplete in the sense that they cannot specify the responsibilities of each party in all eventualities. The consequence of any matching by employer and worker tends to be idiosyncratic in that it has dimensions that cannot easily be quantified or communicated. For example apart from certain minimum working hours it is difficult to make explicit what the responsibilities of employees are in a given workplace. Dimensions such as attentiveness or creativeness cannot be specified in the contract, and as a result agency problems result. Similarly training investments may be too complex or multidimensional for a court to verify whether they have been carried out as specified in a contract. Finally, a lack of information about the risk of accidents or incidence of occupational diseases makes fully contingent contracts costly or perhaps unattainable.

An agency problem results when a principal, an employer in this context, hires an agent, the worker, to produce output. Given their different self-interests, a principal wishes to design mechanisms that encourage the agent to behave in a manner consistent with the employer's interests. A complete employment contract would be one that solves this agency problem. Since the employment contract is incomplete, opportunistic behaviour is possible for both parties. That is, they can exploit changes in the employment environment for their own advantage. For example consider where parties have agreed to share the costs and returns from an investment in firm-specific training. If a new, unanticipated production technology reduces the demand for this type of trained labour, then the firm may have an incentive to renege on the deal and fire the worker. Alternatively if workers with high firm-specific skills quit, they impose high turnover costs on firms, in the form of high recruitment and training costs. In changed market conditions, they may be able to use the threat of leaving, this 'insider-power', to force employers to renegotiate existing arrangements. This fear of opportunistic behaviour by either party may prevent mutually beneficial training investments from taking place. In general, any contract between employers and employees can be renegotiated by mutual consent. Reputation effects may resolve this 'hold-up' problem, since breaking an agreement now may prevent parties from making mutually beneficial agreements in the future. However reputation by itself may be insufficient, given asymmetric information and the difficulty and costs of gaining reliable information on previous behaviour. Hence government regulations that reduce the incidence of opportunistic behaviour, such as employment protection measures, can once again in principle promote efficiency.

In general it is the dominance of long-term relationships between workers and employers in modern labour markets, quantified in the next chapter, that make the incompleteness of employment contracts such an important issue. The potential for both static and particularly dynamic efficiency losses, associated with the acquisition of firm-specific training, provide a prima facie rationale for government regulation across a range of employment issues.

3.3.3 Externalities

Positive externalities arise when as a result of an employer–employee relationship there are benefits received by others who are not directly party to that contract. For example employer-provided sickness benefits may reduce the burden on general taxpayers of funding centralised income-support policies. Analogously, negative externalities arise when other parties are harmed as a consequence of an employer–employee bargain in which they had no say. Thus firms closing a particular production plant will not have taken into account the negative impact upon the local economy as a whole. Crucially the presence of externalities distorts the relationship between individual maximising behaviour and social welfare. Hence in the case of positive externalities, the social benefit of extending a company's sickness scheme exceeds the private benefits and in this case non-market mechanisms, such as mandates, may assist the beneficial expansion of such schemes. Similarly, on second-best grounds, regulations (or subsidies) that restrict the ability of firms to close plants may prevent or delay plant closures that are socially inefficient. Thus where externalities are significant in an employment-at-will system, some aspects of a worker's total compensation package may be under- or overprovided.

More generally, members of society may gain positive externalities from labour market behaviour that corresponds with their own perceptions of a just society. For instance society as a whole may believe that the costs of child-rearing should be partly borne by society as a whole or shared more equally between partners. In which case the introduction of mandatory maternity benefits, paternity and parental leave may each raise social welfare. However as with all mandates there are likely to be costs involved which need to be offset against any advantages. In a competitive market various adjustment mechanisms are possible to the adoption of mandates. For example mandatory maternity and parental leave may lead to lower wages amongst the relevant high-risk groups or a fall in their employment rates, or a general fall in wages or a rise in unit labour costs resulting in a fall in aggregate employment. These arguments are developed further in our later discussion of anti-discrimination legislation in Chapter 6.

Similarly society may prefer that there are limitations on the rights of employers to monitor their workers. Intrusive surveillance, such as hidden cameras and regular monitoring of electronic messages, may conflict with society's view as to a worker's right to privacy. Thus for example in France even prior to the European Directive on the processing of personal data (95/46/EC), the courts have been very active in declaring certain actions by employers to control and monitor their employees as unlawful (Vigneau, 2002).

The prisoner's dilemma is a special case of externalities. It describes a situation when individually rational behaviour is inefficient because it creates an outcome that is less desirable than when parties co-operate. One important labour market example is worker participation and consultation. Although the extension of industrial democracy may increase overall efficiency, the existence of non-participatory firms may prevent such extensions because they create adverse selection problems or prevent the adoption of the necessary compressed wage structure (discussed further in Chapter 8). In other words, a more efficient system may be unable to compete against less-efficient ones where asymmetric information and externalities exist. Once again, requiring all firms to adopt participation removes this constraint on the adoption of more efficient modes of behaviour.

3.3.4 Imperfect Competition

We have so far examined the rationale for regulation in a competitive market environment. However imperfect competition may exist for a variety of reasons. Dominant employers in particular occupations or in specific local labour markets may be able to use their bargaining power to subvert the competitive process. Similarly trade unions may restrict competition on the supply side of the labour market, preventing employers from negotiating with individual workers and again preventing optimal outcomes. More generally preference heterogeneity (different tastes), mobility costs and imperfect information amongst workers may all contribute to the presence of employer market-power (Bhaskar et al., 2002). In the extreme case, monopsony, we have a single hirer and freedom of contract no longer ensures that joint surpluses are maximised in the matching process. In the case of wage determination, orthodox theory even suggests that government regulation of monopsonists can, in certain circumstances, both increase the size of the joint surplus and raise overall employment. Thus minimum wage legislation may, in theory, raise both wages and employment in markets where high levels of monopsony exist.

In practice determining the extent of monopsony power and choosing the rate at which the minimum wage promotes higher employment are problematic. Monopsony power will be greater in the short run given the higher immobility of labour in that time period, though certain groups, married women with children for example, may also face significant monopsony power in the long run because of their geographical immobility. Given the diversity of market conditions a single nationwide minimum wage would either be chosen too low or must reduce employment in certain local markets. However the relatively small employment responses to both increases in minimum wages and the introduction of a minimum wage, as in the UK (Machin and Rahman, 2001; Stewart, 2004), suggests that monopsony power and other market failures may be significant in modern economies.

In addition to the case of monopsony, imperfect competition may also arise because workers are constrained to a sub-set of labour markets, not on the basis of their labour market characteristics but due to their gender, race, ethnicity or a lack or presence of trade union membership. Such discrimination results in labour market segmentation, reducing the quality of the matches made by both favoured and non-favoured groups, and lowering overall productivity levels. Moreover widespread and costly litigation may result if no general legal framework covering discrimination exists. Equal opportunities regulations, to be discussed in Chapter 6, therefore have both an efficiency and an equity rationale.

Finally, imperfect competition may be due to aggregate market failure and the presence of unemployment. Unemployed workers may have little chance to exercise choice, and their presence puts downward pressure on wages and working conditions. Thus for example industrial accident rates in the UK tend to increase with unemployment (Adnett and Dawson, 1998). Unemployment therefore may be a further source of bargaining inequality, preventing markets from generating socially desirable outcomes.

3.3.5 Public Goods, Equity and Paternalism

In certain cases individual workers cannot exercise the freedom to negotiate their own working conditions, since these have to be agreed at group or plant level. For instance on a production line the determination of the timing of breaks and shifts must be agreed collectively by the relevant workforce. These benefits are said to have public good characteristics in that the same level of benefits has to be provided to all the workers. In competitive markets the level of these benefits will be set by the marginal worker's preferences and workers will be continually moving and searching to make better matches. However this process may be inefficient and some collective mechanism, such as collective bargaining or mandated regulations, may be welfare-increasing by reducing excessive job search and labour turnover.

In practice, as noted above, many workers are subject to monopsony power and/or face heavy losses from changing their employer due to their previous investments in firm-specific training. The resulting inertia may also cause market failures, say in an underprovision of health and safety as the marginal worker places a lower valuation on safety than does the average worker in that employment. This in itself may reflect marginal workers being younger with fewer dependants than the workforce as a whole. Similar arguments may apply to maternity benefits and working time arrangements, though as always the rationale for regulation requires not only that market failures exist but that their correction generates net increases in welfare.

As already discussed in Chapter 1, employment regulations may be justified not only on efficiency grounds but because they redistribute welfare to more-deserving groups of workers from less-deserving ones or from capital. The principal justification in the traditional social democratic and liberal political agenda for employment regulation has been to confer basic human rights upon workers. More specifically, a belief that in the absence of regulation the unequal bargaining power of capital and labour will lead to inequitable outcomes has been influential in determining the historical development of policy in Europe. Indeed a hallmark of European labour markets is the strong emphasis upon redistribution: European trade unions typically compress the wage structure and governments redistribute income from high- to low-income groups (Agell, 2002).

In the competitive model of the employment relation, the initial resource endowments of individuals are taken as given. If individual resource endowments and capabilities are unevenly distributed then so will be labour market earnings. This follows, according to orthodox theory, from real wages reflecting the quality and quantity of a worker's human capital and other productivity-related characteristics. Hence those workers with relatively poor endowments may not be able to generate earning levels sufficient to avoid poverty. In orthodox theory these consequences are ones for the tax and benefit system to address, with due attention being paid to the efficiency costs of distorting market incentives. However if there are forces in labour markets and institutions which prevent some individuals from developing their potential and receiving appropriate rewards, then both social justice and economic efficiency may require labour market intervention (Kitson et al., 2000). If disadvantaged workers are crowded into sectors of the labour market where their limited resources are undervalued then a vicious circle exists, which across time and generations can lead to social exclusion. So for instance if disadvantaged workers are crowded into part-time, agency and temporary employment, as Felsted et al. (2000) argue, then policies that encourage flexible employment may promote greater inequality. Alternatively policies that extend mandatory benefits to part-time, agency and temporary workers can, when coupled with a minimum wage, reduce inequalities.

As we noted above in our discussion of externalities, where members of society have a shared vision of social justice then aggregate welfare can be raised by regulations based upon equity considerations. Thus although the use of child labour may be desirable for some employers motivated by the desire to lower unit labour costs, social concerns about education and health may lead to its prohibition. Similarly, once widespread, so-called 'blue' laws were enacted in the US which sought to encourage church attendance and promote quality family time. In democratic societies it may also be felt that all workers should have the same basic rights in the workplace that they enjoy elsewhere, such as due process and fair treatment. However regulations argued on equity grounds may have perverse effects on labour market inequality. Thus for example health and safety regulations may prohibit unskilled workers from earning relatively high incomes by taking dangerous jobs. Alternatively mandatory maternity benefits or minimum wage legislation may increase unemployment amongst respectively females and the less skilled.

In general, since it is the less-skilled workers who earn lower wages and have inferior working conditions, it is this group who will be most effected by any mandates. For example less-skilled workers, given their low earning-power, will have labour–leisure preferences that are more likely to favour longer working hours and shorter holidays. Similarly it is small organisations that are most likely to be adversely affected by regulation of working conditions. Small firms tend disproportionately to pay lower wages, have higher accident rates and are unable to rely on the laws of large numbers to absorb some of the costs of working time and family-friendly regulations (discussed in Chapters 5 and 6 respectively). This raises a question which impinges upon many current policy debates: whether small firms should be exempt from certain employment regulations. However any exclusion of small firms in employment law introduces a further set of equity issues which have to be addressed. Finally, since regulation does not in practice affect all groups in the labour market evenly, this unevenness may in a democracy have a significant effect on the popularity and therefore the sustainability of such legislation in a democracy.

Individuals cannot always be relied upon to value workplace benefits appropriately, which introduces the 'merit good' or paternalist case for mandatory benefits. Individuals may underestimate the probability and costs of serious illness or may be unable to accurately assess the value of alternative pension schemes (Rabin, 1998). These deficiencies give rise to the 'merit good' argument for mandatory sickness benefits and pension schemes (Summers, 1989). Ideally the political system would ensure that the specific benefits which are mandated reflects society's preferences about which particular merit goods it wishes to be more equally consumed.

We have identified a number of reasons why government regulation may potentially improve the functioning of the labour market. Given the large differences in the structure, organisation and development of the labour markets, as illustrated in Chapter 4, then the extent and importance of these individual market failures will differ between countries. The variations in national labour market behaviour, say between Europe and the US, are both a response to differences in regulatory regimes as well as a cause of those differences. Policies implemented in different countries and different labour markets tend to be clustered in well-defined policy models. This reflects the need to co-ordinate individual regulations because of the presence of complementarities and substitutability as well as national or regional differences in the prevailing political and economic philosophies. Thus equal pay legislation may have a limited impact on gender inequalities in the labour market if not combined with policies which target equality of opportunity, such as equal treatment and family-friendly regulations. It is therefore necessary to assess the total package of regulation to make comparisons with *laissez-faire*, rather than attempt piecemeal comparisons (Bertola, 2000). Further, as Saint-Paul (2002) points out, these complementarities may mean that it is easier to change policy through radical rather than piecemeal reforms.

Both the costs and benefits of regulations will depend upon features of the economic and employment environment in which they are implemented. For example in the US a low minimum wage and weak employment protection generate high employment and turnover amongst low-productivity workers, whilst the high cost of providing private medical insurance has the effect of encouraging American employers to reduce employment by requiring long working hours from their employees and allowing them few holidays. In continental Europe a high minimum wage promotes wage compression and lower, but more secure, employment amongst similar workers.

The process of European economic integration may itself provide a reason for increased regulation. Integration increases competitiveness, see section 3.6.1 below, and therefore causes output and employment to be reallocated in favour of the most successful producers. One consequence is that workers face increased job insecurity as the speed of these labour market adjustments increases with integration. If workers are to maintain their investment in job-specific skills then increased job-security measures may be necessary (Schöb and Wildasin, 2003). Hence the solidarity argument for promoting employment rights, characteristic of the Delors Presidency, as a means of securing workers' political support for European economic integration.

3.4 ARGUMENTS AGAINST REGULATION

As we have seen, in a competitive labour market regulation redistributes well-being and has the potential to promote efficiency. However even in the presence of significant market failures and equity considerations regulation may on balance be harmful. Though we started our analysis with the presence of market failures and developed the case for regulation, we could equally have started with the existence of regulations and pointed out how these distort market behaviour. During the 1990s, public choice theory (Orchard and Stretton, 1997) and the development of theories of government failure have been instrumental, particularly in the US and the UK, in radically changing the nature of debates concerning employment regulation and promoting widespread privatisation and deregulation (Belman and Belzer, 1997).

At its simplest level, if additional government expenditure is incurred as a result of a new regulation, say by the creation of a new enforcement agency, then the resulting collection of additional taxation will generally reduce efficiency. Taxes are likely to distort key relative prices, such as those between work and leisure or between the rates of return on human capital and financial capital. These price distortions cause labour market behaviour to deviate from that consistent with producing socially efficient outcomes. In general they discourage paid employment and therefore lead to too little specialisation or encourage the further growth of the tax-free hidden economy.

Information imperfections may also create government failure as public choice theory has emphasised. The overwhelming desire of governments to be re-elected induces two sorts of problems, Firstly, 'short-termism' where governments are biased in favour of policies where the social welfare gains are likely to be recognised by those voting in the next election. For example policies that require additional short-term expenditure to produce long-term benefits, such as improving occupational health, or requiring higher pension contributions from current workers, may be unattractive to governments facing re-election. Secondly, governments will be prejudiced in favour of approving regulations which produce concentrated benefits and widely diffused costs, since the latter may not be perceived by those affected. In such a case as extending regulations for paid holidays, although this extended mandate may reduce social welfare, it may increase government popularity. At the same time Governments may neglect areas that warrant intervention, such as improving occupational health information flows in the labour market, since the benefits are widely distributed and thus have little attraction to a

Government chasing electoral success. Together these tendencies are likely to generate a status quo bias (Saint-Paul, 2000). That is, a given regulation will create its own constituency ready to defend the gains created by the regulation. In sum, these arguments suggest that employment regulation is not a costless corrective device and Governments cannot always be relied on to intervene in a way that will increase social welfare. It follows that intervening to correct market distortions may at times be counter-productive.

Time-inconsistency arguments have been utilised to extend these criticisms of government intervention. Government policy initiatives designed to promote certain behaviour may be discontinued once that behaviour has been generated. Since decision-makers cannot be repeatedly fooled by such government behaviour, the initiative will tend not to have the intended favourable effects even in the short run. For example consider the increased interest in Europe in offering generous financial incentives to stimulate increased pension contributions amongst younger workers. Those considering taking up this incentive may deduce that once they have taken advantage of the incentive and increased their contributions, the resulting fall in government tax revenue means that governments may be encouraged to treat their pension funds less generously when they mature. In this case unless the government can develop a reputation for pursuing consistent policies over time, policy initiatives will be ignored by forward-looking decision-makers.

The economic theory of regulation provides an alternative interpretation of the sources of government failure. In Peltzman's (1976) analysis regulation is treated like any other good. Regulation confers benefits on certain labour market participants by providing subsidies or restricting competition. In a static framework these policies redistribute wealth towards particular groups, unions or employers' associations, and those groups try to retain or extend the regulations by political or financial support to politicians favouring these regulations. The economic theory of regulation can therefore explain both the introduction and the retention of inefficient regulations in the European labour market (Saint-Paul, 2000). This approach has links with the insider–outsider model (Lindbeck and Snower, 2002) which views the adoption of mandatory rights in Europe as a mechanism which restricts the ability of those without jobs (outsiders) to compete with those currently in employment (insiders). In other words employment regulation in practice empowers employees to the detriment of those not working.

Since both free markets and governments are likely to produce inefficient outcomes, the desirability of *laissez-faire* or intervention will depend upon a comparison of the relative inefficiency of the two. The resolution of this comparison will depend upon comparative advantage. In addressing this issue, Snower (1993) stresses that government is a unique economic organisation in four major respects. Firstly, governments can require universal membership of any scheme; this in principle implies that the problems of free-riding and asymmetric information can be avoided. For example they can avoid adverse selection problems by imposing a universal and uniform unemployment insurance system. Secondly, governments have special powers of compulsion, which allow them to tax or penalise those evading regulations. These same powers mean that governments may face too few incentives to use their powers efficiently, especially in a changing environment. Additionally, as we have noted, the ability of governments to redistribute income and wealth leads to the creation of pressure groups to further group interests and this again diverts resources from wealth creation. Thirdly, governments have a multiplicity of objectives, which means in principle they can implement policies that favour the public interest rather than just profits or individual utility. One consequence of this multiplicity of objectives is that citizens have difficulty in accurately assessing government performance, since governments have an incentive to emphasise any individual target that they are achieving and neglect those where they are unsuccessful. Finally, governments have restricted powers to make future governments continue existing policies and agreements. The sovereignty of each specific government has the advantage of making governments responsive to changes in the public interest. However the inability of governments to make credible long-term contracts worsens the time-inconsistency problems raised earlier.

Governments may themselves be the victims of asymmetric information and incomplete employment contracts. For example where European governments seek to reassure citizens against their abuse of power by employing a non-political civil service or establishing an independent regulatory agency for health and safety at work, then additional dangers of a self-perpetuating bureaucracy are created. If civil servants or regulators cannot easily be dismissed, rents are created for these workers as well as administrative inertia. Since productivity is often difficult to measure in the public sector, such policies create additional agency problems that cannot always be resolved by the adoption of efficient contracts.

Finally, consider the relative merits of alternative interventions into the employment relationship. Mandated benefits have two specific advantages over public provision: they allow workers more choice and they create fewer distortions of economic activity. Mandated benefits allow individual employers to offer more than the minimum entitlement and therefore partly tailor their total employment package to respond to the preferences of their current employees. In Britain for example the government's provision of universal free health care, but at minimal level, means that employees are reluctant to pay the costs of higher-quality provision even though they may have done so in the absence of government provision. Moreover mandatory benefits generate a lower deadweight loss than government-provided benefits since they only represent a tax at a rate equal to the difference between the employer's costs of providing the benefit and the employee's valuation of it (Summers, 1989). However mandated benefits only assist those with jobs and in the face of wage rigidities, which prevent wages from falling when new benefits are mandated, employment will fall. In the latter case this employment contraction will be concentrated amongst those workers most likely to receive the benefit. Hence mandatory benefits may harm those groups whom they target.

Our arguments above indicate that there can be no presumption that government intervention at either European or national level will always be harmful or beneficial. Each case has to be considered on its individual merits and the relative size and distribution of the costs and benefits compared.

3.5 COMPLIANCE

We now need to consider the factors which determine whether employers and employees actually comply with government regulations. Compliance is automatic when both employers and employees benefit from a particular regulation. When this is not the case then some combination of monitoring and penalties will be necessary to achieve compliance. The greater the costs of compliance to one party, and the smaller and more diffuse the benefits to the other, then the greater the need for an enforcement agency and the higher the likely enforcement costs. Whilst initially economists argued that fines should be set as high as possible to enhance compliance with regulations (Becker, 1968), in reality high rates of compliance are often observed when expected fines are low. This can be explained by the existence of reputation effects, and costly monitoring and litigation. Thus setting high fines may induce less compliance and reduce social welfare because more resources have to be spent on detection and prosecution (Rodríguez-Ibeas, 2002).

Sunstein (2001) examined compliance in the case of the introduction of an unfair dismissal regime. As long as the regime contains a low-cost resolution process, such as arbitration, then employers can discharge workers at a low cost whenever just cause exists. If arbitrary discharges are infrequent, then employers will be likely to comply with such a regime. Employees clearly benefit from protection against employer malice or mistakes, especially older workers who may fear opportunistic discharges in violation of implicit contracts. Hence job security legislation should be largely self-enforcing as long as a low-cost (to both parties) resolution process exists. Health and safety regulations are less likely to be self-enforcing. New regulations may have a significant impact upon a firm's profitability and may reduce the wages of workers most tolerant of risk. Moreover even those workers who may benefit from the lower risk may lack the information, or ability to interpret it, thus requiring the agency to initiate enforcement proceedings. Here an enforcement agency is likely to be needed to conduct education and dissemination, as well as monitoring and prosecution. The optimal behaviour of such agencies is further discussed in Chapter 5.

3.5.1 Derogation and Alienable Rights

Our discussion above has mostly assumed that regulations involve granting inalienable or non-waivable rights to workers that contain fixed entitlements or default rules. As we discussed above, many combinations are possible. As Collins (2002) points out, British working time regulations created a maximum working hours standard (48) which is inalienable by workers. Similarly the right to four weeks of paid holiday is inalienable, though the timing of the holiday is subject to individual agreement or management direction. However rights in relation to night work, daily rest, the weekly day of rest and rest periods are alienable by contrary agreements through collective bargaining or workforce agreements. More generally, as we noted in Chapter 1, a recent tendency in European social policy has been to allow the social partners flexibility in adapting Directives by enabling derogation through collective bargaining. In this sub-section we analyse the economic rationale for such an approach.

In principle, conventional economic analysis suggests that alienable or waivable rights should be preferred. This preference rests upon the Coase theorem which states that if transaction costs are zero then the initial allocation of any entitlement does not matter (Coase, 1960). That is, parties will bargain to an efficient outcome regardless of the legal rule. For example consider the case of employment protection considered by Sunstein (2001). If an employer wishes an at-will contract and workers are largely indifferent, the actual contract will provide for at-will employment regardless of the property rights established by employment law. If the waivable legal rule is at-will then it has no effect, whilst if it is for just cause then the parties will eventually bargain to an at-will contract.

As we noted above, when a mandatory provision is imposed then the associated costs are largely borne by workers in the form of lower wages or benefits or employment. Hence mandatory regulations have uncertain effects on the distribution of income and wealth, in the presence of significant insider-power these costs may be borne disproportionately by outsiders (the unemployed and entrants). Waivable employment rights may therefore have a superior distribution effect. However if workers gain waivable rights, can they be relied upon to exercise those rights effectively? While this remains an empirical question, our earlier discussion of the extent of ignorance regarding workers' existing rights, together with significant evidence of excessive optimism and myopia (Rabin, 1998), suggests caution. Since trade unions provide an information-synthesising role and have access to expert advice too costly for individuals, union waivers seem preferable to individual ones in general. Hence a further rationale for trade unions is that they may help to solve the public goods problem inherent in workplace regulation and reduce the marginal costs of exercising the rights conferred upon workers (Weil, 2003). An alternative argument is for constraints, or floors, on the extent to which employees may bargain away their employment rights (Sunstein, 2001). Thus in the US, a 1994 amendment to the Age Discrimination in Employment Act (1967) allows a waiver as long as it is 'knowing and voluntary'. Or alternatively, the price at which rights may be traded may be specified. Again in the US, the Fair Labor Standards Act (1994) allows workers to waive their right not to work more than 40 hours per week, but only at a Government-determined premium rate (time and a half). Finally, Government could issue rules determining minimum non-waivable employment rights and allow workers to bargain away their rights to additional provisions (Rose-Ackerman, 1988).

The attractions of derogation when there are third parties involved who would not be a party to the bargaining away of a specific mandate are less evident. Health and safety requirements and job-security measures that prevent employers from firing workers where the consequence would be harmful to outsiders provide examples of such areas. Similarly where the mandate is derived from a desire to change social norms, such as equal opportunities or parental leave, allowing waivers in European employment laws is likely to legitimise practices often deemed undesirable by society as a whole.

3.5.2 Targeted Mandates

Most governmentally mandated benefits are intended to cover all workers (universal mandates), though they often impact upon certain groups more heavily than on others. A few mandates are directed at specific groups of workers, such as the disabled, in order to accommodate their particular needs. These 'accommodation' or targeted mandates though initially aimed at protecting certain groups have sometimes proved to be more comprehensive. For example anti-discrimination policies introduced to offer protection to women and racial minorities have frequently been used by white males facing perceived discrimination because of race or sex. As we have noted above, critics of universal benefits argue that either they are redundant in that employers would have provided the benefit anyway or they generate benefits which are valued less than the costs of providing them. The analysis of targeted mandates differs from that for universal mandates in that employers are legally constrained in how they respond to targeted mandates in ways which do not apply with universal mandates. It is this feature which allows well-designed and carefully implemented targeted measures to be particularly effective.

Jolls (2000) argues that where anti-discrimination law ensures that protected workers do not suffer wage and employment disadvantages, and when the targeted benefit is worth more to the worker than it costs the employer, then both the wage and employment of the targeted group will rise. If distributional considerations favour these beneficiaries, these laws may be desirable even given that some costs are borne by non-disadvantaged workers and/or employers (Donohue, 2001). Moreover this assessment can hold even when, say because of poverty, the disadvantaged worker values the benefit at less than its cost. However when the legislation is only partly effective in preventing wage or employment discrimination, targeted mandates hurt their intended beneficiaries. Jolls notes that disabled workers are spread throughout the employed workforce, whereas females tend to experience occupational crowding into specific segments. Moreover it is usually easier to police wage discrimination than employment discrimination. When a targeted mandate is introduced for disabled workers, since employers have protected and unprotected workers in similar jobs who can readily compare their salaries, then the employer will shift some of the costs of compliance by reducing their employment of disabled workers. In the case of female workers, occupational crowding may prevent an accessible reference group, and avoidance of the targeted mandate predominantly takes the form of increased wage discrimination that obviates the need for employment adjustment. Hence when targeted mandates are unable to prevent the beneficiaries from suffering wage or employment discrimination, their overall impact upon the well-being of the targeted group remains uncertain.

3.6 KEY CURRENT ISSUES

In this section we consider two issues that have aroused much recent debate. Firstly, we consider whether modern globalisation limits the ability of both national states and the EU to regulate labour market behaviour. Secondly, we examine the extent to which employment rights should be individual or collective.

3.6.1 Flexibility and Competitiveness

The Lisbon Strategy, discussed in Chapters 1 and 4, seeks to ensure that the regulation of the employment relationship is consistent with maintaining EU competitiveness in the knowledge-based global economy. In this sub-section we explore the implications of targeting employment regulation at achieving international competitiveness rather than at directly raising the welfare of those in employment. The economic rationale for European integration is based upon the creation of a common market to increase the level of competition in national markets. Increased competition ensures that relatively efficient European producers gain market share, whilst the less-efficient producers contract. The extension of European integration therefore requires that factors that distort the competitive process, especially nation-specific ones, be gradually eliminated. Hence the adoption at EU level of policy in areas such as competition and the implementation of the single currency. Indeed the inclusion of an equal pay for female workers clause in the Treaty of Rome was initially inspired by French concern that their more extensive gender equality legislation would put their domestic producers at a competitive disadvantage.

As European integration has progressed there have been, as we noted in Chapter 1, changing priorities attached to economic and social objectives in policy-making. In recent years the relatively weak performance of European economies together with the growth of globalisation has raised concerns as to whether current levels of labour market regulation in the EU are compatible with global competitiveness and the emergence of the knowledge-driven economy (Collins, 2000, 2002). This increased global competitiveness has generated a new 'systems competition' which is based upon locational advantage primarily driven by the international migration of capital and labour (Sinn, 2001). This process involves a growing number of firms shifting their locations to low-wage, low-tax and less-regulated countries to gain competitive advantage. In addition, as Schöb and Wildasin (2003) argue, integration leads to a general increase in labour market flexibility that may effectively redistribute wealth away from workers towards employers.

These are hardly new phenomena: the same pressures led to competition within national states such as the 'Delaware effect' where local, regional or state governments sought to attract footloose employers by offering low levels of regulation. However what has changed is the size and number of multinational companies together with the relatively low barriers to mobility and trade that characterise the current global economic environment manifestation. As a consequence tax burdens have been shifted away from mobile companies, with labour's share of total tax revenue having risen by a third over the last 50 years (Sinn, 2001). A similar logic applies to labour market regulation, again with labour having to bear a higher proportion of the costs. This means that the incidence of the costs of regulations has changed in this new environment. Where new regulations initially impose costs on employers, a higher proportion of these is now passed on to workers in the form of lower wages or greater effort levels. Where this is not possible or is incomplete, say because of minimum wages, then the employment contraction is now greater as some multinationals switch production to less-regulated locations.

In systems competition, employment laws and labour market regulation in general have to be continually reassessed in terms of their impact on the mobility of workers and capital. Moreover socially efficient regulations, such as unemployment and sickness insurance, may not be sustainable in such a system as countries skim off anticipated net contributors by offering lower taxation regimes and deter net recipients by less-generous benefits. Hence globalisation and the associated greater systems competition threaten the existence of social welfare systems with redistributive elements (Tanzi, 2002). Whilst, as we argue throughout this work, selective regulation at the European level can reduce some of these harmful consequences of systems competition, only global agreements and harmonisation can eliminate them. Moreover as Agell (1999, 2002) argues, globalisation increases the degree of risk and uncertainty that workers face and is therefore likely to increase their demand for social insurance. Hence median voters may be prepared to pay a higher price for social insurance and regulatory protection. Thus since globalisation raises both the costs of many regulations and workers' demand for them, the preferred response of policy is unclear.

At the same time, the growth of the knowledge-based economy has also created a perceived need for more flexible employment relations. As we discuss in the following chapter, jobs now have greater uncertainty or discretionary components, are more likely to involve teamwork and multitasking, and are subject to rapid change over short time periods. Hence the need for a more co-operative relationship between employers and employees and implicit, rather than explicit, contracts backed by a mutual trust that neither party will behave opportunistically (Collins, 2000).

In summary, as Collins (2002) argues, globalisation and the knowledge-based economy, or their threat, has been used to justify a radical new agenda for employment law. Instead of regulation being an agent for promoting industrial democracy or fairness, or conflict resolution, the dominant concern becomes the promotion of competitiveness. As such this 'regulation for competitiveness' approach favours partnership rather than an adversarial approach to industrial relations, and derogable rather than mandatory employment rights. In this new economic and organisational environment legal regulation needs to avoid rigid entitlements, whilst raising workers' confidence that they will be treated fairly in the increasing flexible and idiosyncratic employment relation.

3.6.2 Individual versus Collective Rights

Recent decades have seen the displacement of collective procedures by a growth in individual rights. For example in Britain, the jurisdiction of Employment Tribunals has more than doubled over the last 20 years while the coverage of collective bargaining in the workforce has halved (Hepple and Morris, 2002). One consequence of the decline of collective bargaining has been to strengthen the unilateral power of employers, in part by an extension of individual contracts on employers' standardised terms (Deakin, 1999). In countries where these trends have been most prominent, such as the UK, there has been an expansion of individual rights, nominally within a social partnership framework. However this expansion increases the costs of enforcing these rights; specifically they increase the costs of industry and firm restructuring, a favoured response to the increase in global competitiveness discussed above. Hence the tendency to encourage employers to adopt and formalise dispute resolution procedures in the workplace, and for all parties to favour such low-cost mechanisms in resolving disputes. As Hepple and Morris (2002) point out, such concerns with the costs of enforcing worker rights ignore the social costs of protecting the property and contract rights enjoyed by employers, and the need to compensate workers for the inequality of outcomes in the employment relationship.

We have reviewed arguments above that suggested that the new economy and globalisation have encouraged a movement away from rigid mandatory rights that impede co-operation and flexibility. Instead regulation should now encourage employers to make credible commitments, though not prescribe the precise content of those commitments. Collins (2002) argues that this credibility can be increased by the adoption of clear procedures regarding disputes resolution, and that legislation should provide a general structure for such systems and incentives to adopt. For example legislation on pubic interest disclosure encourages employers to create their own internal procedures to avoid public disclosure by their employees.

One further consequence of the growth of the knowledge-based economy has been increased disputes over the ownership of human capital in the workplace. More accurately, it is the growth of the new economy together with increasing employee mobility, the decline of internal labour markets and the evolution of new relational contracts, discussed in Chapters 4 and 5, which together have caused the emergence of new ownership disputes. Most firms believe that the knowledge possessed by their employees is now both their most valuable asset and their main source of competitive advantage (Stone, 2002), whereas human capital remains the dominant asset in most workers' wealth portfolios.

Conflicts about the ownership of human capital often reflect very different perceptions of the employment relationship, and in particular property rights. Employees typically assume that the skills and knowledge they acquire in a particular job belong to them and they are free to take them with them when they leave. Employers however may believe that if they enabled their employees to gain valuable skills and knowledge then they should own them and ensure that they are used to the benefit of the firm. Hence employers may impose and enforce post-employment restraints preventing former employees from using their knowledge to benefit a competitor. Stone (2002) argues that where an implicit contract promised employees access to training and networking, but also an ability to use newly acquired skills in subsequent employment, then attempts by employers to renege should be prevented. In essence this new debate about the ownership of employee capital resurrects our earlier discussion concerning how in the presence of incomplete contracts supplementary mechanisms may be required to prevent opportunistic behaviour. More generally, this debate is typical of a whole new range of issues in employment regulation in the modern flexible, boundaryless workplace (Stone, 2004).

3.7 CONCLUSIONS

This chapter has considered the rationale for employment regulation, concentrating upon behaviour in the labour market. However we should recognise that the impact of individual employment regulations is felt across the whole economy. That is, labour market policies will also affect behaviour in product markets and vice versa. Thus for example employment protection legislation appears to reduce research and development intensity in countries with decentralised industrial relations systems but encourages it in countries with centralised or co-ordinated wage-fixing systems (OECD, 2002a). Hence whilst the prime criterion for assessing employment regulations is their impact upon labour market efficiency and equity, their cross-market effects should also be considered.

We have identified a number of reasons why regulation of labour market behaviour may be desired. However we have also noted that regulations distort behaviour and are subject to government failure. The persistence of very different regulatory regimes in the US and Europe indicates that nations have found different solutions to achieving a balance between these costs and benefits of regulation. In the following chapter after a review of recent trends in European employment, we identify these differences and consider whether there are factors causing national regulatory regimes to converge. The subsequent chapters then discuss specific areas of employment regulation employing the framework introduced in these preliminary chapters.

4. Trends and issues in the European labour market

4.1 INTRODUCTION

In this chapter we analyse recent trends in the European labour market and identify the most important employment issues currently facing European policy-makers. As labour markets evolve new policy issues emerge, whilst some issues which previously concerned policymakers have either been successfully addressed or become less important. Moreover changes in the way in which the employment relationship develops will effect the effectiveness and efficiency with which previous legislation achieves its objectives. Of particular concern in this chapter is the extent to which national labour market behaviour in Europe is converging or diverging, and its implications for the application of the principle of subsidiarity.

In this chapter we provide a broad summary of labour market behaviour in the EU25, though often data availability leads to a concentration on the previous 15 Member States. Vaughan-Whitehead (2003) provides a more detailed review of labour market developments in the new Member States and their implications for the future development of Social Europe. In the following section we analyse the patterns of employment found in European labour markets. We identify the impact that both the continuing process of de-industrialisation and the growth of the knowledge-based economy have had on employment patterns. The recent growth of atypical, contingent or flexible employment is quantified, as is the changing age and gender profile of employees. In section 4.3 we explore the wage-fixing processes at work in EU labour markets and identify the pattern of wage differentials. We identify the relatively low wages of temporary workers and persisting gender wage gaps, issues that we consider further in Chapters 5 and 6. In section 4.4 we briefly examine the nature of Member States' social protection systems. Here we identify factors that are threatening the sustainability of current levels of social protection, and the adequacy of recent reforms in Europe. Section 4.5 considers the systems of industrial relations prevalent in the EU.

In section 4.6 we discuss the current key issues. This section starts with an examination of the Lisbon Strategy, introduced in Chapter 1. We critically discuss its rationale and consider what progress is being made towards its

2010 targets. In section 4.6.2 we look at recent developments in Member States' employment policies following the revision of the European Employment Strategy, also introduced in Chapter 1. The following sub-section considers mobility and immigration and how these have become more important issues with monetary union and the recent enlargement of the EU. The final sub-section brings the previous discussion together and considers whether the commitment to modernise the European Social Model taken at the Lisbon Summit will inevitably result in a convergence on the American employment-at-will model outlined in the previous chapter. In the concluding section, 4.7, we review the key trends emerging in European labour markets, re-emphasising the continuing diversity of behaviour. We then consider the implications of this chapter's main findings for the detailed examination of European social policies contained in the following chapters.

This discussion of labour market developments will also help us to explain how the different traditions of labour market regulation, introduced in the previous chapter, have evolved in the US and Europe. We will be interested to discover to what extent, if at all, the global increase in economic integration has caused cross-Atlantic convergence in labour market behaviour. Both the employment to population ratio and the annual hours worked per employed person are much higher in the US than in the EU. These differences, together with the higher productivity of American workers, explain the higher material living standards found in the US. The orthodox view is that the greater regulation of European labour markets has created rigidities which have led to Europe's relatively poor employment performance, and that in turn this regulation is a reflection of the preferences of the median voter in Europe (Saint-Paul, 2000). We critically assess this proposition in the concluding sections of this chapter and favour Blanchard's (2004) alternative interpretation that increases in productivity in Europe have led to increased leisure rather than the higher income favoured in the US.

4.2 TRENDS IN EMPLOYMENT

Following the recent enlargement the total population of the EU is over 450 million, two-thirds of whom use the same currency. Of the 1.3 million new EU15 residents in 2002 about a million of these were immigrants. Back in the mid-1970s the employment rate (the proportion of those of working age in employment) in the EU15 was 64 per cent, a percentage point above that found in the US and Japan. However by 2002 the US employment rate had risen to 72 per cent and Japan's to 68 per cent whilst in the EU15 it remained at 64 per cent and in the new Member States it was just 56 per cent. In part the lower rate in the EU15 reflected a higher unemployment rate (still 8.1 per cent in 2003), but it also reflected a slower growth of female employment in the EU and a faster rise in early retirement, especially amongst males. However between 1997 and 2002 total employment in the EU15 increased by 11.5 million, though a further 15 million net new jobs were required to hit the 2010 Lisbon Strategy target of an employment rate of 70 per cent.

Overall employment is sensitive to the phases of the business cycle, but less so than in the past (European Commission, 2003a). One cause of this change has been the continuing increase in female participation rates: in the three years up to 2002 female participation rates rose by 2.7 percentage points to 60 per cent, ten times the increase for males. This increase was reflected in a higher female employment rate that reached nearly 56 per cent in 2002 (though in the new Member States this figure was just over 50 per cent on average). The female employment rate is still 17 percentage points lower than for men and in Greece, Italy and Spain it is 30 points lower. In part the increased female employment rate reflected the marketisation of previous home production, such as meal preparation and childcare. We discuss the causes and consequences of the growth of female employment more fully in Chapter 6.

Another long-term trend has been de-industrialisation, as the relative decline of employment in the manufacturing sector is termed. By 2002 the service sector accounted for 68 per cent of total employment in the EU15, with the industrial sector employing just 28 per cent and agriculture the remaining 4 per cent, though in Greece the latter sector still accounts for 15 per cent of employment. In the new Member States the service sector is smaller and several still have sizeable agricultural sectors. Across the EU job creation is concentrated in the service sector with nearly 90 per cent of recent employment growth being in this sector, with 'real estate, renting and business activities', and 'health and social work', being the fastest-growing sub-sectors. Employment in both high-technology and knowledge-intensive services has also grown rapidly in recent years.

Partly as a result of these sectoral shifts, but also because technology is biased, there has been a decline in low-skilled employment and a demand shift favouring more-educated workers. By 2001, low-skilled workers accounted for just 39 per cent, medium-skilled for 43 per cent and high-skilled 19 per cent of European employment. A further feature of recent European employment growth is the increased use of new contractual arrangements such as part-time and fixed-term contracts. Overall 18 per cent of workers were part-time in 2002 in the EU15, though in the Netherlands the percentage was much higher at 44 per cent of total employment, reflecting the strong growth in female participation (Euwals and Hogerbrugge, 2004). Around 40 per cent of all jobs created in recent years have been part-time. The majority of part-time workers in the EU15 prefer part-time to full-time working. This reflects the increasing participation of mothers and the recent preference of young people to combine work with education and training.

About 30 per cent of the total employment growth in recent years has taken the form of new fixed-term contracts, now covering about 13 per cent of EU15 employees, though in Spain this percentage reaches 31 per cent. Amongst these workers, around a half would have preferred a permanent job but had been unable to find one, and only a tenth actually wanted temporary employment. Transitions out of temporary work and into permanent employment differ markedly across Member States with about a half achieving this transition within a year in Austria, the Netherlands and Ireland, and less than a third doing so in Italy, Greece, Spain, France, Finland and Portugal. In contrast with part-time workers, temporary workers also generally receive lower wages, by up to 15 per cent in the Netherlands, and they also receive less training. The growth of temporary working in Europe raises particular issues for policy-makers concerned with both efficiency and equity implications of more flexible working patterns. Whilst for employers the expansion of temporary employment may generate greater numerical flexibility, for most workers on such contracts it represents greater insecurity and worse prospects for progression.

The greater availability of flexible working hours arrangements, such as shift-working and annualised-hour contracts, has stimulated higher participation as well as raising productivity. Again there is wide variation in the incidence of these arrangements, with a quarter of employees in Finland and Sweden working shifts compared to just 5 per cent in Denmark. Whereas a fifth of UK employed regularly work in the evenings, less than 5 per cent of Belgians do so. Overall about 60 per cent of EU15 employees have fixed starting and ending workdays, though this proportion is only around 40 per cent in the UK where working time banking is much more common. In Chapter 5 we provide more details of these developments and examine how employment law has responded to the new challenges created.

Much has been written in recent years about the need for more flexible working practices in Europe, but it is important to distinguish between the different means of securing flexibility. The expansion of part-time and temporary employment reflects an increased ability of European firms to achieve numerical flexibility. These are part of what Michie and Sheehan (2003) call 'low-road' labour flexibility practices: they may maintain competitiveness in the short term but do not create the high innovation and training required for sustained improvements in competitiveness. For the latter, greater internal functional flexibility is required in the form of a multi-skilled and multitasking workforce able to exploit the economies of scope targeted by modern holistic organisations (Lindbeck and Snower, 2000).

The growth of part-time working is the major reason why average working hours have been declining at 0.5 per cent per year since 1990 in the EU15. This is in contrast to the US where average annual working hours have been rising even though they are already around 20 per cent higher than those found in the EU. The average number of hours usually worked by full-time employees in the EU15 was 40 hours per week in 2002, significantly higher than the 38.5 hours collectively agreed. The average hours worked amongst the EU15 ranged from over 43 hours in the UK to fewer than 38 in France, with the new Member States having longer working hours. Indeed in the UK more than 20 per cent of full-time employees regularly work more than 48 hours per week. About 15 per cent of EU15 workers normally work overtime; half of that is unpaid. Additional analyses of working hours are provided in Chapter 5.

As we discuss in section 4.6.1 below, raising the quality of European employment has become an important policy aim in recent years. Recent figures indicate that the intensity of work is increasing, with a rising proportion of European workers reporting that they are working at very high speeds or to tight deadlines. These respondents also report a greater number of stress-related health problems and greater problems in reconciling work and family life (OECD, 2003). Green and McIntosh (2001) find some evidence that these changes may be related to increased computer usage, increased competition between firms and weaker trade unions. However as yet we know little about the overall processes causing this increase in the intensity of work.

Unemployment in the EU15 declined to 8.1 per cent in 2003, though in the acceding countries the average rate is much higher at 15 per cent. Again there has been a wide divergence of experience in the EU over time; we illustrate with two examples. First, over the last 25 years unemployment in Spain has gone from 3.5 per cent to 24 per cent of the labour force and then back to 12 per cent. Second, during the 1990s Ireland moved from having the highest unemployment amongst Member States to having the lowest. Unemployment rates in the EU15 are typically higher for females, the young, the unskilled and the less educated. Long-term unemployment, those unemployed for over a year, has declined in recent years and affected just 3 per cent of the EU labour force in 2002, though this group still accounts for 40 per cent of the unemployed compared to just 7 per cent in the US. The employment rate of older workers, those between 55 and 64, was 40 per cent in 2002, though in the new Member States rates are much lower at 30 per cent. Indeed in the EU15 there are large differences in the employment rates of older workers, at one extreme there is Belgium (27 per cent) and the other Sweden (68 per cent). The changing position of older workers is discussed further in Chapter 6.

The dynamism of a labour market is not measured solely through job creation but also in terms of the speed of both labour and job turnover. Over the period 1995–99 just over 53 per cent of the male EU population of working age were continuously employed, whereas 19 per cent were unemployed for some of the period. However there is only weak evidence to support the proposition that employment insecurity has recently been increasing in Europe, with a greater disparity between the experience of workers in core and peripheral employment. Average employment tenure in the EU was 10.4 years in 2000 compared to just 6.6 years in the US (Auer and Cazes, 2003). In Britain the typical job currently lasts for around ten years, though the typical new job lasts for only 15 months (Gregg and Wadsworth, 2002). This apparent contradiction occurs because separations are much more likely in the early stages of tenure. This profile of tenure has obvious relevance to our discussion of employment protection in Chapter 7. The turnover of jobs, as opposed to workers, is also much lower in Europe than in the US, largely due to low job-creation in new enterprises.

4.3 THE PATTERN OF WAGES IN EUROPE

While overall employment growth is an important aspect of labour market performance, we have argued above that the quality of that employment is becoming increasingly important. Perhaps the most direct measure of the overall quality of jobs is average earnings; in this section we briefly review the patterns of wage in the EU.

The wage-fixing process differs across Member States, though most have a mixed, multilevel wage bargaining structure, with centralised bargaining at the national or regional level in the first stage and subsequent company- or plant-level bargaining. In general wage determination has become more decentralised, with only Belgium, Finland and Ireland having highly centralised wage formation, but only in the UK is the company the dominant level of bargaining. In contrast to most accession countries, Slovenia apart, the formal coverage of collective bargaining remains relatively high in the EU15. The collective bargaining ratio for employees varies from over 90 per cent in Belgium to fewer than 40 per cent in the UK. Since all EU15 states, apart from Sweden and the UK, have provisions for extending collective agreements to other firms, sectors or regions, coverage rates are higher than the collective bargaining rate. In general, union density is falling in Europe, especially in the accession countries, with density ranging from around 80 per cent in the three Nordic countries to under 20 per cent in Estonia, France, Hungary, Lithuania, Poland and Spain.

Nine of the EU15 and almost all of the accession countries have minimum wage laws to target low wages, whereas in the remaining countries collective bargaining is utilised for this objective. Minimum monthly wages in late 2003 were set in a range of 1000 euro or more in the Benelux countries, France, Ireland and the UK to below 200 euro in Bulgaria, Latvia and Romania. As a percentage of the median full-time wage the minimum wage varies from around 60 per cent in France to just 32 per cent in Spain. One trend apparent in many OECD countries has been growing wage inequality between the highest- and lowest-paid workers. In contrast most European countries, apart from Britain, have so far managed to avoid significant increases in wage inequality, largely because of relatively high minimum wages and the bargaining behaviour of European trade unions (Blau and Kahn, 2002). Relatively compressed wage distributions are found in Austria, Belgium, Denmark, Finland and Italy. Thus the adjustment to the changing pattern of demand for labour in Europe has been predominantly through greater employment inequality with low-skilled workers, and particularly the young, suffering high unemployment. In contrast, in the UK the decline in demand for low-skilled labour increased pay dispersion and reduced work experience amongst the 20 per cent of working age population with very low skills (Nickell, 2003a).

In line with the growth of more flexible patterns of working there has been a growth in variable pay schemes. Performance-related systems of pay have become more popular as wage systems become more decentralised; indeed profit-sharing is compulsory in France amongst companies with over 50 employees. Overall bonuses now account on average for about 11 per cent of total remuneration in the EU25.

European employers face significant non-wage labour costs such as employers' social contributions and payroll taxes. Expressed as share of total labour costs these vary from over 30 per cent in France, Hungary, Italy, Romania and Sweden to less than 15 per cent in Denmark and Ireland. The implicit tax rate on labour has been steadily rising since the early 1970s whilst that on capital and business income has been decreasing, though the most recent data suggest that rates on labour have now stabilised (European Commission, 2003a). The tax burden on labour in the EU is high by OECD standards, with over 60 per cent of the implicit tax on labour consisting of social contributions by employers and employees. This high tax burden on labour has been coupled with high unemployment and inactivity amongst the low-skilled in Europe. However there is no simple relationship between non-wage labour costs and total labour costs: the two countries with the highest gross hourly labour costs in Europe, Denmark and Sweden, are the countries with respectively, the lowest and highest shares of non-wage labour costs.

Overall in 2002 EU average monthly gross wages ranged from over 3000 euro in Denmark and the UK to 950 euro in Portugal and 150 euro in Bulgaria and Romania. Adjusting these figures for differences in price levels, that is taking the wages in terms of their domestic purchasing power, causes these gaps to become smaller by between 20–40 per cent. Apart from differences in price levels, wages crucially differ across Member States due to differences in productivity. For example productivity in Portugal remains below 75 per cent of the EU average when expressed in purchasing power and for Bulgaria and Romania it is just 20 per cent.

In terms of wage differentials, there are important inter-industry differentials in Europe, with average wages generally higher in the services sector than in industry, especially in the accession countries. There are in general significant wage premiums for working in the public sector and in larger firms, though regional differences are relatively small, with the exception of France, Germany, Greece, Portugal, Spain and the UK. Male earnings are about 16 per cent higher than are those of women; the nature and sources of this gender pay gap are explored in Chapter 6, and there is an upward age–earnings profile until the 40–50 age range. Notwithstanding compressed wage structures, returns to education are generally relatively high in the EU, and especially so in Portugal. Adjusting for workforce characteristics, part-time workers receive lower wage rates in Denmark, Ireland, Germany, the Netherlands and Portugal, but in France, Greece, Italy and Spain they receive a higher hourly rate for given worker characteristics. As mentioned above, the position of temporary workers is less ambiguous with studies consistently finding that they receive significantly lower wages in all Member States.

4.4 SOCIAL PROTECTION IN EUROPE

Social protection consists of a set of collective transfer mechanisms that protect citizens against a series of social risks from old age and disability to sickness and unemployment. High levels of social protection are one of the distinguishing features of the European Social Model, though currently this system is frequently described as being under threat (Buti et al., 2002). We outline the main internal and external threats to this system below, but initially we examine recent trends.

Member States of the European Union are autonomous when it comes to the design and operation of their social protection systems, subject to the requirement discussed previously that nationals of all Member States receive equal treatment. However they are subject to a recommendation accepted by the European Council that there should be a convergence of social protection objectives and policies. Levels of social protection generally peaked towards the end of the twentieth century, with average national social expenditure accounting for around 27.5 per cent of GDP in the EU in 2000. Whilst there has been a longer-term trend towards relative convergence, only in the last two decades have increases in social expenditure in Southern Member States promoted some long-run convergence of social indicators in the EU (Cornelisse and Goudswaard, 2002; Sosvilla-Rivero et al., 2003).

Although there are large national differences, benefits linked to old age and bereavement account for over 46 per cent of total social benefits in the EU, sickness and health 27 per cent and disability and family or children-related benefits both account for 8 per cent with unemployment benefits contributing just over 6 per cent. These benefits are largely financed by social contributions (approximately two-thirds of which comes from employers' contributions), with general government contributions funded through taxation accounting for most of the remainder.

Notwithstanding this high level of social protection, significant pockets of deprivation survive in the EU, though in general the more-developed European system is much more effective at combating poverty and discrimination than the US system (Buti et al., 2002). A conventional measure of the incidence of the risk of poverty is the proportion of the population in households having an income below 60 per cent of the national median income. In 2001 15 per cent of the EU population was so classified, corresponding to 55 million, and more than half of these lived persistently on low relative income (European Commission, 2004a). Once again there is considerable variation across Member States with the share at risk of poverty falling below 10 per cent in Sweden and rising above 20 per cent in Ireland. The Commission's 2003 Joint Report on Social Inclusion estimated that in the absence of all social cash transfers and pensions the 'at risk of poverty' share would rise from 15 per cent to 39 per cent. Unemployment was a major cause of poverty risk and a reflection of its high concentration is that over 10 per cent of individuals aged 18–59 reside in households in which no member is in employment.

At the Lisbon Summit in 2000 the European Council agreed the need to reduce the number of people living below the poverty line and in social exclusion. National Action Plans on poverty and social exclusion have been drawn up by Member States since 2003 to assist achieving this objective. However during this same period a series of factors have emerged that threaten the sustainability of even current levels of social protection. The main internal threat is the rapid increase in the dependent elderly population. Given the current age distribution of the EU population, this brings pressures for increased expenditure on retirement pensions and health care yet reduces the proportion of the population who are making social contributions and producing wealth. Over the next 30 years, if the average pension remains unchanged relative to average income, then the growth in the numbers aged over 65 in the EU alone will add 5.5 per cent of GDP to the costs of social protection. Population ageing in combination with the Stability and Growth

Pact has put pressure on Economic Monetary Union (EMU) countries to reduce government deficits and has thus increased governments' interest in reducing the generosity of retirement benefits. We examine these issues further in Chapter 6.

External threats include the greater likelihood of social dumping as a response to the need to attract mobile capital in the increasingly globalised economy. As previously mentioned, one consequence has been a gradual shift in the burden of funding social expenditure towards employees and the general taxpayer and away from capital. In addition the recent enlargement of the EU has significantly increased the diversity of social welfare policies in the EU, raising new pressures for greater co-ordination and harmonisation leading to a possible levelling-down of social protection levels. However De Grauwe and Polan (2003) find that countries with well-developed social security systems do not necessarily face a trade-off between social spending and competitiveness. On average, countries with high levels of social expenditure tend to score well in any league of competitiveness. De Grauwe and Polan interpret this empirical finding as indicating that high levels of social protection may raise the efficiency of production in the private sector. A well-functioning system of social protection makes workers feel less insecure, promotes social cohesion and encourages risk-taking. Each of these effects promotes competitiveness and in turn shields high social protection economies from externally generated risk.

Welfare-motivated migration poses a further external threat, one that the recent enlargement has highlighted. Migration to equalise labour market pressures and rewards is part of the adjustment process needed in the modern flexible labour markets. However migration that merely seeks to exploit higher welfare levels threatens the sustainability of high levels of social protection (Sinn and Ochel, 2003) and hence was a major concern of many Member States in the bargaining related to accession. We discuss this issue in more detail in section 4.6.3 below. The high levels of unemployment in the EU have also had a significant impact on the reform of Social Europe. The prevailing system of social protection was not designed to deal with persisting long-term unemployment. Both the increasing costs of unemployment benefits and their disincentive effects have motivated widespread fundamental reforms. In most Member States welfare policies have been reformed to 'Make Work Pay'. Benefit entitlements have been weakened and payments switched from unemployment benefits to 'in-work benefits' where those in low-paying jobs receive additional state payments (OECD, 2003).

Make Work Pay policies are particularly important in a European context in which employment is becoming less secure for those workers with low levels of education and skills. Such workers need to have financial incentives to retain or regain employment in the face of a deteriorating demand for their labour. Make Work Pay policies complement the previous range of policy initiatives in Europe which favoured activation of passive policies. Here the emphasis was upon creating pressure on the unemployed to increase the intensity of their job search and participate in training and job-creation programmes seeking to increase their probability of finding employment (Adnett, 2001). Make Work Pay policies complement activation policies in making the welfare support for targeted groups of the jobless, say single parents, more work-orientated (OECD, 2003).

The reasons for the much greater redistribution of income in Europe than in the US relate back to our discussion of different models of social policy in Chapter 1. However as Alesina et al. (2001) argue, it is difficult to explain this difference purely in terms of political and economic factors. Pre-tax income in the US has more variance and is more skewed than in Europe, whilst the volatility of income is lower in Europe. One possibility, discussed by Alesina et al., is that racial animosity in the US makes redistribution to the poor, who are disproportionately black, unappealing to many US voters. Alternatively surveys find that Europeans' happiness is more affected by inequality considerations due to lower social mobility and/or weaker faith in the link between individual effort and reward (Alesina and Angelotos, 2002). Since low current income is more strongly associated with low future income in Europe, it may also be that the poor put relatively greater pressure on European governments to redistribute income.

4.5 INDUSTRIAL RELATIONS

As already noted in Chapter 1, each of the EU Member States has its own system of industrial relations, providing for varying levels of worker participation and social dialogue (Blainpain and Hendrickx, 2002). These national systems are often grouped into Anglo-Irish, Romano-Germanic and Nordic systems. However as we noted in Chapter 1, due to enlargement we now have a further category: the Central and the Eastern European models of employment relations. It is important that we understand these systems and their impact upon the EU labour market as a whole. Most particularly in order to predict the consequences of the challenges, identified by Conaghan et al. (2002), facing the enlarged Europe transforming itself to a New Economy. As Supiot (2001) observes: 'new forms of organization of work, employment and collective participation are emerging' (pp. 127–8) and understanding both customs and rules of these industrial relations systems will assist us in understanding the challenges which lie ahead (Marsden, 1999). Consequently we now examine these variant systems of industrial relations by way of generic group models.

4.5.1 The Anglo-Irish Model

The UK and Irish systems of employment relations are unique, insofar as they promote a bargaining model, yet support it with voluntarist practices. Consequently in the UK there exists a mix of practices culminating in both recognised trade unions and elected representatives. In the UK a default statutory system for trade union recognition has existed since 1999, where workers can apply to have their union recognised. This system is surrounded by a plethora of ballots and agreements regarding structures, or 'bargaining units' as they are termed. As a result a union must obtain a majority in the part of the business where the union recognition is being sought. Should workers not seek statutory recognition, then British employers are free to choose, in terms of their employment relations' style, between voluntary recognition and none at all. The current UK employment relations system is now far removed from that of the 1960s to 1970s, characterised by highly active and involved trade unions, reflecting the recent dominance of deregulation and privatisation.

The Irish Trades Unions Acts of 1941 and 1975 and the 1990 Industrial Relations Act provide the basic framework for employee relations in the Irish Republic. Under Irish law, trade unions can only be active and lawful where they hold a negotiation licence granted by the Registrar of Friendly Societies. An obligation now exists for employers to recognise a trade union under its Trade Union Recognition Act 2000. Where Irish employees strike (withdraw their labour) and enter into an industrial dispute, including picketing, with their employer, in relation to the employer's refusal to 'recognise' their trade union, that dispute under Irish common law constitutes a valid trade dispute and confers certain protection on the trade union and its members. Under Irish Constitutional law, employees have a right to join a trade union and at the same time a right not to join a trade union. The law on 'closed shops' remains lawful in Eire, which ensures a level of trade union membership and activity, although a Code of Practice on Dispute Procedures exists to assist in dispute resolution and arbitration through the Irish Labour Relations Commission. Ireland, unlike the UK, has a strong tradition of tripartite agreements on pay, working conditions and social policies. For example in January 2003 the social partners and the Irish Government agreed on the terms for a new national agreement providing for a 7 per cent pay increase over 18 months, further measures on union recognition and increases in statutory redundancy pay entitlement (EIRO, 2003).

4.5.2 The Romano-Germanic Model

The French and German industrial relations systems provide more formal mechanisms for worker involvement. For example France has a complex arrangement for collective employment regulation. Typically consultation between the social partners – trade unions, employer organisations and government – is required by law. The 1982 Trade Union Law abolished the minimum threshold of 50 workers for the creation of a trade union branch. None of the five major unions represents a specific industry, sector or profession. Moreover they can establish a branch in any company and consequently several unions can be represented within one company. These nationally recognised trade unions must be consulted in all negotiated agreements and as a result all French employees are entitled to belong to a trade union. Under French law only recognised trade unions can present candidates for elections to works councils or as employee representatives. To be a recognised French trade union, principally it must show its size of membership, independence, experience and influence. Since 1936, French companies with more than 11 employees are required to annually elect employee representatives (*délégués du personnel*). Their main function is to negotiate collective agreements and present complaints to management. The recognised trade unions within a French company can also appoint representatives (*délégués syndicaux*). Since 1945, all companies with more than 50 employees have been required under French law to have a works council (*comités d'entreprise*), members of which are elected by staff and appointed by trade unions. Works councils in France act as an intermediary between the company and its employees on matters relating to the improvement of conditions of employment and of work. In particular the works council must be consulted when the company encounters economic problems. It is also the works council that is responsible for managing welfare and social funds within the company. Under French law the works council must meet at least once a month, and members of the works council are treated as protected employees and a special procedure must be followed for their dismissal.

According to the German Constitution all workers have the right to join a trade union. German Collective Agreement Law (*Tarifvertragsgestez*) requires agreements between employers and employees to be concluded regionally for each trade. This means that salaries, working time, holidays and other conditions are agreed locally. Consequently the conditions of the collective agreement are usually applied to all employees in that company within a specified region. Beyond the condition set out in these collective agreements, the general provisions of German labour law apply.

The Romano-Germanic model provides more formalised opportunities for worker involvement: since 1972 German enterprises with five or more employees must establish a works council (*Betriebsverfassungsgesetz*). The works council has the responsibility to supervise the enforcement of labour legislation and to negotiate improvements. German works councils have co-determination rights and duties in social, personnel and economic matters. Works councils have some responsibility for fixing the terms of working hours, pay, hiring, firing and holidays and settling disputes and complaints between employers and employees. Where the works council exists with more than 20 employees a German employer must inform the works council of any major operational changes brought about by economic conditions (for example redundancy situations).

The 2001 New Works Constitution Act generally strengthened the role of works councils. Councils can exist across undertakings (that is, can be company-wide) and where 200 or more workers exist a permanent works council with permanent, full-time, paid works councillors is established. Furthermore where 2000 or more workers exist, the works councillors must elect representatives to sit on the company's board of directors. Wherever agreement cannot be reached between the employer and the works council, a conciliation committee is appointed to resolve the dispute. The latter committee consists of an even number of employer and employee representatives and a neutral chair elected by the other members or appointed by the local Labour Courts. A simple majority makes the decisions of this committee.

4.5.3 The Nordic Model

The Swedish employment relations model reflects the high coverage (around 90 per cent) and unionisation rates (nearly 80 per cent) of its workforce. To that end, since the 1920s and 1930s, but now under the 1976 Joint Regulation of Working Life Act, each workplace must establish a scheme for workplace consultation. This requires the election of worker representatives, and under the legislation unions in the private sector must elect two union members to the corporate board, where 25 or more workers exist. Danish labour law, whilst steeped in collective regulation, has two central elements in terms of employment relations: the employer's managerial right and the no-strike agreement (the so-called 'peace obligation'). The main agreement exists between the key Danish social confederations, which seek to make industrial action illegal, whilst the standard rules for handling industrial disputes seek to promote mediation. Throughout, the Danish system of employment relations ensures consultation and negotiation, monitored by the National Labour Council.

4.5.4 The Central and Eastern European Models

Poland, Estonia, Slovenia and many of the new Member States, as noted in Chapter 1, adopt a union bargaining model. For example in Poland since 1991 trades unions have been permitted to organise and register with the Polish courts. In state-owned enterprises worker self-government (*samordzad zalogi*) exists which involves the establishment of a workers' council. In Estonia little collective bargaining exists, whilst in Slovenia minimum standards are enforced through codes by worker representatives. The approaches of the ten new EU Member States provide a fourth model, a hybrid of collective and minimum standards provided in codes, either enforced voluntarily or by worker bodies, unions and/or labour inspectors.

These variant models, both well established and newly developed, whilst demonstrating diverse economic and social arrangements also pose a dilemma for workplace democracy. The dilemma will be discussed in Chapter 8. Such varying models of industrial relations also evidences national differences in approach to labour law, as well as compliance and implementation methods of EU social policy. To that end, in the next section we assess the impact of these national systems on the current key issues in the EU labour market.

4.6 KEY ISSUES IN THE EUROPEAN LABOUR MARKET

In this section we assess recent developments in employment policies at both EU and Member State levels. Firstly, we examine the evolution of the Lisbon Strategy introduced in Chapter 1. We then consider how the European Employment Strategy has developed since Lisbon. Next we address the issue of geographical mobility and immigration in the enlarged EU. This section concludes with an assessment of to what extent the current modernisation of Social Europe requires convergence with the US at-will approach.

4.6.1 The Lisbon Strategy

In explaining relative employment performance across nations, sectoral factors such as the share of employment in agriculture seem to be unimportant. Instead a policy package of low taxation and low dismissal costs has been claimed to account for most of the difference between continental Europe and the high-performing non-European countries (Garibaldi and Mauro, 2002). Since the early 1970s there has been a series of shocks to which national labour markets in Europe have been exposed. These range from the oil-price increases of the 1970s and early 1980s, the fall in the relative demand for unskilled labour since the 1980s, to disinflation during the 1980s and 1990s

(Blau and Kahn, 2002). It has been hypothesised that the less-flexible labour markets of the European Union would be less able to respond to these shocks than that of the US. More particularly the system of wage bargaining in Europe largely prevented the necessary absolute and relative wage adjustments, and unemployment sharply increased. It was this failure to match the job-creation performance of the US economy, together with the fear that Europe was losing its competitiveness in the technological and knowledge-intensive sectors, which stimulated the Council of Ministers in 2000 to adopt the Lisbon Strategy.

The Lisbon Strategy was not just a response to the failure to match US performance in job creation, but also to the so-called 'demographic time bomb'. By 2030 there will be 110 million people over the age of 65 in the EU25, an increase from just 70 million in 2000. This will cause the old-age dependency ratio, the percentage of those aged 65 and over compared to those of working age 15–64, to rise from 23 per cent in 2000 to 39 per cent by 2030. As the old-age population rises the working-age population will decline from 303 million in 2002 to just 280 million in 2030. This has a direct impact on the ability of the EU to sustain its economic growth and hence maintain rising living standards, since any overall decline in employment has to be accompanied by much faster productivity growth to match the 2–2.5 per cent annual growth of recent decades. In addition to the Lisbon Strategy these demographic changes have also led to new regulations on age discrimination which we analyse in Chapter 6.

At the Lisbon Summit there was a concern about not only the quantity of European jobs being generated but also, as mentioned above, their quality. Improving the quality of European jobs was seen as important not just because of the well-being of workers but also to promote social inclusion and attain the ambitious employment targets set. Relatively high degrees of labour market flexibility seem to be associated with high shares of employees in insecure and poorly paid employment and without prospects of career advancement. To monitor these developments the European Commission identified ten indicators of job quality, covering aspects such as occupational health and safety, job security and access to training. Around a quarter of Europeans remain in jobs classified as low quality (in terms of job security and access to training), though in recent years this ratio has been stable. Interestingly this percentage is similar to the 20 per cent of employees who declare themselves dissatisfied with their job (European Commission, 2003a). Transition from low-quality jobs remains low, with around two-thirds staying in them between two consecutive years, whilst in the UK only one-third improved the quality of their job between 1995 and 2000.

The strategic goal set at the Lisbon conference was to 'become the most competitive and dynamic knowledge-based economy in the world, capable of sustainable economic growth with more and better jobs and greater social cohesion'. The overall aim of the associated economic and employment policies was to raise the overall employment rate in the EU to approach the US rate. The initial target agreed at the Lisbon Council was an overall 6 per cent rise in the employment rate to 70 per cent by 2010, nearly two-thirds of which would be additional female workers.

At the Stockholm Council, intermediate targets for 2005 were added together with a new target for the employment rate of older workers (ages 55–64): specifically it was to rise from 38.6 per cent to 50 per cent by 2010. The initial slow progress towards the latter target led to calls at the 2002 Barcelona Council for greater incentives for older workers to remain in the labour market. These were to take the form of more gradual retirement formulas and improved access to lifelong learning, and by 2010 lead to a rise of about five years in the average age at which people in the EU stop working. This emphasis upon retaining older workers in the labour market represents a dramatic change for many European countries. In most Member States early retirement and lax disability insurance schemes were, until recently, politically acceptable responses to the (then) key objective of reducing measured unemployment, especially among the young (OECD, 1994; Conde-Ruiz and Galasso, 2003). The Barcelona Council also introduced, as means of removing disincentives to female participation rates, new targets for the provision of childcare for those below the age of mandatory schooling.

With an overall employment rate of just 64.3 per cent in 2003 and unemployment returning to over 8 per cent, it became clear that the 2005 overall target of 67 per cent would be missed (though that for female workers should be met). More than 6 million jobs have been created since 1999 and long-term unemployment has been significantly reduced; however achievement of the overall 2010 target also seems unlikely with a further 20 million jobs being required. Though the recent rise in female employment rates is consistent with hitting the 60 per cent target in 2010, a ten-point increase in the employment rate of older workers is still needed (European Commission, 2004a). There has been a diversity of progress across Member States in meeting these targets. Whilst Denmark, the Netherlands, the UK and Sweden had already reached or exceeded the overall 70 per cent target by 2002, Belgium, Greece, Italy and Spain had rates below 60 per cent. Of these, Spain had managed to raise its rate by over nine points since 1997, largely through a much higher female rate, whilst Greece had made little progress, with its older workers' rate actually falling.

The emphasis in the Lisbon Strategy on raising overall employment rates represents a radical departure for European employment and social policies. Previous concerns with full employment and underemployment are now replaced by a new emphasis on the employment rate. Given that nobody has as yet suggested raising the employment rate by reducing participation in post-compulsory education, the emphasis is upon increasing the participation of mothers and elderly workers, and those amongst the 14 per cent of working-age population classified as having some form of disability. However economic theory makes no clear link between employment rates and economic and social welfare. Indeed for the individual, voluntary early retirement or full-time care of dependants may represent a welfare-increasing decision since the conventional presumption is that the main purpose of employment is to generate income to enable optimal combinations of consumption and leisure over the life cycle. Hence there is no clear rationale why marketisation of home production, such as childcare, should raise social welfare. As Freeman and Schettkat (2002) show, increasing the employment–population rate to US levels requires substantive changes in the way Europeans allocate their time and lives. There is as yet no evidence that Europeans want the longer lifetime working hours and marketisation of home production associated with higher employment rates. Only when we consider the issue of the sustainability of existing levels of social protection in Europe does a rationale for the Lisbon Strategy become clear. It is the rationale that has been reflected in the new focus for the European Employment Strategy and the Luxembourg Process.

4.6.2 Trends in European Employment Policies

As explained in Chapter 1, the Luxembourg Process has evolved into a target-based European Employment Strategy (EES). The EES was designed to be the main tool of co-ordination of, and give direction to, the employment policy priorities of Member States. Following a review in 2002 of the first five years of the EES, new guidelines and recommendations were agreed at the 2003 Thessaloniki European Council. The Council had also invited the Commission to establish a European Employment Taskforce under the chairmanship of Wim Kok whose report was integrated into the 2003/2004 Joint Employment Report. The new EES pursues three overarching objectives: full employment, promotion of quality and productivity at work, and the fostering of cohesion and inclusive labour markets. In contrast to the previous system of annual revisions to guidelines, it is intended that the new guidelines for National Action Plans remain until a mid-term review in 2006. More emphasis is placed on the results achieved and monitoring implementation together with a clearer co-ordination with the EU's broad economic policy guidelines.

The new employment guidelines consist of a more concentrated set of priorities, often supported by quantified targets. A first concern is active and preventative measures for the unemployed and inactive, with an overlying concern to 'Make Work Pay' and reduce the extent of undeclared work. The

2003/2004 Joint Employment Report documents the current emphasis on such policies in Member States but points out weaknesses in the targeting of the inactive, the evaluation of the effectiveness of activation measures and the development of comparable performance indicators. The Report also identifies a need to tackle disincentives to take up low-paid jobs, to encourage older workers to remain longer in work and address regional disparities in employment and unemployment. In addition, policies to integrate the disadvantaged need to be extended to cover the low-skilled, social benefit recipients and lone parents.

Fostering job creation and entrepreneurship are the second concern, and the Joint Employment Report documents some progress in facilitating start-ups and reducing administrative burdens on business. Access to funding for start-ups and small and medium-sized enterprises (SMEs) in general remains a weakness of current national policies, as does the stimulation of higher levels of innovation and R&D. The third concern is with the promotion of adaptability whilst avoiding the emergence of a two-tiered labour market. Greater flexibility through changes to working time patterns and the working environment are evident as documented above, though weaknesses remain in the promotion of geographical mobility and the management of restructuring.

The pursuit of the knowledge-based economy has further raised the importance of increasing the effectiveness of education and training. Currently the EU appears unlikely to meet its 2010 targets of 85 per cent of 22-year-olds completing upper secondary education and 12.5 per cent of the adult population participating in education and training. Whilst some Member States are making efforts to develop a more demand-led system of lifelong learning, and to improve the recognition and certification of non-formal or workplace learning, the Joint Report identifies the need for a greater concern with increased and more efficient investment in human capital.

Increasing the labour supply, as we noted in the previous section, has become a key concern of employment policies and the recent emphasis has been upon older workers. National ageing strategies embrace a range of policies from increases in the standard retirement age for state pensions to improving older workers' access to training and improving their working conditions. Reducing gender gaps in employment, unemployment and pay are a further key element in achieving higher employment rates. Whilst improving childcare provision has been adopted as a priority across the EU, the Joint Report identifies a failure amongst Member States to focus on the quality and cost of that provision. Gender mainstreaming has been a feature of the Employment Guidelines for several years, though the 2003/2004 Report identifies a continuing failure to assess the impact of existing systems and new policies on gender gaps in the labour market.

There have been some notable successes in employment policies in recent years. For example Denmark managed to reduce its unemployment rate from 13 per cent in 1993 to just 6 per cent by the end of that decade. Andersen (2003) attributes this achievement in part to the turn in the business cycle, but also to structural changes induced by shifts in employment policies. The activation of passive policies, introduction of employment-increasing measures and reform of the Danish unemployment insurance system have made important contributions to achieving this success. More generally, Nickell (2003b) analyses the reasons for the uneven performance in reducing unemployment in the EU. He points out that though average unemployment in Europe is relatively high compared with other OECD countries, the majority of EU states have lower unemployment than any OECD country outside Europe, including the US. The explanation for this apparent contradiction is that the Big Four continental Western European countries (France, Germany, Italy and Spain) have very high unemployment rates. In turn, Nickell (2003b) and Saint-Paul (2004a) explain the poor performance of the Big Four as indicating their failure to follow the successful reforms introduced elsewhere in the EU since 1990. More specifically, their failure to reduce the generosity and duration of unemployment benefits and police the intensity of job search amongst those receiving benefits. In addition, greater use of Active Labour Market Policies, such as targeted training and employment subsidy programmes, and improved co-ordination of wage bargaining have also been associated with successful unemployment reductions.

The above concerns are reflected in the individual guidance provided to Member States in the employment recommendations for 2004 (European Commission, 2004b). The four common recommendations concentrate upon the perceived priorities for reform: increasing the adaptability of workers and enterprises; attracting more people to enter and remain in the labour market; investing more (and more effectively) in human capital and lifelong learning; and ensuring the effective implementation of reforms through better evaluation and governance. The country-specific recommendations, first introduced in 2000, identify the most pressing issues to be addressed in each Member State. With the increasing diversity of labour market situations and behaviour following enlargement (the new Member States submitted their first National Action Plans in 2004), these individual recommendations clearly reflect the rejection of 'one-size-fits-all' solutions discussed in the opening chapter.

4.6.3 Mobility and Immigration

The creation of EMU with the abandonment of exchange rate variability as a policy instrument places greater reliance on labour market flexibility as a response to shocks. Specifically increased labour mobility, both occupational and geographic, can help to eliminate persisting imbalances in regional, national and European labour markets. At the same time the adoption of the Lisbon Strategy transformed EU-level debates about immigration, culminating in the Commission adopting a Communication on Immigration, Integration and Employment (European Commission, 2003b) in June 2003. A key element of this was the recognition that the recruitment of migrant workers and targeted immigration were necessary both to achieve the Lisbon targets and adjust to the longer-term demographic changes in the EU discussed above.

National policies amongst the Member States have been much slower in responding to this changing context. For example all of the EU15 adopted measures to restrict free entry of workers from the ten 2004 accession countries. The ten newcomers will have to wait until 2011 for the full implementation of the EU principle of the free movement of people, goods and capital.

The immigration of foreign nationals increased steadily over the 1980s to reach an absolute annual level of immigrants higher than that of the US, an estimated 1 million in 2002 (European Commission, 2003a). Overall there were around 13 million non-EU nationals in the EU15 in 2002, accounting for about 3.4 per cent of the total EU population. Whilst in many countries immigration for employment still dominates, in Denmark, Finland, France and Sweden family reunion (secondary immigration) was the single most important factor generating immigration. Whilst nearly two-thirds of the total foreign population of the EU live in Germany, France and the UK, Austria (10.3 per cent) has the highest share of people with a foreign nationality. Notwithstanding the objectives identified above, currently the employment rate of non-EU nationals is on average much lower, by nearly 14 points in 2002, than that for EU nationals. Unemployment rates of non-EU nationals are double those of EU nationals and there are large gender and pay gaps. The higher skill-levels of recent immigrants have not translated into an improved relative position in the labour market. The extent of integration of immigrants varies widely between host countries and by countries of origin (European Commission, 2003a), though in all Member States the position of women, older workers and the high rate of school drop-out of non-EU nationals has been noted.

The 2003 Communication concluded that immigration was increasingly necessary to fill the needs of the labour market as EU employment was likely to fall from 2010 even if the Lisbon targets are met. Immigration was therefore a potentially important source of additional labour supply, thereby removing a key future constraint on economic growth. The Communication argued that without a better integration of immigrants into European society sustained immigration flows would not be achieved. As a consequence it was argued that the European Employment Strategy, the Social Inclusion Process and the strategy to combat discrimination should each be revised to place greater emphasis upon the integration of immigrants. The 2004 Brussels Summit broadly adopted this strategy.

About 6 million EU citizens are resident in a Member State other than that in which they are a national. Although EU citizens have the right to reside and move freely, this figure is equivalent to only 1.6 per cent of the total EU population. In general, forecasters have grossly exaggerated the likely extent of cross-national movements of population in Europe. As Puhani (2003) shows, the sensitivity of regional migration to changes in unemployment and income are relatively low in Europe. Regional labour mobility is highest in Germany, though even here the accommodation to a rise in unemployment takes several years. Similarly the anticipated massive emigration of Spanish and Portuguese after their accession in 1986 failed to materialise. More recently, whilst the UNCHR anticipated that 25 million people would emigrate from the ex-communist bloc to the West in the 1990s, fewer than 10 per cent of this number actually moved. Currently Britain anticipates that fewer than 13 000 people a year from the new Member States would take advantage of an open door policy, though this did not prevent it tightening entry conditions immediately before enlargement. This low mobility appears to reflect the general unwillingness of Europeans to relocate both within and between national economies. Estimates of geographical mobility suggest that Americans are ten times more likely to relocate to another region than are Europeans within their current country of residence. Whilst language may explain the low cross-national mobility, identifying the sources of the very low regional mobility in the EU are more problematic. Various explanations have been advanced related to social and cultural factors and the strong negative effect of home ownership on regional mobility.

4.6.4 Americanising the European Social Model?

The last 20 years has seen a continuing debate about the contribution of European and US labour market institutions to their respective economic and social performance. The sustained superior employment record of the US, and its recent superior productivity growth, has frequently been attributed to the beneficial effects of its less-regulated employment relations. As we explained in the previous chapter, the convention has been to contrast the market-orientated, employment-at-will policies in the US with the more neo-corporatist European Social Model and its establishment of diverse, non-waivable worker rights. There have been persisting disagreements about the overall relative performance of these alternative institutional arrangements (OECD, 1994; Buchele and Christiansen, 2000; Blau and Kahn, 2002; Freeman, 2002) and their consequences for unemployment (Nickell, 1997; Siebert, 1997), human capital formation (Wasmer, 2002; Krueger and Kumar,

2003), technology adoption (Acemoglu, 2003) and wage inequality (Freeman, 2000). The Amsterdam Treaty and the adoption of the Lisbon Strategy, with its commitment to a modernisation of European social policy, have been interpreted as representing a pivotal movement towards a more competitiveness-orientated approach to social and employment policies (Adnett, 2001; Chapon and Euzéby, 2002).

Previously in this chapter we have recorded the EU's attempt to match the high US employment rates and reduce the incidence of long-term unemployment to US levels. There had been a tendency to attribute the faster job creation of the US in general, and of its service sector employment in particular, to its ability to create low-productivity 'burger-bar' jobs. In part this faster service sector, employment growth is indeed due to the greater marketisation of previously household-produced services in the US, such as food preparation and childcare. Indeed Freeman and Schettkat (2002) find that German women work as many hours as US women, once adjustment is made for the greater home production of the former. However studies have shown that the US is also more successful than the EU in creating high-productivity service sector jobs and that the proportion of the latter is increasing (OECD, 2001a, 2003).

Whilst it is difficult to establish a causal link between structural policies raising employment rates and the creation of low-pay, low-productivity jobs, such policies may have contributed to growing wage inequality. US wage dispersion has increased strongly over the last 20 years, notwithstanding that it started from an already high level. US policies encouraging flexibility and decentralised wage-setting have similarly been associated with growing wage inequality, whilst comparable trends can be observed in many Central and Eastern European countries, albeit they inherited a more egalitarian wage distribution. Elsewhere in the EU, collective bargaining and relatively high minimum wages have prevented the influence of globalisation, technological and structural changes from reducing the relative wages of low-skilled workers, though sometimes at the cost of high unemployment.

As we examine below, a significant part of the superior productivity performance of the US economy disappears when adjustment is made for the relatively low annual levels of working hours in Europe. Whilst European politicians have been eager to close the employment rate gap with the US, few have been willing to suggest a need to increase weekly working hours, or reduce public and paid holidays. Here it seems the utility of leisure is recognised, and this may be related to concerns about how the dominant work culture in the US is related to social fragmentation, as evidenced by the much higher rates of imprisonment and relative poverty in the US (Freeman, 2000). Moreover whilst productivity growth has declined dramatically in the EU over the last 40 years, both absolutely and relative to the US, Finland, Sweden and

Ireland have all managed to outperform the US in both employment and productivity growth.

At the start of this chapter we reintroduced the arguments of Saint-Paul (2002, 2004b) outlined in Chapter 3. He argues that European labour market institutions mainly reflect the rent-seeking activities of unions and employed insiders. That is, existing employees utilise their voting strength to support legislation that favours their interests at the cost of reduced employment opportunities for the unemployed and labour market entrants. Agell (2002) provides an alternative economic interpretation for the continuing popularity of the European Social Model based upon the desire for social insurance. He argues that many characteristics of the European labour market identified previously, such as employment protection, compressed wage structures and collective bargaining, can be thought of as second-best instruments of risk-sharing in the face of market failures. That is, the 'at-will' employment model creates too much risk for employees whose portfolio of wealth is dominated by their human capital. Van der Ploeg (2003) similarly challenges the supposed superiority of the *laissez-faire* approach to labour market regulation. He points out that in the real world of imperfect labour markets, social policies such as progressive taxation, conditional unemployment benefits or facilitating corporatism may induce beneficial wage moderation and hence stimulate employment growth. If, as we suggested above, aspects of elements of these protective institutions are not sustainable in the 'New Economy' then the implication is that employees will demand new ways of risk sharing.

Blanchard (2004) provides a critical examination of the fundamental proposition underlying the loss of confidence in the European Social Model: its supposed inferior performance. In Table 4.1 we reproduce some of his data. The first two columns indicate that the gap between US Gross Domestic Product (GDP) per capita and that of the EU15 has remained roughly constant since 1970. However in the middle two columns we can see that the EU15 has significantly closed the gap in productivity, as measured by output per hour

Table 4.1 Comparison of productivity and labour inputs: EU15 and US (US = 100)

	GDP per capita		GDP per hour		Hours per capita	
	1970	2000	1970	2000	1970	2000
US	100	100	100	100	100	100
EU15	69	70	65	91	101	77

Source: Extracted from Blanchard (2004).

worked. The explanation for this apparent contradiction is provided in the final two columns. The data here shows that Americans have taken the increased productivity in the form of higher incomes and material living standards. However in Europe the higher productivity has been associated also with increased leisure. If these outcomes reflect a difference in preferences between American and European workers, then neither performance is superior to the other.

In summary, whilst there are features of the US labour market which appear attractive, such as high rates of job creation, there are others which European labour markets would not wish to emulate: high levels of wage inequality for example. We return to this question of the relative attractiveness of US-style labour markets in our concluding discussion of the modernisation of Social Europe in Chapter 9. Regardless of the feasibility of transplanting US-style employment policies, the desirability of such reforms seems as yet unproven. Well-designed welfare systems providing high levels of social protection can generate sustained levels of international competitiveness (Sakellaropoulos and Berghman, 2004). The secret appears to be the periodic reform of these systems to ensure that all labour market participants have incentives to support continual restructuring to support job creation biased towards high-productivity and high-quality employment.

4.7 CONCLUSIONS

We set ourselves an ambitious target in this chapter. We have provided an outline of key recent trends in European labour markets and introduced some of their policy implications that will be examined in detail in the following chapters. In this concluding section we briefly summarise our major findings and then re-emphasise the extent and implications of diversity in the labour markets of the EU25.

A major part of this chapter has addressed the current dominant policy aim of raising European employment rates. We noted how this, in practice, means increasing the employment rates of mothers, the partially disabled and older European citizens. We identified the demographic forces that have led to this objective and the problems and disadvantages of introducing policies to achieve it, such as the further marketisation of home production and later retirement. We recorded the continuation of de-industrialisation, the intensification of work, and identified a new concern with the quality of employment opportunities in Europe. The latter in part reflected a concern that the previous stress on greater flexibility of employment had led to a neglect of issues related to the insecurity of work and marginalisation of those unable to attain permanent full-time employment.

Our review established the overall success of policies to reduce the concentration and level of European unemployment, but the need for further progress in targeting the causes of social exclusion. We noted the tendency of globalisation, new technology and structural changes to widen gaps between the low- and high-skilled workers, and the weakness of forces promoting regional and national labour market convergence. Whilst the overall decline of trade union membership was established, we noted the continuing dominance of collective bargaining in many Member States together with a trend towards more decentralised bargaining. The sustainability of high levels of social protection was considered and the nature and effectiveness of the reforms taken to ensure their survival was examined.

In presenting this review we have tried to review developments across all 25 Member States, though data availability led to a certain concentration on the previous 15 members. A danger that such a brief survey faces is the tendency to identify common trends and ignore the diversity of labour market behaviour in the EU. A common feature of our following review of employment policies is the diversity of practice in the EU and the inappropriateness of uniform EU-wide policy-making.

5. Terms of employment and workplace health and safety

5.1 INTRODUCTION

At the heart of the European Social Model is the notion that all citizens can share in the wealth that is created and hence participate fully in society. Having a job is, for most citizens, a precondition to wider social and political participation, while losing or finding a job is still a key factor in moving in and out of poverty (European Commission, 2001b). In this chapter we examine an issue central to social inclusion in Europe: workers' rights to fair employment, a safe working environment and job security. To that end, we explore and evaluate the current provisions covering the free movement of workers, health and safety (particularly working time) and future provisions in relation to atypical workers' rights. Overall the two central themes of this chapter are the drive towards the 'humanisation of work' embodied in Article 13 of the Amsterdam Treaty, and the achievement of the free movement of workers throughout the enlarged EU, initially discussed in Chapter 1. The former theme is reflected in the Working Time Directive. This places a duty on Member States to ensure that

> an employer who intends to organise work according to a certain pattern takes account of the general principle of adapting work to the worker, with a view, in particular, to alleviating monotonous work and work at a pre-determined work-rate, depending on the type of activity, and of safety and health requirements, especially as regards breaks during working time. (Preamble, Working Time Directive)

Beyond health and safety considerations lies the general principle of adaptation of work to the worker when organising the working pattern. The construction of the provision indicates that the employer is obliged to take into account these principles not solely when the employer alters patterns of work, but also at the initial organisation of working time. Consultation between the employer and the workers on the organization of working pattern is regarded as the most appropriate means of achieving the aim of the provision, especially in the case where the employer intends to organise work according to a certain pattern.

This chapter is constructed as follows. In the next section we examine the link between the free movement of workers and posted worker rights. An economic analysis of EU contractual employment rights is provided in section 5.3. Here again we identify conflicting pressures between hard law and soft law. Section 5.4 examines EU legislation being developed to address the consequences of the growth of atypical work identified in the previous chapter. The original hard law dominance of EU social policy is revisited in section 5.5 where we consider workplace health and safety regulations. In section 5.6 we concentrate upon the Working Time Directive, and the following section contains our conclusions. These case studies illustrate the continuing policy dilemma, that whilst hard law achieved minimum standards, soft *acquis* is now increasingly relied upon to deliver EU social policy goals. In drawing conclusions we will assess how effective is the 'humanisation' process of EU social policy that has emerged, considering both its social and its economic facets.

5.2 THE CASE FOR EUROPEAN WORKERS' RIGHTS

In this section we examine how the EU's categorisation of workers – fixed-term, part-time, posted – represents, in practice, varying levels of protection. As we explained in Chapter 1, a fundamental element of economic integration is the existence of free mobility of resources between Member States. The elimination of national barriers to capital and labour mobility is a key requirement in fostering increased competition based upon relative efficiency rather than protection. Enabling free movement of workers between Member States, by say mutual recognition of professional qualifications, in theory promotes convergence of productivity levels and fosters overall economic growth. However at the same time increases in the mobility of capital, especially at a time of increasing globalisation of production, increase the potential for social dumping, a process explained in Chapter 2. The movement towards defining European workers' rights represents an attempt to reconcile these conflicting pressures within an economic union. As previously discussed in Chapter 1, European citizenship was established with the Treaty of Maastricht. According to Article 17(1) of the EU Treaty, being a national of a Member State implies citizenship of the EU. EU nationals benefit by the rights established by Articles 17 to 22 of the Treaty. One of the central principles of the EU is the freedom to go from one Member State to another to work; this is also a concrete realisation of European integration. Although geographical mobility remains low in the EU, legislation encourages the posting of workers. Posted workers result when companies established in one Member State relocate their employees to a host Member State in order to supply particular services to comply with the contract they have signed. Such relocations have led to fears of social dumping as the service provider may be considered as taking advantage of cheaper labour standards in their own State to win contracts in the host State. A certain degree of protection has been considered necessary for these posted workers. Directive 96/71/EC deals with the terms and conditions of employment of such workers, ensuring that their rights are respected and that they are not subjected to unfair treatment. Regulation 1612/68 is a central text when dealing with the question of free movement of workers and their families. Various notions have been expressed throughout this Regulation. The text deals in fact with employment conditions, reiterating in Article 1 the right of free movement of workers. It is concerned with the issue of equality of treatment, as Title II provides a specific example of the application of the principle of non-discrimination on the ground of nationality. Another central issue addressed by the Regulation is the question of a worker's family. The Regulation recognises the right of the family to join the worker in the host Member State. The European Commission was still taking infringement proceedings in 2004 against Member States to ensure these rights to free movement and non-discrimination. In one 2004 case proceedings were instigated against the Netherlands, following the exclusion from the Netherlands social security system of a posted worker. In the same year the Commission asked the Court of Justice to impose a daily fine on Italy for the non-execution of a previous 2001 judgment. This had held that Italian universities had treated non-Italian foreign language assistants differently from equivalent Italian nationals in a way that amounted to discrimination on the grounds of nationality. Clearly establishing the rights to free movement and non-discrimination on the basis of nationality is a slow process.

In accordance with Council Directive 91/533 on proof of employment contract, an employer shall be obliged to notify an employee of the essential aspects of the contract or employment relationship including the place of work, the title, nature or category of the work, a brief description of work and the amount of paid leave. However Member States may provide that this Directive shall not apply to employees having a contract with a total duration not exceeding one month or if an employee has a contract of a casual and/or specific nature. In the next section we examine how these contractual terms seek to maintain a high level of employment and social protection in the extended EU. Social protection represents a fundamental component and a distinguishing feature of the European Social Model. It has been increasingly realised at EU level that social protection systems need to be adapted to the changing nature of work, where a new interplay is called for between policies designed to improve flexibility and those designed to provide security; to change in the gender balance in working life, where equal opportunities bring new issues and requirements in terms of social protection; to the ageing of the population in Europe, where the rapid growth of the dependent population is creating new needs as well as forcing the pace of pension reform; and to the need to reform the co-ordination of national social security schemes for people moving with the EU.

5.3 THE ECONOMICS OF EMPLOYMENT CONTRACTS AND RIGHTS FOR ATYPICAL WORKERS

In this section we utilise our analysis in Chapter 3 to examine the efficiency arguments for requiring explicit contracts of employment and extending rights for those in atypical employment.

5.3.1 Employment Contracts

In the conventional 'employment-at-will' model outlined in Chapter 3, employees are within a hierarchical structure in which a manager controls, monitors and assesses their performance. Contracts are largely implicit, with workers being managerially controlled *ex post* and paid largely fixed wages. In the US, the general belief is that common law defaults are generally effective at regulating contractual relationships of this kind. Employment is here preferred to the use of independent contracting due to lower total production, transaction and management costs, these latter reflecting lower search, contracting and monitoring costs for employers, as well as potential uncertainty and team production externalities. However in employment law, unlike contract law in general, typically workers who leave their employment earlier than anticipated do not have to compensate the employer for lost profits or wasted training and transaction costs. De Geest et al. (2001) provide an explanation for this anomaly based upon the efficient breaching of contracts.

The prevalence, even in the US, of explicit contracts can be explained by the presence of agency problems in an implicit contract regime. Many employed workers are granted a wide degree of autonomy to take decisions on behalf of the firm and act free of day-to-day supervision of firm owners. Formal employment contracts may facilitate this granting of discretion by making workers agents. Typically agency relationships require the creation of specific property rights enabling firm owners more fully to exploit economies of scale and scope. As James and Johnson (2001) point out, explicit contracts may involve the allocating of rights to employees, such as rights to act on behalf of the owners or internal property rights over company assets. In addition explicit contracts create and allocate specified employment and post-employment rights such as termination for 'just cause' (see the discussion in Chapter 7 below) or limitations on post-employment opportunities. Such covenants in employment contracts typically prevent an employee from working for a competitor after termination, perhaps to safeguard trade secrets or to recoup a firm's investment in general training. These covenants are becoming more common as disputes over the ownership of human capital become more frequent, reflecting the growth of the knowledge-based economy (Stone, 2002).

In the European context there has been, as noted in Chapter 3, greater recognition of the limitations of employment at will. In particular the harmful consequences of unequal bargaining power and ability to seek common law protection in such a system have been much debated. Given these concerns, the right to explicit contracts can dissuade opportunistic behaviour by both employers and workers, and prevent cognitive dissonance concerning the scope of contractual employment rights such as sickness benefits and holiday entitlements (Sunstein, 2001). These benefits from improved information flows between employers and workers are more fully examined in Chapter 8, where we explore recent directives that target improving consultation between workers and their employers.

We have so far ignored how the growth in non-standard forms of employment is effectively challenging regulatory capacity in the labour market based on the traditional dichotomy between employers and employees. For example, recently the emergence of 'economically dependent workers' (EDWs) has raised new concerns about the nature of employment contracts and the definition of the term 'employee'. Such workers do not have an employment contract as a dependent employee, but they are economically dependent upon a single employer. In other words by typically having a service contract with a single employer they are somewhere between the status of self-employment and dependent employment. EDWs do not generally benefit from the legal protection available to employees or that provided through collective bargaining, indeed this may be the attraction to employers in fostering such patterns of employment (EIRO, 2002a). Similar contractual uncertainties apply to project-based workers whose numbers are expected to grow as the 'network' economy expands in the media and other sectors (Marsden, 2004).

5.3.2 Atypical Employment

In Chapter 4 we analysed the growth of atypical employment in Europe. Perhaps the most debated aspect of this growth has been the rapid expansion of temporary employment in some Member States. In economies where permanent workers have high levels of employment protection, such as France and Spain, fixed-term contracts provide firms with a mechanism to achieve increased labour flexibility. Indeed by 1998 nearly a third of Spanish employees were on temporary contracts. In other countries with relatively low levels of employment protection, such as the UK, workers on fixed-term contract employment represent a stable and much lower share, around 7 per cent, of total employment (Booth et al., 2002a).

Whether the advantages of temporary employment in terms of increased employment flexibility outweigh their disadvantages has been much debated. Booth et al. (2002b) find that in the largely unregulated British labour market such jobs are less well paid, provide less training and are filled by less-happy workers. For men, but not women, in temporary jobs there is a 'scarring' effect. This takes the form of experiencing income penalties long after moving into permanent employment. Even in Member States with high levels of employment protection for permanent jobs, as in France, an expansion of temporary employment may be undesirable as this leads to high turnover amongst younger workers as they struggle to enter paid employment permanently (Blanchard and Landier, 2002). Spain provides the most interesting case study: here an unwillingness to dismantle Franco-era employment protection legislation created a segmented labour market. Two-thirds of Spanish employees enjoyed permanent employment with a high degree of the security whilst the remainder experienced fixed-term contracts intermitted by frequent and lengthy spells of unemployment. Overall, Dolado et al. (2002) conclude that temporary contracts led to an increase in employee turnover; a fall in training and labour productivity; a widening of the wage distribution in favour of higher-educated workers; and reduced long-term but largely unchanged overall unemployment.

Agency workers represent another key group of atypical workers. Outsourcing and the growth of compulsory competitive tendering in the public sector have caused a growth of such workers, particularly in areas of business services. In some occupations, particularly unskilled manual labour such as cleaners, this has led to significant deteriorations in relative earnings as firms have contracted out certain services. We consider these particular activities in Chapter 7 below. However firms often use temporary agencies to screen workers for permanent positions. Moreover because temporary agencies lower the cost to employers of using workers with poor work histories or other undesired characteristics, agencies may have an important role in assisting social inclusion policies in Europe. It is hence not surprising, given their various impacts on labour market behaviour, that the growth of agency working in Europe has prompted widespread debate about the desirability of their growth and the extent of regulation required.

5.3.3 Working Time Regulations

Around the middle of the twentieth century a long-term process of working-time reduction began in Europe (Bosch and Lehndorff, 2001). Annual and weekly hours worked per worker in European countries have declined, though the growth of part-time working distorts both aggregate figures and cross-national comparisons. In the long run, reductions in working time are one means of distributing the benefits of higher productivity, since most models of employee motivation assume that the demand for leisure should rise as living standards increase. However in recent years both the legal and agreed working hours have not changed substantially in Member States (Sousa-Poza and Henneberger, 2002) and there have been suggestions that the intensity of work may have been increasing. In addition there have been fierce debates in Europe as to whether reductions in working time should be adopted to reduce aggregate unemployment through work-sharing.

International comparisons suggest that Portugal and the UK have a particularly high proportion of their employees working long hours (OECD, 1998). However the growth of intra-EU and global competition has increased pressure on employers to increase working time flexibility and make existing working time structures cheaper. New manufacturing technologies, a 24-hour service economy, the 'just in time' model and the globalisation of organisations, production and competition are leading employers to create more flexible working hours practices (Hepple, 2002), such as continuous breaks, staggered working time and variable daily shift lengths. The increased focus on unit costs and the conditions for the optimum use of plant and equipment is leading in turn to a broader diversification of working time arrangements. In the service sector, restrictions on opening hours in the retail sector have been reduced or even eliminated in some countries and the trend is towards an open-all-hours working day. Working time is becoming more differentiated and variable as a consequence of these economic, technological and cultural changes. The line between work and leisure hours is becoming increasingly blurred, as employment moves toward more knowledge-based jobs and traditional factory-work declines. The 'standard' working week based on the Taylorist form of work organisation is vanishing, and there is a trend towards flexible hours, the annual averaging of hours of work, working on-call, teleworking, irregular employment and pseudo self-employment. As such the sorts of social rights as defined in the regulation concerning working hours appear somewhat dated and the need now is to distinguish more clearly between work and free time (Supiot, 1999).

Although the Working Time Directive (WTD) was introduced as a health and safety measure, the empirical support for this rationale is limited. We now consider how economic rationales relevant to health and safety might affect contemporary EU labour market behaviour. We concentrate upon recent research related to three arguments: work-sharing, incomplete employment contracts and family-friendly employment policies. For example in France, Germany, Italy and the Netherlands, reductions in working hours have in recent years become a key element in employment policy (see Bosch and

Lehndorff, 2001). In competitive labour markets conventional economic analysis suggests that arguments for work-sharing suffer from the 'lump of labour fallacy'. That is, proponents of work-sharing assume that the total amount of work to be done is constant. However reducing working hours may increase unit labour costs by raising hourly wages, as employees seek to avoid income-sharing and also face less competition from the unemployed. In addition employers' fixed costs may rise due to additional hiring and training costs. In turn, any higher unit labour costs are likely to lead to both a substitution of capital for labour, and reduced international competitiveness, which together will lower domestic employment. Demand theory thus suggests that work-sharing could have either a negative or a positive (through higher productivity) effect on employment, and hence empirical studies are needed to resolve the debate.

Freeman's (1998) survey of time-series and production function studies concludes that reductions in working hours generated by market forces have generally created additional employment, whilst those generated by government policy have, at best, only a small positive effect. Bauer and Zimmermann (1999), using German data, find that skilled and unskilled workers are largely complements in production. Since overtime is concentrated amongst the skilled and unemployment amongst the unskilled, then a general reduction in overtime working lowers production and unskilled employment. Similarly, Crépon and Kramarz's (2000) analysis of the 1982 mandatory reduction of working hours in France indicates large employment losses, especially amongst the lower-paid. In summary, labour supply factors, including the different skills composition of the employed and unemployed, and a reluctance of those in employment to income-share, severely limit the effectiveness of work-sharing policies. Although where work-sharing can be combined with increased capital-sharing, for example through increased weekend and shift-working, then this form of increased labour market flexibility may, as Freeman (1998) and perhaps the most recent French experience suggest, be more effective in raising employment levels. Using hours restrictions, such as a more restrictive WTD, is also likely to increase inequality. Only hourly-paid workers are required to income-share, since as we still see, most workers with 'autonomous decision-making powers' are excluded from the Directive.

Recent developments in the economic analysis of firms, contracts and institutions have led to both explanations for the high incidence of unpaid work (Bell and Hart, 1999), and a more general reappraisal of the economic rationale for labour market regulations (Hardy and Adnett, 1999b). Bell and Hart provide a range of uncertainty, asymmetric information and team-working explanations for the existence of widespread unpaid working. Their associated empirical work suggests that unpaid work is negatively related to union coverage and positively to manager, foreman or supervisor status. In addition to traditional arguments concerning sources of individual and aggregate market failure, carefully designed regulation may be welfare-enhancing in the presence of incomplete employment contracts and asymmetric information.

As we noted in Chapter 3, US-style 'employment-at-will' policies may create 'opportunistic behaviour' by employees and employers who seek to exploit short-term bargaining advantages to the detriment of both static and dynamic efficiency. Specifically, if more flexible labour markets create greater employment insecurity, then workers' ability to resist employers' attempts to extend working hours, paid or unpaid, is reduced. Workers may be forced to agree to extend their current working hours to provide insurance against unstable work futures. Working in excess of their long-term desired hours allows them to accumulate income reserves in anticipation of future spells of unemployment (Bluestone and Rose, 1998). Such increases in the volatility of an individual's working hours are unlikely to be privately or socially efficient. The decentralisation of both pay and working-time determination has also contributed to this tendency (Arrowsmith and Sisson, 2003). However as Sousa-Poza and Henneberger (2002) point out, working-hours restrictions also prevent some employees from supplying all of the hours they wish. Indeed their study of 21 countries found that the large majority of workers were satisfied with their hours of work, and of those dissatisfied more wished to work longer hours than wished to work fewer, with Denmark being an exception to this latter finding. Boheim and Taylor (2003) found in Britain that a majority of the 40 per cent of workers who preferred to work a different number of hours wished to work fewer hours.

The concern to encourage 'family-friendly' employment policies (see also Chapter 6) has in part emerged from a concern with the growth of extensive unpaid-for overtime working. This seems to be a common feature of managerial and professional work, whilst working long hours seems to have a strong effect upon future earning prospects (Bell and Freeman, 2001; Pannenberg, 2002). Landers et al. (1996) argue that these characteristics may reflect an inefficient 'rat-race' equilibrium. These are characterised by a tendency for promotion to be on the basis of commitment, ambition and propensity to work hard, which given asymmetric information may all be proxied by employers as actual working hours. In such circumstances, adverse selection issues may encourage workers who desire short hours to adopt the camouflage of working longer hours at the current wage. Working-hour norms may therefore become inefficiently long and fail to adjust to the changing demographics of the workforce. This selection process may have the effect of discriminating against those groups bearing a disproportionate amount of non-market activities, particularly mothers. If certain types of labour markets do persistently generate excessive working hours, and these are becoming more prevalent, then policies such as the WTD have further potential advantages to those traditionally recognised. Firstly, they may prevent employers screening on the basis of actual hours worked. Secondly, by forcing firms to adjust working patterns at the same time, they spread adjustment costs across all firms (Landers et al., 1997). Thirdly, they complement maternity and parental leave policies in combating employment discrimination against mothers, and encourage a more equitable distribution of non-market work and income. We return to these latter issues in our discussion of anti-discrimination legislation in the following chapter.

5.4 EU SOCIAL POLICY AND ATYPICAL WORKERS

Atypical work can be defined as including: (1) part-time employment involving shorter working hours than statutory, collectively agreed, or usual working hours; and (2) temporary employment relationships in the form of: (a) fixed-term contracts, including seasonal work, concluded directly between the employer and the employee, where the end of the contract is established by objective conditions such as reaching a specific date, completing a specific task or the occurrence of a specific event; and (b) temporary employment which covers any relationship between a temporary employment business (a temp agency), which is the employer and its employees (the temps), where the employees have no contract with the user undertaking where they perform their activities. In other words, the employees have a contract with the temp agency, which sends them to work as a temp for a user company needing staff. Part-time work, temporary (or fixed-term) work, seasonal work, casual work, homework, self-employment and family work are therefore all forms of atypical work. Atypical employment still principally affects women and young workers but, as noted in Chapter 4, it has been steadily increasing in Member States. The Community Social Charter of 1989 first identified a need for action to ensure the improvement in living and working conditions as regards 'forms of employment other than open-ended contracts, such as fixed-term contracts, part-time working, temporary work and seasonal work'. Barnard (2000) argued that traditionally, employment legislation has been geared towards individuals with regular full-time jobs working under open-ended contracts of employment. We now turn to consider the cases of part-time workers and those on fixed-term contracts. Since 1984, as examined in Chapter 4, there has been an increase in part-time relative to full-time employment. In some cases this is the result of a government decision to promote part-time work, particularly in countries suffering from high unemployment. Indeed there has been much support by the new EU Member States for its supposed merits as a means of reducing unemployment as well as of its benefits for workers and employers alike. It is suggested that facilitating part-time working is in line with good equal opportunities practices by helping people to match their work and domestic commitments to help meet their needs. It also gives employers greater flexibility in adjusting working hours to business requirements while achieving higher productivity. But where these policies fall down is in generalising from measures that help individual workers and employers to a national employment policy to increase the number of part-time jobs as a solution to unemployment; in a sense this just amounts to a redistribution of work, as we discuss in section 5.4.3 below. Within these limitations it is increasingly realised at the EU level that part-time work offers an opportunity for the creation of new and additional jobs.

On 6 June 1997 the social partners (UNICE, ETUC and CEEP) agreed the European Framework Agreement on Part-time Work which, following the procedure under Article 139 (2) of the Amsterdam Treaty, was later implemented by Council Directive 98/23/EC. The aim of the Directive is twofold. Firstly, to provide for the removal of discrimination against part-time workers and to improve the quality of part-time work. Secondly, to facilitate the development of part-time work on a voluntary basis and to contribute to the flexible organisation of working time in a manner that takes into account the needs of employees. Specifically, clause 4(1) of the Framework Agreement provides that: 'in respect of employment conditions, part-time workers shall not be treated in a less favourable manner than comparable full-time workers solely because they work part-time unless different treatment is justified on objective grounds'. The less-favourable treatment of part-time workers is sometimes indirectly discriminatory on the ground of sex since the majority of part-time workers are women. Under the Directive on part-time work, any discrimination against the part-timer is unlawful without having to prove that a full-time work requirement has a negative impact on women. Moreover to seek to challenge it a worker will no longer have to show that she cannot comply with a full-time work requirement. Lastly, male part-timers enjoy the protection afforded by the Directive.

The term 'part-time worker' refers to 'an employee whose normal hours of work, calculated on a weekly basis or on average over a period of employment of up to one year, are less than the normal hours of work of a comparable full-time worker' (clause 3 of the Framework Agreement on part-time work, which was later implemented by Directive 97/81/EC). According to clause 3(2) of the same Agreement, 'comparable full-time worker' means a 'full-time worker in the same establishment having the same type of employment contract or relationship, who is engaged in the same or a similar work/occupation, due regard being given to other considerations which may include seniority and qualifications/skills'.

Similarly, despite the growth in the use of fixed-term contracts, many employment rights have been confined to individuals with traditional working arrangements, resulting in a less-favourable treatment of fixed-term workers. As Rubery et al. (2000) have shown in their studies, an abuse of fixed-term work may arise from the use of successive fixed-term employment contracts ('chain contracts') or relationships, that is, when there are no limits imposed by national legislation on the number of occasions on which fixed-term contracts can be renewed. These employees often suffer from lower levels of employment protection and of work-related benefits. This danger of using fixed-term contracts rather than permanent contracts as a way of excluding employees' rights with no objective reason led the Council to adopt Directive 99/70/EC of 28 June 1999 concerning the Framework Agreement on Fixed-term Work concluded by UNICE, CEEP and the ETUC.

The purpose of the Directive is to improve the quality of fixed-term work by ensuring the application of the principle of non-discrimination, and to establish a framework to prevent abuse arising from the use of successive fixed-term contracts. The Directive applies to fixed-term workers, defined (Article 3) as 'a person having an employment contract or relationship entered into directly between an employer and a worker where the end of the employment contract or relationship is determined by objective conditions such as reaching a specific date, completing a specific task, or the occurrence of a specific event'. Article 4 defines the principle of non-discrimination. This states that fixed-term workers are not to be treated in a less favourable manner than comparable permanent workers solely because they have a fixed-term contract, unless the different treatment is justified on subjective matters relating to business needs. It also states that period-of-service qualifications relating to particular conditions of employment should be the same for fixed-term workers as for permanent workers except where different length-of-service qualifications are justified on objective grounds. Article 5 requires Member States to introduce measures to prevent abuse arising from the use of successive fixed-term contracts. One or more of the following measures should be introduced:

- objective reasons justifying the renewal of fixed-term contracts
- the maximum total duration of successive fixed-term contracts
- the maximum number of renewals of such contracts.

By 2001 EU Member States were supposed to determine under what conditions fixed-term contracts would be regarded as 'successive' and be deemed contracts of indefinite duration. Article 6 requires employers to inform fixed-term workers about permanent vacancies and other employment opportunities; Article 7 contains provisions on information and consultation. In particular a fixed-term employee has the right not to be treated less favourably by his or her employer as regards the terms of his or her contract or by being subjected to any other detriment by any act, or deliberate failure to act, of the employer. The Directive gives an entitlement to receive a written statement of reasons for any less-favourable treatment. The Directive limits the use of successive fixed-term contracts by stating that an employee on a fixed-term contract will be regarded as a permanent employee if (1) the employee is currently employed under a fixed-term contract and that contract has previously been renewed, or the employee has previously been employed on a fixed-term contract before the start of the current contract; (2) the employee has been continuously employed under fixed-term contracts for four years or more, discounting any period before 10 July 2002; and (3) at the time of the most recent renewal (or, where the contract has not been renewed, at the time that the contract was entered into) employment under a fixed-term contract was not justified on objective grounds. Where these conditions apply, the provisions in the contract that restrict its duration will cease to have effect and the contract will be regarded for all purposes as being a contract of indefinite duration.

On 20 March 2002 the European Commission issued its proposal for a Directive on working conditions for temporary workers. This arose from the failure of the EU-level social partners (the ETUC for trade unions, UNICE for private sector employers and CEEP for public sector workers) to negotiate an agreement on temporary work. The proposed Directive's aim is to improve the quality of temporary work by ensuring that the principle of non-discrimination is applied to temporary workers, and to establish a suitable framework for the use of temporary work to contribute to the smooth running of the labour market. Furthermore Article 5 of the proposal states that temporary workers are to be treated at least as favourably as a comparable worker in the user enterprise in respect of basic working and employment conditions, including seniority. Any differences must be justified by objective reasons. Basic working and employment conditions are defined as:

- the duration of working time, rest periods, nightwork, paid holidays and public holidays;
- pay;
- work done by pregnant women and nursing mothers, children and young people; and
- action take to combat discrimination on the grounds of race, sex, or ethnic origin, religion or beliefs, disabilities, age or sexual orientation.

It should be noted that the Directive leaves the issue of pay unclear, as it does not define what this constitutes and whether or not it covers elements such as pensions. The Directive defines a comparable worker as a worker in the user undertaking who occupies an identical or similar post to that occupied by the worker posted by the temporary agency, taking into account issues such as seniority, qualifications and skills.

Casual workers, who may also be described as temporary workers, generally supply a short-term or specific need, and typically will have periods of employment with breaks in between where no work is performed. Casual employment may be the working person's only job, or his or her second or even third job. The relationship will often be short-term but it can also be long-term, and the type of work may be skilled or unskilled. The work may involve arrangements whereby the individual agrees to be available for work as and when required, but no agreement is made on the particular number of hours or times of work. This type of work may suit individuals who want earnings on an occasional basis. A worker who works 'on-call' for one or more employers may also be a casual worker. Casual workers play an important role by filling in for permanent employees who are off for disability or other leave, or by working for relatively short time periods on one-off projects or during periods of unusual needs. Blue-collar female workers are among those most frequently hired for casual jobs. They are often employed in hotels and restaurants, retail, building maintenance, transport and public health-care, where casual work is common. However casual workers (those on fixed-duration contracts or on temporary employment agency contracts) have less-secure working conditions than permanent workers (those on open-ended contracts) due to the nature of the work and/or post. For example related to the protection of casual workers, on 16 July 2002 the EC social partners signed a general framework agreement on teleworking following a similar teleworking agreement relating to the commerce sector signed in April 2001. However the Directive 91/533/EEC on proof of the employment contract does not seem to extend its application to those employees of a casual and/or specific nature, provided, in these cases, that the non-application is justified on business needs-related matters.

In EU labour law terms, an 'agency worker' is the shorthand used to refer to workers who contract with an agency, but carry out work not for the agency but for the agency's client with whom they have no direct contractual relationship. Agency workers range from unskilled manual workers to highly qualified professional people. Temporary agency work is a conceptually interesting form of employment, since it combines elements of both commercial and employment contracts, and brings a third party – the agency – into what was previously a two-party relationship. A definition of temporary agency work (although not fully applicable to all Member States) is one whereby the temporary agency worker is employed by the temporary work agency and is then, via a commercial contact, hired out to perform work assignments at the user firm. There are two main legal aspects to agency work: the regulation of the agency business itself and labour law regulation of contracts and assignments. The business is primarily regulated by means of licensing and monitoring procedures, and some countries curtail the scope of agencies' activities by, for example, prohibiting recruitment services. In most countries, labour law regulates not primarily the contract of employment, but rather the assignment at the user firm. This is typically the case in continental Europe. Collective agreements may also play a role in regulating assignments and contracts.

These changes to traditional employment structures within the EU present challenges for an enlarged and modernising Europe. In this section we have shown examples of the 'humanising face' of EU social policy which formed the basis of the ESM. However it often produced negative 'humanisation' regulations, reacting to social inequalities and/or fears of social dumping and discriminatory practices, rather than proactive promotion of desired outcomes. In this section we have discovered a high reliance on measures to combat the potential exploitation of atypical workers in recognition of their recent growth in numbers. In the next two sections, we examine an example of the latter, occupational health and safety, assessing whether a positive 'humanising face' has been attained by the EU policy-makers under the ESM.

5.5 THE REGULATION OF HEALTH AND SAFETY IN EUROPE

We identified in Chapter 3 several reasons why the market cannot be relied upon to allocate industrial and occupational safety efficiently. Firstly, we mentioned the problem of asymmetric information and the temptation that employers may not disclose the true risk faced by workers in dangerous employment. Whilst reputation effects may partially offset this temptation, these may be ineffective in sectors characterised by a high turnover of workers and firms. In addition the presence of externalities means that employers and firms are unlikely to negotiate optimal levels of safety, since some of the costs of occupational disease and industrial accidents are borne by the general taxpayers in the form of hospital and disability pension costs. Moreover given the presence of cognitive dissonance and myopia we cannot always rely upon individual workers to enter contracts that are in their best interests. Hence all countries regulate health and safety at work, normally combined with some monitoring process with penalties for non-compliance.

Whilst the arguments for some regulation of occupational health and industrial safety are generally accepted, the level at which regulation should be conducted is less apparent. Whilst application of the principle of subsidiarity might suggest devolving responsibility wholly to national governments, the fear of a race to the bottom suggests a case for European-level regulation. As we have noted previously, the promotion of both the free movement of labour and capital in an economic union makes the location of production more sensitive to divergences in national costs. Hence a more lax level of regulation of occupational health and industrial safety could be a source of competitive advantage and distort the process of economic convergence in the Community. Differential standards of heath and safety may also distort patterns of labour mobility and provide further justification for regulation at the European level.

The influence of EC-derived legislation in the health and safety field is both vast and substantial. The Treaty of Rome, as amended by the Single European Act, the Treaty on European Union and the Treaty of Amsterdam recognises the need for worker protection in terms of health and safety in Articles 137 and 138. Article 137(1) in particular provides that 'the Community shall support and complement the activities of the Member States in the improvement of the working environment to protect workers' health and safety and working conditions'. Such Directives are subject to the co-decision procedure whereby the European Parliament jointly adopts proposals with the Council of Ministers. A surge in European health and safety legislation occurred following the adoption of the so-called Framework Directive (89/391), implemented on 1 January 1993. The Directive imposes a number of general obligations upon both employers and employees. Whereas much English legislation on workplace health and safety uses the standard of what is 'reasonably practicable' (that is, a series of economic considerations), the EU approach is to set absolute standards and to permit a defence of *force majeure* for non-compliance (see Article 5(4) of the Directive). That means that here social factors predominate over economic issues.

Consequently every employer must also make, and give effect to, adequate health and safety arrangements, including the effective planning, organisation, control, monitoring and review of the preventive and protective measures. Where there are five or more employees, these arrangements must be recorded in writing. Every employer must ensure that all employees are provided with appropriate health surveillance and must appoint one or more competent persons to assist him in undertaking the preventive and protective measures. Where there is a 'competent person' in the employer's employment, then that person must be appointed as the competent person to assist in undertaking health and safety measures, in preference to a competent person from another source. Every employer must, *inter alia*:

1. establish (and where necessary, give effect to) procedures to be followed in the event of serious and imminent danger to persons working in his undertaking; and
2. nominate a sufficient number of competent persons to implement such procedures in relation to the evacuation of the premises.

The procedures referred to in (1) above must:

a. so far as is reasonably practicable, require persons at work who are exposed to serious and imminent danger to be informed of the nature of the hazards and the steps to be taken to protect them from it;
b. enable the persons concerned to stop work and proceed to a place of safety in the event of being exposed to serious, imminent and unavoidable danger; and
c. require the persons concerned to be prevented from resuming work where there is still a serious and imminent danger.

Article 12 of the Framework Directive (89/391) provides that all workers must receive adequate health and safety training. This must be given on induction and should also be ongoing throughout their employment. Special training must also be given to safety representatives. Training must be at the employer's expense and during working hours. Article 10 of the Framework Directive (89/391) imposes requirements on employers in respect of the information to the workers on health and safety risks and protective and preventative measures, and measures to deal with first aid, fire-fighting and evacuation (Article 10(1)). Article 11(1) and effective consultation with relevant persons and authorities further provides that employers must consult workers, in order to allow them to take part in questions of health and safety, including 'balanced participation' in accordance with national laws and practices. The Directive therefore presupposes the existence of unionised workforce involvement. The issue of consultation will be further discussed in Chapter 8.

As Wright (1999) explains, five further Directives laying down detailed requirements were initially adopted pursuant to the Framework Directive. They relate to minimum requirements for safety and health in the workplace (89/654), the use of machines and equipment (89/655), the use of personal protective equipment (89/656), the use of visual display units (90/270) and the handling of heavy loads (90/269). In addition, Directives have been adopted on, *inter alia*: carcinogens (90/394, 97/42, 99/38), biological agents (90/679), construction sites (92/57), health and safety signs (92/58) and the protection of pregnant workers (92/85). For example the EC Directive relating to the use of display screen equipment (for example VDUs) (90/270) requires every employer, after making a suitable and sufficient analysis of each workstation (that is, display screen equipment, its accessories and the surrounding work environment), to ensure that it meets the detailed requirements set out in the Schedule to the Regulations. Users of display screen equipment must: (1) be provided with eye and eyesight tests on request, both initially and at regular intervals thereafter; (2) be provided with adequate health and safety information relating to the equipment; and (3) have their daily work routine planned in such a way that they have periodical interruptions from using the equipment.

The ECJ has given a ruling on the application of Directive 90/270 in *Dietrich* (C-11/99). It ruled that Article 2(a) of the Directive provides that 'display screen equipment' means 'an alphanumeric or graphic display screen, regardless of the display process involved'. The Court concluded that the term 'graphic display screen' had to be interpreted broadly and therefore included screens that display film recordings, whether in analogue or digital form. A film cutter in a television production studio was therefore entitled to the protection of the provisions of the Directive.

The EU is assisted by a European, supranational body – the European Agency for Safety and Health at Work. This EU Agency aims to make Europe's workplaces safer, healthier and more productive. The European Agency acts as a catalyst for developing, collecting, analysing and disseminating information that improves the state of occupational safety and health in Europe. The Agency is a tripartite European Union organisation and brings together representatives from three key decision-making groups – governments, employers and workers' organisations – in each of the European Union's 25 Member States. The Agency is based in Bilbao, Spain. Evidently health and safety in Europe remains one of the few sanctities where social rights prevail. In the next section we turn to the issue of working time regulation across the EU.

5.6 IS THE ESM WORKING SAFELY? THE WORKING TIME CASE STUDY

In 1993 the Directive on the organisation of working time (93/104) was adopted as a health and safety measure, for implementation in national legislation by 23 November 1996. With exceptions made for certain types of worker, the Directive regulates maximum working weeks, rest periods and paid annual leave. Additional protection for night workers is laid down. As Adnett and Hardy (2001) note, the UK unsuccessfully challenged the legal basis of the Directive in the ECJ and the Directive was only implemented in the UK on 1 October 1998 (amended in 1999). One of the most important provisions in the Directive, and the one which has attracted the most attention, is the 48-hour limit on weekly working. Article 6 provides that 'the average working time for each seven-day period, including overtime must not exceed 48 hours over a reference period of four months'. The strength of the maximum weekly working time contained in Article 6 is significantly weakened by a complex set of derogations. The legal basis of the Directive is Article 118a (now Article

138) of the EC Treaty, which allows the adoption of health and safety measures by qualified majority vote and provides that: 'the Member States shall pay particular attention to encouraging improvements, especially of the working environment, as regards the safety and health of workers, and shall set as their objective the harmonisation of conditions in this area'.

In March 1994 the UK Government launched a challenge on the basis that the Directive's legal base was defective; that the measure had been adopted in breach of the principle of proportionality; that it further constituted a misuse of powers; and finally, that it infringed on the essential procedural requirements to state reasons. Both the Advocate-General and the Court rejected the arguments advanced by the UK, except one, namely that the Directive went beyond the scope of Article 118a in specifying that the minimum weekly rest period should include Sunday. In the most important passage of the decision regarding the appropriateness of Article 118a, the Court adopted a broad interpretation of the notion of 'working environment' based on the Nordic countries' concept of physical, psychological and social aspects of working time such as monotony and lack of social contact at work. It accepted the definition of health as construed in the Commission's Explanatory Memorandum.

Member States can derogate from the 48-hour limit and the specified reference period in the case of 'autonomous decision-takers' or self-managed executives, as identified in Article 17(1) – another example, as discussed in Chapter 3, of flexibility rebutting the social rights presumption. However with regard to cases specified in Article 17(2) and (3), derogation is only possible in the case of the reference period, which may not result in the establishment of a reference period exceeding six or twelve months. More importantly Article 18(1)(*b*)(i) states that a Member State need not apply Article 6, providing certain conditions are satisfied. This constitutes a general derogation from maximum weekly working hours and gives to workers the right of the so-called individual opt-out. Collective agreement cannot substitute the requirement for an individual agreement concluded between the employer and the worker in order for the derogation to be valid. Despite the fact that the level of requirements imposed on employers, such as the obligation to keep records, is considered as being so onerous that it may discourage both Member States and employers from making use of this derogation, it is questionable to what extent the worker decides individually to opt out from the maximum working time limit, or whether instead this is a result of pressure by the employer. Nonetheless, based on the inclusion of the above-mentioned derogation in the final provisions, the Council regarded Article 18(1)(*b*)(i) as a temporary derogation facility subject to review in 2003. Indeed the Commission has already indicated that it would prefer this Article to be removed when it finally launched the consultation process in January 2004.

The Working Time Directive regulates:

- the maximum working week
- rest periods
- paid annual leave
- additional protection for night workers.

The Directive provides for a maximum 48-hour working week averaged over a four-month period, a rest break after six hours' work, a daily rest period of 11 hours, a weekly rest period of 11 hours plus 24 hours, and statutory holidays. There are restrictions on nightwork. Working time regulation has historically constituted a highly controversial subject. At the EU level, the matter of working time regulation was confined until recently within the limits of national regulation in the form of either legislation or agreements between the social partners, providing consequently for a wide spectrum of divergence across Europe. In 1993 however, the adoption of the Working Time Directive (WTD) signalled the end of exclusive regulation at national level and a new era of working time organisation, based both on national measures and on standards set by the EU.

The Working Time Directive applies to all sectors of activity, both public and private, as determined by the 1989 'Framework' Directive on health and safety and to 'workers' as defined in Article 3 of the latter Directive. While self-employed persons are not within the scope of the Directive, casual, temporary, seasonal, home and teleworkers enjoy the protection afforded by the Working Time Directive. The concept of 'working time' underpins the limits and entitlements imposed by the Directive. Under the latter, working time is defined as 'any period during which the worker is working, at the employer's disposal and carrying out his activities or duties, in accordance with national laws and/or practices'. Any other time is designated as a 'rest period'.

The crucial question is how Article 2(1) should be interpreted. The case of 'on-call' workers highlights the difficulty with the definition of working time and the interpretation of the criteria in Article 2(1). Adnett and Hardy (2001) noted, in the *SIMAP* case (C-303/98), where the issue was whether the periods the doctors spent on-call were within the scope of 'working time', the ECJ ruled that the three criteria within Article 2(1) WTD apply conjunctively; hence if a worker is on-call at his or her workplace, all of the on-call time will constitute working time. Moreover the definition of 'working time' in the WTD may lead to controversy as regards other particular situations, such as lunch breaks, travelling or training time, working from home, zero-hours contracts, the right to time off work for trade union activities, health and safety responsibilities and public duties, and work-related activities. It is obvious thus that in order to determine the exact scope of the limits and the entitlements conferred by the WTD, the term 'working time' in these cases will have to be resolved by the courts and the tribunals. Finally, the possibility of using practices as a method of national implementation of the term 'working time' may cause further difficulties for its definition. The different transposition of the term in the various Member States may have the effect of excluding some categories of workers and creating differences among the protection afforded to workers across Member States.

Article 3 lays down the obligation of Member States to ensure that every worker is entitled to a minimum daily rest period of 11 consecutive hours per 24-hour period. While it seems that the effect of Article 3 is a 13-hour working day, less the employee's rest break entitlement, the general principle of humanisation of work, contained in Article 13, ensures that this is not the case. In addition to the daily rest period, Article 5 provides for a minimum uninterrupted rest period of 24 hours for each seven-day period worked, plus the 11 hours' daily rest. Since the weekly rest period must follow from one of the 11-hour daily rest periods, this equates to a minimum uninterrupted rest period of 35 hours. However if objective, technical or work organisation conditions justify it, a minimum rest period of 24 hours may be applied. This means that in these specific circumstances a worker's daily rest period may be incorporated into his weekly rest period, rather than that it qualifies a worker's right to an uninterrupted period of rest.

There is no definition in the Directive of the conditions which allow the application of a minimum rest period of 24 hours, though the limit on average weekly time, and the need of regular justification from the employer in case he or she makes use of the exemption, will have an impact on the application of the provision. Finally, the provision that the minimum weekly rest period 'shall in principle include Sunday' was annulled by the ECJ in the *UK* v. *Council of the European Union* case. Nonetheless the above-mentioned entitlements are considerably undermined by specific derogations provided by the WTD. Specifically Article 17(1) and (2) stipulates that Member States may derogate from the requirements as to daily and weekly rest periods as regards certain activities. In respect of unmeasured working time, while there is the general obligation to take account of the general principles of the protection of the health and safety of workers, no specific requirement exists for provision of equivalent compensating periods. Article 17(2) permits derogation in the case of some other activities 'by means of laws, regulations or administrative provisions', but also 'by means of collective agreements', without hence the need for authorisation by the Member State. In this case 'equivalent periods of compensatory rest or … appropriate protection' must be afforded. The same applies in case of derogations from daily and weekly rest periods through collective agreements between the social partners. Finally, as regards daily and weekly rest, derogations are possible in the case of 'shift work activities' and 'activities involving periods of work split up over the day, particularly those of cleaning staff'.

If the working day is longer than six hours every worker is entitled to an in-work rest break, the details of which, including the duration of the break and the terms on which it is taken, must by preference be laid down by collective agreement between the two sides of industry or, failing that, by national legislation. The Directive does not lay down conditions for the application of this entitlement, such as its duration, timing and nature. As regards the duration of the rest break, the Preamble of the Directive just states that workers should be granted 'adequate' breaks. Furthermore Article 4 does not specify when the rest break should be taken or if a worker is entitled to multiple rest breaks. Equally the provision does not clarify whether rest breaks constitute working time as defined in Article 2(1) of the Directive, nor does it make any reference as to whether the worker is entitled to be paid in respect of rest breaks. Nevertheless it has been argued that the principle of humanisation of work, as accepted in Article 13, can play a positive role in clarifying the above-mentioned uncertainties.

A significant feature of Article 4 is the preference for collective agreements as a means of transposition of the provision into national law. In order to fill the gap as regards the duration of the rest break and the extent of the employer's obligation to organise working time so as to include work breaks, Bercusson (1999) proposed the use of the criteria employed in the case of indirect sex discrimination. He further argued that if it could be shown that working time could be reorganised in such a way as to ameliorate health and safety according to the principle envisaged in Article 13, it would be for the employer to justify his failure to do so on objective grounds.

According to Article 7, every worker is entitled to paid annual leave of at least four weeks, in accordance with conditions for entitlement to, and granting of, such leave laid down by national legislation and/or practice. Therefore it is for the Member States to set the conditions governing the way in which annual leave should be granted. Part-time workers and those on other atypical contracts are considered to be included in the categories of workers enjoying the right to paid annual leave. Additionally, under Article 18(1)(*b*)(ii) the possibility of a three-year transitional period during which workers need only be granted three-weeks' paid annual leave, was given to Member States. It is important to note that the right to annual leave is not subject to any exception or derogation and cannot be replaced by an allowance in lieu, except where the employment relationship is terminated.

The Working Time Directive defines 'night work' as any period of time of not less than seven hours, as defined by national law, but must include the hours between midnight and 5 am (Article 2(3)). 'Night workers' are defined as those workers who work at least three hours of their working time during the hours of midnight and 5 am, as well as those who are likely to proportionally work more during night-time. The Directive provides special arrangements for the health surveillance of these workers, due to the exceptional hazards they may face due to the nature and time of their working time. Despite the Commission's intention that the Directive should apply to all economic activities, the Council initially excluded from its scope the sectors of air, rail, road, sea, inland waterway and lake transport, sea fishing, other works at sea and the activities of doctors in training. The 1997 issuance of the Commission's White Paper on Sectors and Activities excluded from the Working Time Directive however culminated in the adoption of the so-called Horizontal Directive 2000/24, which sought to cover the sectors and activities excluded from the ambit of the present Directive. Consequently by 2003 all EU Member States applied the 1993 Directive to non-mobile workers, including doctors in training, and provided basic protection for mobile workers and those engaged in 'other work at sea'. Directive 2000/24 sets a maximum number of hours to be worked annually and guarantees adequate rest periods, paid annual leave and health assessment for night workers.

The original 1993 Working Time Directive was reviewed in 2004. After much controversial debate, the EU Ministers agreed that the opt-out from the Directive, in terms of working time applying to certain types of workers, could remain, except for those relating to transport and doctors (see Barnard et al., 2003). More recently the ECJ in *Landeshauptstadt Kiel* v. *Jaeger* (C-151/02), held that German doctors resting on hospital premises could count such sleeping time as working time, due to being on-call, as in the *SIMAP* case. In any event the Framework Directive (89/391) encourages sectoral agreements. Examples include Council Directive 2002/15/EC on the organisation of the working time of persons performing mobile road transport activities which was adopted on 11 March 2002. A further landmark in the progress of sectoral social dialogue occurred with the EU social partners reaching an agreement on 30 September 1998 on the organisation of working time of seafarers, providing for either a maximum number of working hours or a minimum rest period. In September 2004 the Commission finally adopted a proposal to update the Working Time Directive. The individual opt-out from the 48-hour week remains, but is to be subject to slightly stricter conditions.

In this section a true EU myth has been highlighted and a paradox demonstrated, surrounding working time. Even when workers have rights, and social protection is afforded by the EU legislators, flexibility under the auspices of economic rights emerges to undermine the social rights provided. Hence the myth that all EU workers are protected. With extensive use of derogation the paradox is that in trying to address competing economic and social rights EU social policy effectively provides less protection to the most vulnerable groups of workers. The EU places much credence in its strong line on safety across the EU, but is this another myth? Again soft law prevails in order to buttress failing hard law approaches to the rebuilding of the ESM.

5.7 CONCLUSIONS

This chapter has provided further evidence of the extent to which soft law is being used to assist, if not supplant, hard law in achieving the aims of EU social policy. We have seen that the ESM initially provided uneven levels of protection for different categories of workers; with the rise in atypical working such discrimination was not sustainable and recent Directives have addressed some of these discrepancies. We have seen that workplace health and safety regulation largely reflects the predominance of social rights, whilst regulation of working conditions has become governed more by economic rights in the guise of supporting greater flexibility. In an attempt to reconcile these competing rights, the EU has sought to further develop the role of social partners in the formulation of labour standards and more importantly in the introduction of flexibility in working time. For example in the earlier drafts of the Working Time Directive, collective agreements were seen merely as a possible means of implementation and as vehicle for agreeing a limited amount of derogation from the standards set. However the final text included a large number of new provisions that effectively charged the social actors with the responsibility for realisation of the EU standards on working time.

In the example of working time regulation in this chapter, we have shown how substantive standards may be set through hard law, but modified by soft law. For example collective agreements have been given the ability to provide definitions for what constitutes work involving special hazards relating to night work. They can also specify the conditions for the grant of annual leave and are given priority over legislation in setting the EU standard for rest breaks. While as we have seen there is no possibility for derogation from the 48-hour weekly working time limit, the definition of the reference period for its calculation can be given by agreements between the social partners, provided that this period does not exceed in any event 12 months. Lastly, Article 15 allows 'the application of collective agreements or agreements concluded between the two sides of industry which are more favourable to the protection of the safety and health of workers'. Another example was Article 11 of the Framework Directive (89/391) which requires that workers and/or workers' representatives should be consulted in advance and in 'good time' with regard to any measure that will substantially affect health and safety. Hence social protection is increasingly being devolved; whether the institutions facilitating such negotiations between the social partners at the local level are sufficient for this role will be considered in Chapter 8.

6. Equality in Europe

6.1 INTRODUCTION

The principles of equal treatment and non-discrimination are at the centre of the European Social Model. These principles provide a cornerstone of the fundamental rights and values that support the European Union. Prior to the Amsterdam Treaty, Community anti-discrimination law had a remit limited to discrimination on grounds of gender and EU nationality. This limited remit was subject to criticism (Bell, 2000) and Article 13 of the EC Treaty opened up the prospects of further Community action in the areas of discrimination based upon racial or ethnic origin, religion or belief, disability age or sexual orientation. This resulted in Directive 2000/43/EC implementing the principle of equal treatment between persons irrespective of racial or ethnic origin, and Directive 2000/78/EC establishing a general framework for equal treatment in employment and occupation, both of which were required to be transposed by Member States during 2003.

Equal pay for women and men for work of equal value was a fundamental principle of the EC treaty, the Equal Pay Directive of 1975 being the first Directive adopted in the area of equal treatment for women and men. However as we noted in Chapter 4, substantial pay gaps by gender still persist in most Member States and recently an indicator of the gender pay gap has been added to the structural indicators established to monitor progress to achieve the Lisbon objectives. The Lisbon Strategy attaches prime importance to raising the employment rate in the EU. In turn, as explained in section 4.6.1 above, this has focused attention on the specific need to raise both overall female employment rates and those of older workers. The large gender gaps found in the labour markets of most of the new Member States and the problems faced by the Roma community in several of them, stimulated new policy debates. In summer 2004 the Commission launched a consultation to gauge opinion as to how it should better combat discrimination and promote the positive benefits of diversity. The delayed response to addressing the position of older workers was surprising given the ageing European society, the growth of early retirement, especially amongst males, and the emphasis upon active ageing policies in the post-Lisbon development of the Employment Strategy. Similarly action against race and ethnic origin discrimination was limited to soft law measures prior to the

Amsterdam Treaty establishing a legal basis for the Commission to present proposals.

In this chapter we examine the rationale for, and development of, Community equal opportunities legislation before assessing its effectiveness and considering current issues. In section 6.2 we trace the development of that legislation from the early social dumping concerns of the French Government which led to an equal-pay clause being included in the Treaty of Rome. The following section explores the relative position of females, older workers and racial and ethnic minorities in European labour markets. We concentrate upon gender gaps in employment and pay and investigate their origins and the reasons for their persistence 30 years after the adoption of anti-discriminatory legislation. In section 6.3.4 we investigate the appropriate definition of discrimination in the labour market and this is followed by an examination of the economic rationale for anti-discriminatory legislation. Section 6.4 concentrates upon recent legislation and current issues. In section 6.4.1 we critically examine the equal treatment directives and assess their likely impact upon labour market behaviour and outcomes. In section 6.4.2 we trace the emergence of work–life balance issues and the initial EU responses to developing a legislative framework to tackle emerging problems. Our final issue in this section concerns age discrimination in the labour market. Here we consider the special considerations that make the definition and recognition of age discrimination problematic and raise fundamental concerns about the desirability of such measures. In our penultimate section we address key challenges which Community legislation faces and assess the prospects for reducing inter-group differences in labour market experiences. In particular in section 6.5.1 we discuss the new challenges raised by the enlargement process and in section 6.5.2 we address the causes of the persistence of gender gaps in the European labour market. In section 6.6 we present our conclusions.

6.2 THE DEVELOPMENT OF EUROPEAN EQUAL OPPORTUNITIES LEGISLATION

The EU's model of equality is based on the idea that true equality cannot be achieved if individuals begin from different starting points. The main objective of European equal opportunities policy has been to achieve equality of access through a combination of formal and substantive equality measures. Once individuals enjoy equality of opportunity the problem of institutional discrimination has been overcome, and fairness demands that they be treated on the basis of their individual merit, without regard to sex or race or other personal characteristic. This approach has largely rejected policies to correct imbalances in the workforce by quotas or targets whose aim is one of equality of outcome. However granting equal access to men and women fails to address inequalities arising before entry into the labour market, since equal treatment of individuals who are not socially equal perpetuates inequalities. Hence the EU's approach favours those women whose cultural experience, family circumstances and share of domestic responsibilities are similar to those of men as a group. The ECJ has adopted a positive stance towards substantive equality, accepting that the mere fact that a male candidate and a female candidate are equally qualified does not mean that they have the same chances. Therefore as we explain below, carefully targeted affirmative action programmes were in line with Article 2(4) of the Equal Treatment Directive.

In an EU context, direct discrimination occurs when a person is treated less favourably due to their sex than a person of the opposite sex would be in similar circumstances. The motive or intention to discriminate is not a necessary element of direct discrimination; it is enough that the effect of the measure is discriminatory. There is no defence to a claim of direct discrimination unless an express derogation is provided. While the Equal Treatment Directives 76/207 and 79/7 contain such derogations, there are no equivalents in the field of pay. The European Court has confirmed that pregnancy discrimination is direct discrimination. Their recent decision of *Jiminez Melgar* v. *Ayuntamiento de Los Barrios* (C-438/99) restates this position in holding that the non-renewal of a fixed-term contract is direct discrimination, which cannot be justified.

In sex discrimination cases it has been recognised that the prohibition on discrimination also included unintentional indirect discrimination. This is where the employer does not intend to discriminate but the effects of any policy are discriminatory (*Bilka-Kaufhaus* case, C-170/84 [1986] ECR 1607). In order to establish indirect discrimination, the ECJ requires detailed evidence of disparate impact rather than merely a potential impact (*Hill* case, C-243/95 [1998] ECR I-3739). Seymour-Smith (C-167/97 [1999] ECR I-623) dealt with the issue of whether a two-year service requirement prior to bringing a claim for unfair dismissal in the UK was indirectly discriminatory against women. Here the ECJ suggested that there were two tests for disparate impact. First, whether 'considerably smaller proportions of women than men' were able to satisfy the two-year requirement. Secondly, there would be evidence of apparent sex discrimination 'if the statistical evidence revealed a lesser but persistent and relatively constant disparity over a long period between men and women who satisfy the requirements of two years' employment'.

Indirect discrimination occurs where a condition or requirement that appears to be sex-neutral conceals an unjustified disproportionate adverse impact on women (or men). The notion of indirect discrimination is designed to target those measures that are discriminatory in effect. The Directive on the burden of proof states that indirect discrimination takes place where an apparently neutral provision, criterion or practice disadvantages a substantially higher proportion of the members of one sex unless that provision is necessary and can be justified by objective factors unrelated to sex. This definition mirrors the views expressed in the case law of the ECJ. In *Bilka-Kaufhaus* the ECJ held that the EC Treaty is infringed where the contested measures affect a far greater number of women than men, unless the undertaking shows that the exclusion is based on objectively justified factors unrelated to any discrimination on grounds of sex. In *Boyle*, the ECJ held that indirect discrimination arises where a national measure, albeit formulated in neutral terms, works to the disadvantage of far more women than men.

In the field of equality law, affirmative action is a management approach intended to identify and remedy situations which lead to or perpetuate inequalities in the workplace. It aims at putting women in the position to be able to compete equally with men, but does not interfere with the selection process, as is the case in positive discrimination. Therefore its objective is to complement legislation on equal treatment and includes any measure contributing to the elimination of inequalities in practice. Affirmative action is accepted in EC labour law. Specifically in Article 2(4) of the Equal Treatment Directive it is stipulated that the Directive shall be: 'without prejudice to measures which promote equal opportunity for men and women, in particular by removing existing inequalities which affect women's opportunities'. The provision is designed to allow measures which, although discriminatory in appearance, are in fact intended to eliminate or reduce actual instances of inequality which may exist in the reality of social life. It thus permits measures relating to access to employment, including promotion, which give a specific advantage to women with a view to improving their ability to compete in the labour market and to pursue a career on an equal footing with men. During the 1990s this gradual acceptance of positive action continued and indeed accelerated. The European Commission in particular pressed forward with a series of specific, positive actions on behalf of women, both within and outside the workplace, ranging from childcare and affirmative action to questions of women in leadership and violence against women. The EU has witnessed a lively debate over positive discrimination, stimulated by the European Court's decisions in the *Kalanke* and *Marschall* cases. Its resolution is a reaffirmation of the member states' right to adopt positive discrimination schemes under EU law, as expressed in Article 141(4) of the Treaty of Amsterdam.

Positive discrimination refers to measures that specifically favour a particular category of people in order to make up for their consistent under-representation in society. They are usually applied in relation to employment, but also to public office and other positions of representation. Examples of positive discrimination include setting a quota of women for specific jobs. Sometimes positive discrimination quotas go as far as preferring women even if they are less qualified than men. But usually less-rigid quotas are used, where women are only preferred if they are equally qualified. As far as the EU is concerned, equal treatment between men and women is a fundamental principle, though the EU has focused more on positive action than on outright positive discrimination. Consequently since 1984 EU Member States adopted a resolution on the promotion of positive action 'designed to eliminate existing inequalities affecting women in working life and to promote a better balance between the sexes in employment'. But in a leading 1995 case, known as the *Kalanke* case, the European Court ruled against a Bremen law (Germany) that 'required' women to be preferred in the selection process in employment if they had the same qualifications as men applying for the same post. The Court's decision put the more direct forms of positive action into disarray, though the EU Treaty specifically permits EU countries to adopt positive action measures that give a specific advantage to women in order to make it easier for them to pursue a job or profession. Positive action measures may also be taken to compensate women for disadvantages in professional careers. This means that it is up to each individual country to decide whether it wants to impose special measures of positive action or positive discrimination.

In 2001 a four-year Community Framework Strategy for Gender Equality was implemented. A 2002 amendment to Directive 76/207/EEC on equal treatment in employment incorporated sexual harassment as a form of sex discrimination. The amended Directive also seeks to define more clearly direct and indirect forms of discrimination and strengthen enforcement and sanctions. Member States have until 2005 to comply with the directive. The former clarification reflects decisions of the ECJ concerning the position of part-time workers, and where statistical evidence revealed a difference in pay by gender the onus is now placed on employers to justify this on factors unrelated to sex.

Alongside this 'hard law' framework provided by the Equal Treatment Directive and its accompanying sister Directives, there has recently been a considerable amount of 'soft law' measures dealing with gender equality (Bercusson, 2002). In some cases, such as with parental leave, initiatives have eventually resulted in the adoption of a collective agreement between the social partners and a new Directive (Hardy and Adnett, 2002). Soft law approaches arise due to the need for specific measures to strengthen opportunities for people in disadvantaged groups, which has been an element of European Union debate since 1994 and was reiterated at the Barcelona Summit in March 2002. Improved access to employment and increased investment in people are now a main concern of the EU in terms of both policies and budgets. The general consensus across the Union is that social policy towards the unemployed, as well as others not in work, should shift away from passive income support towards active measures to help get them into employment. The European Social Fund (ESF) is the main tool through which the EU translates its employment policy into action. With aims that are both preventive and remedial, the Fund uses its resources to develop prospects for those who face the greatest obstacles in finding, keeping or regaining work. The Nice European Council of December 2000 underlined the need to support employment, particularly among the long-term unemployed, disabled workers, older workers and ethnic minorities. It set objectives particularly to facilitate participation in employment for the most vulnerable. The Council underlined the need for an integrated and multidimensional strategic approach.

Gender mainstreaming prevailed as a policy initiative to revitalise EU objectives to combat gender discrimination under the Swedish Presidency of the EU in 2001. Gender mainstreaming incorporates:

> the systematic integration of the respective situations, priorities and needs of women in all policies and with a view to promoting equality between women and men and mobilising all general policies and measures specifically for the purpose of achieving equality by actively and openly taking into account, at the planning stage, their effects on the respective situation of women and men in implementation, monitoring and evaluation. (Bell, 2000)

Mainstreaming does not mean simply making Community programmes or resources more accessible to women, but rather the simultaneous mobilisation of legal instruments, financial resources and the Community's analytical and organisational capacities in order to introduce in all areas the desire to build balanced relationships between women and men. The 1997 Amsterdam Treaty identified gender mainstreaming as a general competence of the EU.

6.3 AN ECONOMIC ANALYSIS OF EQUAL OPPORTUNITIES LEGISLATION

In this section we build upon the analysis provided in Chapter 4 to summarise the current position of female and older workers in the EU. We concentrate upon these two groups both because of the greater knowledge we have about their labour market position, but also because EU legislation has until recently concentrated upon the former, whilst the latter have now been targeted in the Lisbon Strategy. After this summary we address the problems of defining and identifying discrimination in employment, and critically examine the economic rationale for equal opportunities legislation.

6.3.1 The Current Status of Female Workers

In Chapter 4 we outlined both the growing role of female workers in Europe and the persisting gender gaps. Here we draw out some more details of these trends and explore the relative status of female workers. There are indications that some of the traditional gender gaps are being addressed. Females have filled about 60 per cent of the new jobs created in the EU in recent years and they now outperform males at school across most of the EU. However the review of the first five years of the European Employment Strategy found uneven progress across the Community within the equal opportunities pillar. The guidelines for that strategy advocate the gender mainstreaming approach outlined above, the tackling of gender gaps and the reconciliation of work and family life. The gender gaps in employment, unemployment, pay and representation have become areas of specific action for Member States and reconciliation of work and family has recently become a policy priority (Hardy and Adnett, 2002).

Over the period since 1997 women have benefited from the majority of new jobs created and their overall employment rate has risen from 50.6 per cent of those of working age to 55.6 per cent in 2003 (European Commission, 2004a). The gender gap in employment has fallen from 20 per cent to 17.2 per cent since 1997 and the gap in unemployment rates has fallen to just 1.8 per cent, though the much higher proportion of females working part-time distorts these comparisons. Despite this increase in female market employment in the EU there remains a substantial employment gap in many of the Southern Member States, particularly Greece (31 per cent), Italy (27 per cent) and Spain (30 per cent), though in these countries male employment rates are relatively low, suggesting that the gender gap is the product of the overall employment system as well as gender relations (OECD, 2002b). In many of the new Member States gender gaps are small, notwithstanding their very low rates of part-time working (5 per cent or below in the Czech Republic, Hungary and the Slovak Republic), though participation rates are higher and unemployment rates lower for the age groups between 35 and 49 years of age. This seems to be the result of increasing barriers to female participation during the transition period, partly related to cutbacks in benefits supporting female employment which have disproportionately affected the younger age-groups (Eurostat, 2000).

Employment rates are generally much higher, and the gender gap much lower, among women with higher educational qualifications. For example in Ireland, Italy, Greece and Spain low-educated females have employment rates of around 40 per cent, half those for similarly educated males. Dolado et al. (2001) suggest that about half of the difference in female employment rates between the EU and the US can be explained by differences in educational attainments. The employment rates of less-educated European women are much lower than those found in the US, even amongst those aged 25–34. Given these findings it is important to note that gender gaps in educational attainment are narrowing or even reversing; for example in 2002 women accounted for 55 per cent of all EU graduates, and the educational level of the EU female population is slowly converging on that of the US. Indeed in the transition countries and the Scandinavian Member States there is no gender gap in educational attainment for all age cohorts currently in the labour force (OECD, 2002b). This closing of the gender gap is stronger in tertiary education, and especially so in Austria, Greece, Hungary and Spain. However important gender differences remain in the fields of study undertaken at tertiary level (Eurostat, 2001), with female students still concentrated in the arts, humanities and education, and accounting for just 36 per cent of graduates in sciences, mathematics and informatics. These differences appear to explain some of the female–male wage gap. Gender gaps in employment also reflect the asymmetric gender effects of parenthood. As the number of children rises, mothers' employment rates generally fall and the incidence of part-time working increases.

While participation and employment rates of women and men are converging, the distribution of employment by occupation or sector is still significantly gender-segmented. Women are over-represented in clerical and selling occupations, and the life science, health and teaching occupations. They remain under-represented in managerial and top administrative occupations and in manual and production jobs. Indeed in the EU, men are twice as likely as women to be in managerial positions and three times as likely to be senior managers. The degree of occupational segregation tends to be higher in Member States with the highest female participation rate (Anker, 1998; OECD, 2002b). However the younger generation is more occupationally integrated in the majority of Member States, the exceptions being Austria, Belgium, Germany, Greece, Italy and Spain. Gender segregation appears to be positively associated with the incidence of part-time work (Dolado et al., 2002) and is stronger amongst mothers and the less-educated (Dolado et al., 2001).

The extent to which these and other aspects of segregation reflect different preferences and aspirations of male and female workers remains an important issue. When the job content of male and female workers are compared it appears that women's cognitive skills are underutilised (OECD, 2002b). The skill requirements of men's jobs are typically higher than those for women, though survey evidence suggests that few women appear to feel that they could or would like to do a more demanding job. The same OECD (2002b) study reports survey evidence which indicates that men display higher levels of job satisfaction than females in 12 European countries, the UK being an exception. In summary, it is difficult from this evidence to conclude that these gender gaps are the consequence of differences in innate preferences between men and women.

The unadjusted gender gap gross hourly earnings in the EU was 16 per cent in 2002, having hardly changed in recent years (European Commission, 2004b). The pay gap ranges from 6 per cent in Portugal to 24 per cent in the UK (European Commission, 2002a). It has narrowed in most Member States, though there has been comparatively little increase in the Member States with the largest gaps (EIRO, 2002b). Internationally the slow closing of the gender pay gap has been attributed to the increased education and experience of female workers, and the impact of equal-treatment laws (Weichselbaumer and Winter-Ebmer, 2003). In the UK there are indications that the gap widens during mid-life (Makepeace et al., 2002), while changes in industry wage differentials have systematically worked against female workers in Sweden (Edin and Richardson, 2002).

The narrowing of the aggregate gender pay gap may not always be a favourable development for women. In several transition countries a smaller gender pay gap has been the result of less-skilled women being displaced from the labour market (Hunt, 2002). Indeed across all Member States the gender wage gap tends to be wider where the employment rates of less-educated women are higher. There is evidence for Germany and the UK that the different subjects studied by men and women at tertiary level can explain a sizeable part of the wage gap for graduates (Machin and Puhani, 2002). Differences in productivity-related characteristics, such as education, experience and tenure, seem to explain little of the remaining wage gap and there is some evidence that the gender wage gap and occupational segregation are positively correlated (Dolado et al., 2002). For example the large US gender gap is largely due to the large penalty which the US wage structure imposes on groups with below-average skills or who are located in less-favoured sectors (Blau and Kahn, 1999b), and the unequal division of home production between the genders (O'Neill, 2003). Interestingly Ruiz et al. (2002) find that unexplained gender wage gaps in Spain are much larger for involuntary job-movers and disappear for voluntary job-movers. Consistent with our discussion of occupational segregation and the presence of a 'glass ceiling', Dolado and Llorens (2004) find that female graduates face greater wage discrimination at the top than at the bottom of the wage distribution.

In six EU countries there is a significant family gap between the monthly earnings of mothers and childless women, but apart from Austria and the UK this gap is mainly due to the lower hours worked by mothers. However since mothers now appear to be better endowed with productive characteristics, in particular they are on average older, then a family gap becomes a more common experience when the hourly earnings data is adjusted for other characteristics. In particular childless women appear to work in higher-paid occupations than mothers do (OECD, 2002b), though mothers who do not interrupt their employment experience no wage penalty (Joshi et al., 1999). These findings stimulated the Spanish Government for example to introduce in 2003 a tax subsidy for working mothers to encourage their continued employment. Women are twice as likely as men to spend time looking after children on a daily basis, and on average they do this for twice as many hours as men (European Commission, 2002c). The average age at marriage for women was 28.5 in 1999 (compared with 23.5 in 1980) and the average age at the birth of their first child has also risen to 28 in 2000 (25 in 1980). Women have fewer children than before, 1.48 in 2000 (1.82 in 1980), and the steepest falls in fertility have been in the countries with the highest birth rates in 1980 (Ireland, Greece, Spain and Portugal).

In summary, less-educated women and those with children are less likely to be in employment, and those that do work are more likely to be in the female-dominated sectors of the labour market. In addition, significant gender pay gaps persist in the EU which are attributable to earnings differentials between men and women with children, and gender segregation by sectors and occupations – in particular the relatively low earnings of women in female-dominated sectors and occupations that cannot be explained by observed differences in productivity-related characteristics. Together these persisting differences pose a challenge to EU policy-makers since increasing and improving female employment is crucial to the maintenance of existing levels of social protection in an ageing Europe. In addition, increased risks of family dissolution and the persistence of pockets of high male unemployment indicate the importance of women's earnings in combating poverty.

6.3.2 The Current Status of Older Workers

The sudden emphasis upon the importance of retaining older workers in the labour market amongst European policy-makers is predominantly a response to major demographic changes common across the existing Member States. Life expectancy both at birth and at retirement age has been growing, whilst fertility levels remain low in the EU. Thus whilst about a fifth of the EU population was aged 50 or over in 1995, this fraction will reach a third by 2050. Moreover as the number of new entrants drops, the average age of the workforce rises and, as the post-war large cohorts start to retire from around 2010, the labour force shrinks. Overall the old-age dependency rate increases from around 24 per cent in 2000 to over 27 per cent by 2050 (European Commission, 2002c). In the US the effective retirement age for men rose slightly to over 65 in the 30 years up to the end of the twentieth century. In Europe there has been no common trend, though effective retirement is generally earlier, Portugal being an exception, and is below the age of 60 in Finland, France and Italy (OECD, 2002c).

Regardless of its determinants, early retirement results in a growth of unused capacity, a reduced tax base and a heavier load on the fiscal and pension systems. The latter is particularly important in those countries such as France and Germany whose state pension systems were funded on a pay-as-you-go basis, that is, the retirement pensions of one generation are funded out of the contributions of the following one. Herbertsson and Orszag (2001) calculate that the costs of early retirement in 1998 expressed as a percentage of GDP varies from around 13 per cent in Austria, Belgium and Luxembourg to around 7 per cent in Denmark, Ireland, Portugal and the UK. All Member States have higher costs than the OECD average of around 6 per cent. In the face of its ageing population and these costs of early retirement, Europe has sought to increase the effective age of retirement. At the same time, as elsewhere in the OECD, policy has sought to reduce the generosity of state pensions, enhance the role of private pensions and instigate more fundamental changes to government finances aimed at reducing debt levels to allow for the growth of age-related public spending (OECD, 2002c).

Since leisure is a normal good, a rise in early retirements may in part reflect economic growth as well as a response to the fall in the relative price of leisure goods and a change of preferences. However to explain the pattern of early retirement across countries we have to consider labour market behaviour and the operation of social protection systems. Retirement decisions appear to be sensitive to financial incentives (Herbertsson, 2001). The overall fiscal incentive to retire can be separated into two components. Firstly, the replacement rate, that is, the pension an individual receives as a percentage of their working income prior to retirement. The lower this replacement rate, the smaller the financial incentive to retire. Thus tax changes which effectively raised the net earnings of UK elderly workers had a significant positive effect on their working hours (Disney and Smith, 2002). Similarly Ashenfelter and Card (2002) found that professors with higher incomes were less likely to retire after the abolition of mandatory retirement. Secondly, the fiscal incentive to retire depends upon the change in net pension wealth from working an additional year. For example Ashenfelter and Card report that US professors with lower pension wealth were less likely to retire at any given age. Whilst the incentive-based approach has largely stimulated policy responses, discussed above, which concentrated upon the supply-side of the labour market, it is the demand-side of the market that is targeted by age discrimination legislation.

Legislation that raises the demand for elderly workers increases their current earnings or their prospects of gaining better jobs and accordingly reduces their replacement rate. Legislation that reduces the incidence of redundancies amongst older workers may also lower replacement rates, through both higher earnings and reduced pension entitlements. Where pension payments are linked to final earnings, legislation may also increase the incentive to retire later through the positive effect on net pension wealth. However these effects may be relatively small if not supported by the other policy reforms discussed above (Taqi, 2002). This may be especially the case in the EU, since in several European countries the operation of the pension, unemployment, disability and early retirement systems still create significant incentives for early retirement (OECD, 2002c).

The rising proportion of older workers poses a further problem for the achievement of the competitive and dynamic, knowledge-based European economy of the future enshrined in the Lisbon Strategy. A rising proportion of older workers, given their greater sunk-capital and enhanced job-security, slows down the speed of adjustment to shocks in the labour market. Moreover the response to change is, as Herbertsson (2001) argues, more likely to favour reduced participation rates through increased early retirements and discouraged worker effects (involuntary early retirements). These latter adjustments appear to be particularly undesirable given our discussion above, and suggest that the economic arguments concerning the desirability of age discrimination legislation may be particularly complex in Europe.

6.3.3 Understanding Discrimination in the Labour Market

We have seen that establishing equal opportunities is one of the guiding principles of the European Social Model, but this objective is also related to the EU's commitment to extending economic integration. Discriminatory practices distort the competitive process within integrated markets and prevent efficient allocation of resources in both product and labour markets.

How to identify labour market discrimination and individual discriminatory practices remains problematic. Since groups of workers differ both in their productivity-related characteristics (such as education and experience) and their preferences and aspirations, unadjusted employment, pay and occupational gaps between groups cannot be taken as evidence of discrimination. Even when we adjust for differences in productivity-related characteristics between groups, identifying discrimination is still problematic for two reasons. First, those differences in characteristics may reflect discrimination that occurs before entering the labour market (for example access to schooling) or even after entry (for example access to training). Second, if groups differ in their preferences and aspirations, such as willingness to take on supervisory roles, then differences in outcomes are expected for groups with similar productivity-related characteristics. Moreover if preferences and aspirations are in part endogenous, then the existence of discrimination itself distorts inter-group behaviour. One conventional definition is that discrimination concerns unequal treatment for groups with similar productivity-related characteristics, though our discussion above clearly indicates that this provides an inadequate basis both for estimating the extent of discrimination in practice and for the design of correcting legislation.

6.3.4 The Economic Rationale for Equal Opportunities Legislation

The modern economic analysis of discrimination is usually assumed to start with Becker (1957). He assumed that employers have a 'taste' or preference for discrimination and are prepared to sacrifice profits to exercise this taste. Employers, or more precisely managers, may therefore refuse to hire black or female workers in competitive markets, even where it would be profitable to do so. As a consequence white males and other favoured groups of workers receive higher wages than in a non-discriminatory market, since the competing labour supply has effectively been restricted. Black or female workers receive lower wages because they are viewed as inferior substitutes for white male workers of the same quality, and wage reductions are required to induce their employment.

If there is a dispersion of discrimination tastes between employers and common production methods, employers who discriminate the least will have lower unit labour costs and therefore under competitive conditions should be able to eliminate more discriminatory firms from their market. Ultimately only non-discriminatory employers should survive; persisting discrimination is therefore indicative of non-competitive markets or severe transaction costs, reflecting the influence of government, trade unions or monopolists. In general the same conclusions follow if it is employees or consumers, rather than employers, who exhibit a taste for discrimination. In these cases, assuming different groups are perfect substitutes for each other, competition should eliminate wage discrimination but the end result would be segregated workplaces.

An alternative approach to the analysis of discrimination, still within the framework of competitive analysis, is to consider the consequences of employers having imperfect information about an applicant's potential productivity. The increased use of line managers in the recruitment and selection of employees in European companies makes this possibility an important one. In labour markets where it is costly to acquire information, employers will wish to find a proxy to predict the employability of particular applicants. Race and sex being easily observable characteristics, applicants may be considered to have the mean productivity of previous workers hired with these characteristics. If firms for example have in the past observed that on average white males had the highest productivity, or have subjective beliefs to that effect, statistical discrimination can occur against the higher-productivity female or black applicants. Employers react to the anticipated lower productivity of women or blacks by offering employment only at a lower wage. Statistical discrimination against women may also exist if employers view pregnancy, childbirth and child-rearing as imposing direct and indirect costs upon themselves. Women may be viewed as less productive during pregnancy and discontinuities may occur with mothers having to be replaced during maternity leave. Even if such beliefs are warranted, then discrimination occurs against women employees who do not intend to have children since they are unable to signal this characteristic to their employers. Blacks or women will only be hired on equal terms to white males in industries and occupations where their inferred 'inferior' characteristics are unimportant to productivity. This leads to their occupational crowding in jobs with poor access to on-the-job training and a further depressing of the relative wages in those occupations.

The statistical discrimination approach is also unconvincing as an explanation of persisting discrimination. If average group differences are perceived but false, then over time employers should learn about these errors and correct them (Darity and Mason, 1998). Firms with accurate stereotypes will have a competitive advantage and displace those with obsolete stereotypes. Tight labour markets, which force employers to experiment with groups not normally hired for particular occupations, should increase the speed of adjustment of stereotypes. In summary, orthodox competitive theory is unable to explain the persistence of discriminatory behaviour in the labour market. Sustained differences in economic outcomes between different groups must, according to this approach, reflect differences in either preferences or human capital. As Darity and Mason (1998) conclude, the consequence is for orthodox theory to absolve the employment process of a role in producing sustained differential outcomes and to blame pre-market or extra-market processes, a conclusion that is inconsistent with empirical studies showing that schooling, work experience and culture differences by themselves cannot explain the persisting wage differentials and employment patterns. Hence the continuing popularity of non-traditional analyses that reject some of the conventional assumptions concerning behaviour in competitive markets.

One non-traditional approach concerns self-fulfilling expectations where unjustified statistical discrimination generates deterioration in the human capital of the disfavoured group. Suppose that employers only hire females or blacks for dead-end jobs, believing them to have low productivity or high turnover rates, then the behaviour induced by such tasks will conform to that anticipated by employers. Hence where productivity is job-based, stereotypes may be self-perpetuating. More generally, depressed expectations amongst a disfavoured group about their employment opportunities will reduce their willingness to acquire additional education and training, again sustaining differing outcomes.

A second non-traditional theory concerns non-competing groups. Here the dominant group controls access to preferred employment opportunities initially by regulating the required credentials and access to the gaining of those credentials. By introducing elements of power and social control, the presence of racism and sexism are now parts of the explanation of persisting discrimination in employment. According to this approach, if society manages to reduce or eliminate pre-entry discrimination against the disfavoured group then in-market discrimination may increase as the dominant group seeks to retain their position. Goldin (2002) provides a variation on this theme, developing a 'pollution' theory of discrimination. She argues that new female recruits can reduce the prestige, and hence remuneration, of a previously all-male occupation. Hence glass ceilings emerge, which place an effective limit on the advancement of the highly qualified members of the disfavoured group.

The competitive theory underpinning employment-at-will labour markets would also be seemingly tolerant of 'contractual' harassment. That is where female workers accept employment in firms which have a reputation for sexual harassment, or if they were warned to be prepared for such behaviour at interview. Since they accepted the employment then conventional analysis would suggest that they are being sufficiently remunerated to cover any disutility. Basu (2002) argues that there still may be grounds for preventing firms from exposing their workers to such behaviour even when the worker finds the wage sufficiently attractive to submit. It is thus possible to provide a general principle for deciding upon what types of behaviour are obnoxious rather then relying upon *ad hoc* judgements.

Our review of the analysis of persisting discrimination in employment has shown the absence of any general agreement regarding causation. This failure to agree which mechanisms can sustain inter-group differences in outcomes in contemporary labour markets means that any rationale for anti-discriminatory legislation can be disputed. Competitive theories of employment behaviour downplay the role of in-market processes in sustaining differences in outcome. From this perspective, equal pay and opportunities legislation merely raise the hiring and firing costs of the targeted groups and therefore worsen their disadvantage. Alternatively for those who believe that persistent differences in outcomes have their origin in labour market processes, the failure to identify their specific nature makes the design of effective anti-discriminatory policies problematic. If we do not understand the key processes that sustain discrimination, we cannot target policy to eliminate them. Moreover this ignorance implies that more blanket equal pay and equal opportunities legislation will have uncertain and possibly dysfunctional effects.

6.4 RECENT LEGISLATION AND CURRENT ISSUES

In this section we examine four areas of EU equal opportunities legislation. In the following section we review the development of the equal treatment directives, building on our analysis of section 6.2. This is followed by an examination of the EU's attempts to target the work–life balance through legislation. In Section 6.4.3 we consider the use of hard law to target discrimination against older workers, and the section concludes with a short discussion of initial legislation seeking to address racial discrimination in the EU.

6.4.1 The Equal Treatment Directives

In the field of equal treatment, many EU legislative initiatives have been promoted throughout the years. The Social Action Programme saw the adoption of the following directives. Directive 76/207/EEC on equal treatment with regard to access to employment, vocational training, promotion and working conditions, aimed at eliminating all discrimination, both direct and indirect, in the world of work and providing an opportunity for positive measures. Directive 79/7/EEC targeted the progressive implementation of equal treatment with regard to statutory social security schemes. In the 1980s, Directive 86/378/EEC required implementation of equal treatment in occupational schemes of social security, which was later amended by Directive 96/97/EC in light of the *Barber* decision (C-268/88 [1990] ECR I-1889). In addition, Directive 86/613/EEC on equal treatment for men and women carrying out a self-employed activity, including agriculture, was adopted. More recently, the Treaty of Amsterdam explicitly introduced equality between men and women as one of its tasks (Article 2) and activities (Article 3) of the Community. Article 13 also allows the Council, acting unanimously on a proposal from the Commission, to take action to combat any form of discrimination, including that based on gender. The principle of equal treatment is defined by Article 2(1) to mean that 'there shall be no discrimination whatsoever on grounds of sex either directly or indirectly by reference in particular to marital or family status'.

The first important piece of legislation relating to equality in the first Community legal texts was contained in Article 119 (now Article 141) of the Treaty of Rome, which introduced the principle of equal pay for women and men for equal work. This principle was used extensively by the European Court of Justice to ensure equal opportunities between women and men in the labour market. In one of the most significant cases of the ECJ, the Court stated that Article 141 was 'directly applicable' both horizontally and vertically, and 'may thus give rise to individual rights which the courts may protect'. The prohibition of discrimination applies not only to acts of employers, in respect of both the contract of employment and unilateral acts, but also to action by public authorities and collective agreements. Thus Article 3 of the Equal Pay Directive 75/117/EEC requires Member States to abolish all discrimination arising from laws, regulations, or administrative provisions which are contrary to the principle of equal pay.

Men and women are also protected from discrimination, which may occur when they are performing different jobs for the same employer. For this reason Community law now gives the right to receive equal pay for work of equal value. In concrete terms, this means that where a woman (or a man) undertakes work as demanding as that of the other gender, even though the work is different, she (or he) should receive the same pay and benefits unless there is a non-discriminatory explanation for the differential. To determine whether the work performed by a man and a woman is of equal value, a comparison of their work is required. This involves assessing the nature of the tasks and the demands made upon the workers in carrying them out, such as skill, effort, responsibility and so on. Only the nature of the job is relevant to the assessment. So other factors, like the fact that one works part-time and the other full-time, are not relevant, and cannot in themselves justify the wage difference. In each Member State there is an authority with the power to decide if work has the same value as other work, after having obtained the necessary information. The right to equal pay for equal work and work of equal value applies to both the public and the private sector, whether the pay has been decided by collective agreements, wage scales, wage agreements or individual contracts. To determine if the complaint is well founded the two jobs need to be compared, by analysing the nature and demands of the tasks undertaken. Collective agreements must respect the principle of equal pay for equal work and work of equal value. Therefore if collective bargaining arrangements result in lower pay for a group composed predominantly or almost exclusively of women, this will constitute an infringement of the basic Community right to equal pay, unless this difference results from objective factors which in no way discriminate on the basis of sex.

According to Article 141(2) of the Amsterdam Treaty, 'pay' means the ordinary basic or minimum wage or salary or any other consideration, whether in cash or in kind, which the worker receives directly or indirectly, in respect of his employment, from his employer. In Case 80/70 *Defrenne (no.1)* v. *Belgian State* [1971] ECR 445, the ECJ held that pay can be 'immediate or future' provided that the worker receives it, albeit indirectly, in respect of his employment from his employer. Moreover according to C-457/93 [1996] ECR I-243 the pay does not need to be contractual in origin: it can be legislative or voluntary.

As regards equal pay, the European Union has helped to sustain a view that men and women should face equal opportunities in employment. The obvious milestones are the inclusion in the Treaty of the equal pay principle, the Equal Pay Directive, the case law of the European Court of Justice and now more recently, the mainstreaming of equality principles into the European Employment Strategy and the European Social Inclusion Agenda. However in the second *Defrenne* case the European Court of Justice brought life to the concept of equal pay by recognising the direct effect of the then Article 119 EC (now Article 141).

The circumstances in which gender is a genuine occupational qualification for a job are usually: (1) the essential nature of the job requires a man or a woman because of physiology or for authenticity in dramatic performances or other entertainment; (2) the job requires a man or a woman to preserve decency or privacy; (3) the job is likely to involve the employee working or living in a domestic setting and has significant physical or social contact with the person living there; (4) the nature of work or the location of the establishment requires the employee to live in premises provided by the employer and the only available premises do not provide separate sleeping accommodation and sanitary facilities for either sex; (5) the employment establishment is a single-sex establishment or in a single-sex part of an establishment where people receive special care, supervision or attention, and the essential character of that establishment or the part of it requires a person of the same sex to do the job; (6) the holder of the job provides individuals with personal services promoting their welfare or education, or similar personal services, and such services are most effectively performed by one sex; (7) the job is one of two to be held by a married couple; which allows Member States to exclude from its field of application those occupational activities and, where appropriate, the training leading thereto, for which, by reason of their nature or the context in which they are carried out, the sex of the worker constitutes a determining factor.

In this section we have shown that hard law approaches dominate the EU's competence in non-discrimination measures. In the next section we question the effectiveness of such a hard law framework in examining soft law approaches to eliminating discrimination, in terms of work–life balance issues.

6.4.2 Work–Life Balance

The Employment Guidelines for National Action Plans under the European Employment Strategy have included a commitment to reconcile work and family life. For instance Guideline 18 in 2002 required Member States and the social partners to design, implement and promote a wide range of family-friendly working arrangements. Following Evans (2001), we can classify these arrangements into four broad categories. First, leave from work for family reasons. This category includes maternity, paternity and parental leave, but also leave to care for elderly dependants or in cases of bereavement. Second, changes in work arrangements for family reasons. Job-sharing, home-working, flexitime working, a compressed working week, term-time only contracts and a facility to switch between full- and part-time working exemplify this category of flexibility. Practical help with child and elder-person care is a third category, including affordable and accessible nurseries and play schemes in holidays. Finally, there is information, training and networking assistance. This includes assistance for re-entrants and the active promotion of family-friendly benefits and entitlements. In practice the EU legal framework has concentrated on the first of these categories, while the current emphasis in the Employment Strategy is on the third.

There are a number of contextual and policy considerations which have raised the profile of family-friendly employment practices in the EU in recent years. Currently, female employment rates fall below those of males only with motherhood; hence recent increases in the overall female employment rate have been primarily attributable to the increased participation rates of mothers, most recently amongst those with children aged up to four (OECD, 2001b). As we have noted, there are large national differences within the EU in the extent to which new mothers exit the labour market or switch to part-time working. As also recorded above, a substantial component of gender wage gaps reflects the costs of career interruptions through motherhood or care of elderly dependants (see also Davies et al., 2000; Rubery et al., 2000), interruptions that, we concluded, may themselves reflect an unequal division of market work, home production and care of dependants within households. Policies that encourage a more equal division of these activities are thus likely to reduce gender gaps and stimulate female employment both directly and indirectly through increasing female relative wages. Indeed across OECD countries there is a positive relationship between the extent of work–family reconciliation policies and female employment rates, though we should be wary about assuming a unique direction of causation in this relationship (OECD, 2001b). Thus for example family policies in both Denmark and Sweden have been shown to effect the probability of mothers returning to the labour market, though the more generous parental leave provisions in Sweden have been associated with a greater take-up amongst fathers (Pylkkänen and Smith, 2003). Indeed in the generous Swedish system mothers take up to 85 per cent of the total parental leave and new policies are being developed to encourage a more equal division.

The increasing number of households containing a single parent or having no one in employment has been a further stimulus to the advancement of family-friendly working practices. For example in the UK, contrary to the general trend, the employment rate of lone parents and the partners of jobless men hardly changed over the last 20 years of the twentieth century (Desai et al., 1999). Current fashions favour preventing social exclusion through strengthening attachment to the labour market. With that objective in mind, tax and benefit systems have been reformed to increase the financial attractions of market work and reduce obstacles to combining parenthood and working life. More generally, the concentration of European unemployment in jobless households has also promoted social inclusion policies targeting female members. This emphasis reflects the finding that female employment has generally risen only in households where a partner is already in work. In the UK, where the polarisation of work across households has been greatest in recent decades, over 17 per cent of households were workless in 1999, a proportion three times greater than in the 1970s. Moreover as Dickens et al. (2000) point out, worklessness is not generally a temporary state: in 60 per cent of workless households, no resident adult has worked in the previous three years.

In addition the nature of employment has itself been changing in ways that create new problems for those seeking to reconcile work and family life. Most types of 'atypical' working patterns, as analysed in Chapter 4, have risen rapidly in recent years and these changes have disproportionately affected female workers. Indeed as the Commission comments: 'some EU Member States continue to promote flexibility with little regard for the impact on gender equality' (European Commission, 2001a, p. 19). In the EU as a whole, a third of female employees work part-time, a proportion around five times greater than for men. Women also constitute a (small) majority of fixed-term, temporary and casual workers, being almost a third more likely than men to be so employed. Flexible working time often involves patterns that meet employers' requirements to adapt to temporal fluctuations in demand for goods and services, rather than employees' own preferences. One consequence has been increased weekend and evening working, particularly in those services such as retailing that traditionally have disproportionately employed women. Additional problems for workers with dependants have been generated by the increase in the intensity of work in many European countries (Green and McIntosh, 2001), the growth of unpaid overtime and a tendency for many workers to have to work longer hours than desired (Adnett and Hardy, 2001). Mothers employed full-time typically spend over twice as much time as fathers on both childcare and unpaid household work (OECD, 2001b), and therefore face much greater conflicts in their struggle to prosper in contemporary labour markets.

Changing family patterns and demographic changes have also added to the problems of balancing work and family demands. Marriage rates have generally been falling in Northern Europe, though in most Mediterranean countries and Ireland they have risen since the 1960s. Divorce rates have also risen rapidly in Europe, and the general decline of marriage is indicated by the rapid rise in the proportion of births outside traditional marriage. In the UK, 40 per cent of babies are now born outside marriage, mainly to cohabitees. Child-rearing has also become spread out over more of the mother's life, even though overall fertility rates have fallen by around 50 per cent since 1960 (Carnoy, 1999). The birth rate has fallen most rapidly in the Mediterranean and more socially conservative EU Member States. Increasing longevity has extended the length of time during which workers have elderly dependants. Evidence for OECD countries, summarised in Jensen and Jacobzone (2000), suggests that over half of the frail elderly receive care from adult children or grandchildren, with around three-quarters of the primary care workers being female. The same source indicates that the main effects of informal caring work are to reduce the carer's paid working hours and hourly wage rate.

There are complex interrelationships between the growth of female employment, extensions of non-standard working and demographic, social and cultural changes. In turn, national differences in these latter contextual factors contribute to the diversity of experience within the EU, in particular in explaining the speed of the decline in the 'male breadwinner' family model, still dominant in Greece, Spain, Italy and Portugal (Figart and Mutari, 2000), and the extent to which 'one-and-a-half breadwinner' or 'adult earner' models have replaced it. Associated national differences exist in the extent of the shift of caring activity from the family to markets and public provision. Overall if these changes are not to lead to new sources of gender inequalities, then it has become clear that policy must assist the more equal sharing of all forms of work in society, rather than just compensating for unpaid work (Lewis, 2001). However these national differences mean that once again a common EU policy approach towards these labour market developments will not produce uniform effects in national economies (Yeandle, 1999). There has been some attempt to adjust the objectives and provision of employment and welfare policies to reflect these needs, but there have been only limited attempts to adjust EU employment law.

According to Dex and Scheibl (2001), employers that help their employees to balance their work with their family lives see an improvement in their business performance. Presumably the gains in terms of reduced absenteeism and increased motivation offset any additional costs to employers from increased flexibility or direct childcare expenses. If this is the case, then an obvious response is to question why we require any regulation in this area. If family-friendly employment policies are indeed profitable for firms, then orthodox economic analysis suggests that they will automatically be made available to employees. More precisely, the theory of compensating wage differentials suggests that those workers who desire a family-friendly employment environment will be matched with those firms willing to provide such an environment. Even if there are net additional costs to employers of providing such working practices, adjustment should occur through their wage offers falling relative to those of firms not providing family-friendly employment conditions. If workers value the benefits of a family-friendly environment less than the costs of the lower wages, then they will prefer to work for firms not offering these benefits. Mandatory benefits seemingly prevent this mutually beneficial contracting and encourage discrimination and occupational segregation.

The current research evidence on the extent and determinants of family-friendly employment practices, surveyed in Evans (2001) and Wood (1999), provides mixed evidence as to the strength of this mechanism. Wood finds that employers' perceptions of the benefits do influence the adoption of family-friendly practices, though this 'business case' for such practices does not appear to apply, or be perceived to apply, to all firms. Many firms go beyond the legal minimum in making family-friendly arrangements, but implementation is patchy and very few private sector employers provide extra family leave and childcare. Overall, international evidence suggests that firms in countries with high levels of statutory provision tend to rely almost entirely on that provision, whilst where national provision is low, firms do not appear to have filled the gap (OECD, 2001b). Specifically in the EU, outside the Nordic countries, a relatively high proportion of employers provide extra-statutory family leave benefits, but few provide help with childcare. The Netherlands is the exception on childcare provision; here the public authorities have directly involved firms in providing subsidised care to employees. The OECD (2001b) study clearly illustrates the current diversity in the relative importance of statutory policies, employer provision and flexible working arrangements in attempts to reconcile work and family commitments in the EU.

This slow growth of family-friendly practices in the face of the growing need identified above suggests that there are market failures in their provision and implementation. Proponents of mandatory family-friendly employment practices usually focus on market failures associated with human capital, unemployment, asymmetric information and externalities (Ruhm and Teague, 1997). Greater flexibility at work would reduce turnover amongst carers, encouraging both them and their employers to invest more in firm-specific training, and reduce unemployment spells on re-entry to the labour market. Adverse selection under asymmetric information can prevent socially desirable parental leave or shorter working hours from being generally available. Where the costs of revealing to employers one's preference for parental leave or shorter hours are high, workers disguise themselves as having a low risk of requiring such leave or as having a taste for long working hours. The consequence is that all employers offer contracts with no or very limited provisions for leave, and long working hours. In partial support, Figart and Mutari (2000) find that countries with shorter working weeks have a smaller gap between women's and men's labour market behaviour. Finally, externalities may exist such that the costs to carers of forgoing leave are less than those for society as a whole. For example economic disincentives to care for frail elderly dependants may entail that these receive worse care and taxpayers bear higher costs through alternative hospital or nursing home care. Within this category we can include the advantages to society as a whole of a more equal distribution of all market and non-market work and the resulting improvements in gender equality (Rubery et al., 2000).

Strengthening mandatory rights to family-friendly working conditions need not automatically promote gender equality. For example given that in the majority of European families the male's income is higher, increasing statutory entitlements to unpaid parental leave effectively strengthens the 'male breadwinner' model. This follows since mothers, as we saw in Sweden, will be much more likely to exercise the right to parental leave (Bruning and Plantenga, 1999) and as a consequence be more likely to be placed on the 'mommy track' with lower career prospects (Lommerud and Vagstad, 2000). Moreover it is possible that statutory benefits may reduce extra-statutory benefits. Evans (2001) finds that extra-statutory provisions for maternity leave are least common in those European countries, the Nordic countries, where legislation is strongest.

6.4.3 Age Discrimination

In the US the Age Discrimination in Employment Act established a legal framework to promote and protect older workers in 1967. As Issacharoff and Harris (1997) point out, in practice most litigation under this Act concerns claims for unfair dismissal by elderly workers. Hence as suggested in our discussion in Chapters 3 and 4, the absence of employment-at-will in European labour markets provides one explanation for the delayed introduction of age discrimination legislation. Other differences between American and European employment relationships are likely to have contributed to the initial absence of political pressures for age discrimination measures. In Europe the lower overall rates of unemployment in the 1960s and 1970s and the much lower rate of job and worker turnover meant that discrimination against older applicants was much less of an issue. Similarly the greater wage-compression in Europe reduced the importance of seniority or age-related pay and reduced the incentives for employers to indulge in age discrimination. The presence of strong trade unions and the adoption of collectively bargained 'last-in, first-out' rules for redundancies further restricted employers' ability to target older workers when making compulsory redundancies. Moreover the dominance of centralised pension schemes and the other manifestations of

Social Europe, where benefits were often linked to participation rather than employment, limited the costs for those older workers who faced exclusion from employment. Together these differences with the US seem capable of explaining the absence, at least during the 1960s and 1970s, of significant political pressures in Europe for age discrimination legislation at national or supra-national level. We now turn to consider what factors have been instrumental in creating pressures for such legislation in recent years.

A direct cause of age discrimination legislation in Europe has been the adoption of the Lisbon Strategy. This Strategy attaches prime importance to raising the employment rate in the EU to approach the US rate. The initial target agreed at the Lisbon Council was an overall 6 per cent rise in the employment rate by 2010, nearly two-thirds of which would be additional female workers. At the Stockholm Council a new target was set for the employment rate of older workers (ages 55–64), specifically it was to rise from 38.6 per cent to 50 per cent by 2010 (European Commission, 2002a). The initial slow progress towards the latter target led to calls at the 2002 Barcelona Council for greater incentives for older workers to remain in the labour market. These were to take the form of more gradual retirement formulas and improved access to lifelong learning, and lead to a rise of about five years in the average age at which people stop working by 2010. This emphasis upon retaining older workers in the labour market represents a dramatic change for many European countries where until recently early retirement and lax disability insurance schemes were favoured responses to the key objective of reducing measured unemployment, especially among the young (OECD, 1994).

Prohibitions of discrimination in the labour market based upon gender, race, religion and national origin have typically been justified on grounds other than economic efficiency. These prohibitions typically reflect the acceptance by society that systematically different outcomes for groups with apparently similar productivity-related characteristics are inconsistent with the fundamental tenets of a democratic society. Discrimination on the basis of age is different in the sense that the latter has both a temporal and a universal element. As a consequence any distributive gains which legislation achieves for elderly workers results in losses for similar younger workers. Such redistribution is difficult to justify on traditional distributive grounds (Jolls, 1996); we therefore have to look elsewhere for an underlying rationale. Efficiency considerations are an obvious starting point for an attempt to find justification for age discrimination legislation.

Labour market discrimination concerns unequal treatment of groups of workers who have equal potential productivity. Unequal treatment based upon cost considerations and overall economic efficiency would not normally constitute discriminatory behaviour, and much of the reluctance to hire or eagerness to fire older workers would appear to fall under this category of behaviour. It was Lazear (1979) who first pointed out that given asymmetric information and costly turnover then firms and workers might both benefit from implicit contracts where workers get paid by seniority rather than their current productivity. Such contracts reduce the need for costly monitoring or 'low-wage, low-effort' solutions to the effort-elicitation problem. A consequence of such long-term incentive contracts is that older workers get paid more than both their marginal product and their reservation wage. This model can explain the observed rising age–earnings profiles and has found a measure of support in empirical studies (Lazear, 2000). Loewenstein and Sicherman (1991) provide an alternative explanation for age-related earnings based upon a psychological preference for improvement in earnings over time. Both models suggest that given the presence of such efficient contracts, mandatory retirement is required to provide an endpoint to the bargain, since firms are paying wages in excess of the productivity of older workers. Hence as Lazear (1979) originally argued, legislation that abolished mandatory retirement would cause a once-and-for-all small redistribution in favour of older workers but at the costs of large and continuing efficiency losses as these contracts were rendered illegal.

However Neumark and Stock (1999) argue that other considerations suggest that legislation may encourage the formation of Lazear contracts. Specifically, by preventing age discrimination in lay-offs it prevents employers from opportunistically reneging on implicit long-term contracts. That is, legislation can act as a precommitment or hand-tying device that prevents employers from reneging on age-based wages for older workers (Jolls, 1996). As a consequence workers may be more likely to enter into such contracts, especially in the more turbulent labour markets of recent decades, given their greater confidence that employers will comply. Jolls makes similar arguments in support of legal regulations to eliminate 'age discrimination' in hiring, though Issacharoff and Harris (1997) question whether anti-discrimination law is the most appropriate response to any threat of opportunistic behaviour. If Lazear contracts are common, then firms who screen out older workers on a cost basis or refuse to pay age-related earnings may gain a short-run competitive advantage and threaten the sustainability of efficient contracts. By these means age discrimination legislation could raise labour market efficiency. Neumark and Stock's empirical work attempts to evaluate these two effects and they interpret the rising age–earning profile as indicating that age-discrimination laws in the US have led to a greater use of Lazear contracts and hence have most likely increased labour market efficiency.

If mandatory retirement applies to all groups and is the result of an implicit or explicit contract with a long-term employer then it is difficult to term this practice as discriminatory. In Europe the greater proportionate investment in firm-specific training makes Lazear contracts relatively more attractive, since separations are now more costly to both parties. As such the outlawing of mandatory retirement would seem to be particularly undesirable. One remaining potential justification concerns whether the changing demographic circumstances should cause society to intervene to require that contracts be effectively renegotiated, with retirement being postponed. The above arguments have largely been developed by commentators on the behaviour in the at-will labour markets of the US. In Europe existing job security policies effectively provide greater relative protection to older workers. Here, as noted above, corporate restructuring in response to transitory and permanent shocks is more likely to take the form of lower labour-force participation rates. Even in the absence of government encouragement, European firms may opt for early retirement of their older employees rather than costly dismissals (Herbertsson, 2001). Hence strengthening age discrimination legislation related to lay-offs may, in the European context, worsen the early retirement problem as well as redistribute wealth to older workers. Recent policy initiatives to raise the status of part-time and temporary employment in the EU create additional incentives for older workers to choose progressive retirement. Hence our general conclusion that we need to analyse how age discrimination policies interact with other employment regulations before we can identify whether overall their impact is beneficial.

6.4.4 Racial Discrimination

According to the results of a Eurobarometer survey (European Commission, IP/03/840) a fifth of Europeans surveyed had personally witnessed discrimination on ethnic grounds, with the proportion ranging from 15 per cent in Ireland to 35 per cent in the Netherlands. In the same survey two-thirds of respondents were unaware of their rights if they were discriminated against. EU Governments in June 2000 adopted the Racial Equality Directive, barely six months after submission by the Commission. This speedy implementation reflected the desire of the Council to respond to the entry of the right-wing Freedom Party into the Austrian Government. Interestingly most Member States missed the July 2003 deadline for transposition into national law, and none had provided notification to the Commission of complete transposition. In July 2004 the Commission announced that it was taking legal action against Austria, Germany, Finland, Greece and Luxembourg for failure to pass all the necessary national measures.

As Bell (2002) explains, the Racial Equality Directive, being much broader in scope, fits uneasily into traditional European labour law. This Directive prohibits racial or ethnic discrimination in employment and other areas such as training, education and the supply of and access to goods and services including housing. The EU rules on indirect discrimination apply to this Directive. Indeed the first case brought under Sweden's 1999 measure against ethnic discrimination in employment was successfully brought by a Bosnian-born women who failed to get a job at a telemarketing company because she was said to have a foreign accent.

The recent enlargement has focused attention on the position of the Roma population in the Community. By 2007 it is expected that there will be over 8 million Roma living in the EU and the Commission has been drawing attention to the serious problems they face in gaining access to employment, training, education, health care, housing and other social services.

6.5 CHALLENGES AND OPPORTUNITIES

The European Social Model's concern about diversity, as discussed above, provides both a challenge and an opportunity. The challenge lies in the sphere of enlargement and the opportunity with regard to seeking to eradicate the causes of discrimination across the EU workplace. In this section we consider key current issues in the development of equal opportunities policy in the EU. Firstly, we consider the impact of the recent enlargement on equal opportunities, concentrating upon gender gaps in the new Member States. Secondly, we consider the nature and consequences of the extension of equal opportunities policies into the areas of discrimination on the basis of disability, religion and sexual orientation. Our third sub-section considers an important but largely neglected area: equal opportunities regarding occupational social security benefits. We conclude this section by considering the effectiveness and limitations of equal opportunities policies. In particular why, after nearly 30 years of equal opportunity policies targeted at reducing gender gaps in EU labour markets, do these gaps remain so large?

6.5.1 Enlargement

The new Member States of Central and Eastern Europe had high female employment rates during their command economy period. Between 70 and 90 per cent of women of working age were in the labour force in 1989, compared with an average of just 50 per cent elsewhere in Europe. There were similarities in occupational segregation with that found in Western Europe, though a higher proportion of females in the communist regimes were employed in manufacturing and agriculture. In agriculture it was predominantly older females who were employed and there were large regional differentials in the proportion of females employed. A further characteristic of these centrally planned economies was that women had relatively high levels of education as measured in years of completed schooling. Their preference for academic rather than technical and vocational schooling pathways led to women making up 40 per cent of students, lecturers and researchers in higher education (Rangelova, 2002). In this period women had legally guaranteed equal rights and opportunities to work, though even with the compressed wage structure characteristic of these economies, gender pay gaps were similar to those in Western Europe.

The costs of the transition process in Central and Eastern Europe have disproportionately fallen on female workers. Although females still account for between 44 and 50 per cent of the labour force, their share of employment has declined, and in all these countries apart from Hungary their share of unemployment is higher than their share of employment (Rangelova, 2002). To a large extent this reflects that the structural changes have disfavoured female-intensive sectors. The decline in participation amongst younger females is partly due to a rise in enrolments in post-compulsory schooling and partly due to deterioration in childcare provision. Perversely, the tendency of the least-educated females to be displaced from employment prevented the overall gender pay gap from falling due to the growing public–private sector wage differentials.

Accession to the EU required changes in the labour code in these countries to comply with the EU's equal opportunities policies, the principle of non-discrimination being one element in the 'political criteria' for membership agreed at the 1993 Copenhagen Council. Implementation of these changes was not given a high priority in the former communist countries and doubts remain about the effectiveness of monitoring and enforcement mechanisms (EIRO, 2004). In particular the introduction for the first time of legal protection against discrimination on some grounds – disability, sexual orientation and age – has proved controversial in some new Member States.

As the 2004 Green Paper on 'Equality and non-discrimination in an enlarged Europe' pointed out, enlargement changed the political and institutional context for policy-making on non-discrimination and equal treatment. In the absence of any amendment to Article 13 of the EC Treaty, the adoption of legislation in this area requires unanimous agreement by Member States. Whether there exists a strong and shared will to take further legislative action in this area in an EU of 25 Member States remains uncertain.

6.5.2 New Frontiers: Harassment, Race, Religion, Disability

Sexual harassment is an expression of the pervasive social and political secondary position of women that is reflected in, among other things, sex discrimination in the workplace. When women choose to avoid certain jobs based on experience or anticipation of sexual harassment in male-dominated occupations, then sexual harassment constitutes a barrier to equal opportunities for women in the workforce. It is argued that sexual harassment is a dynamic process that develops within the context of specific labour market structures and cultural patterns. It is a process that is influenced by legal rules and frameworks, political decisions, personal characteristics and experiences. Thus short-term and mid-range preventive strategies that eliminate sex segregation in the labour market, and strategies to develop concrete legal guidelines to pursue incidents of sexual harassment, must be adopted. These measures function both as deterrents for potential perpetrators and to allow individual women to pursue their rights to sexual self-determination and equal chances in the labour market.

Under the new Directive, harassment, including sexual harassment, shall be deemed to be discrimination when an unwanted conduct unrelated to racial or ethnic origin takes place with the purpose or effect of violating the dignity of a person and of creating an intimidating, hostile, degrading, humiliating or offensive environment.

A further current concern relates to discrimination on the basis of nationality. Under Council Regulation 1612/68 on the free movement of labour within the Communities, Article 7(1) states that: 'no employee who is a citizen of one Member State but residing in another may on grounds of his/her nationality be treated differently from workers of that Member State as regards conditions of employment and work'. Article 7(2) of the Regulation provides that an employee who is a citizen of one Member State but resident in another shall moreover 'enjoy the same social and tax advantages as citizens of that State'. By virtue of the Court's previous case law the concept of 'social benefits' has developed to embrace all benefits accruing to any national employee chiefly on the grounds of his or her objective status as an employee, or simply on the basis that he or she is resident within the territory of the state concerned. Thus social security benefits also come within their scope. As regards those benefits that fall within Regulation 1612/68, the Court has further extended the principle of equal treatment to apply also to members of the migrant worker's family. A further expression of the principle of equal treatment is to be found in Article 3(1) of Regulation 1408/71 on the application of social security systems when employees, self-employed workers or members of their families move within the Community. Persons who are resident within the territory of one of the Member States and to whom the Regulation applies shall be 'subject to the same obligations and enjoy the same benefits'. However family members and surviving dependants are not accorded any independent right to the benefits to which the Regulation refers. Even if the term 'indirect discrimination' is not explicitly mentioned in any of these statutes, the ECJ has made it clear that the principle of equal treatment laid down in both Article 39 of the Treaty of Rome and in Regulations 1612/68 and 1408/71 prohibit both direct and indirect discrimination.

In addition the Treaty of Amsterdam introduced Article 13 which complements existing powers to tackle discrimination against people on the grounds of specific characteristics, most notably Article 141 (gender discrimination), Article 137 (measures to tackle exclusion from the labour market) and Article 12 (discrimination on the grounds of nationality). Article 13, which was included in the EC Treaty pursuant to the Treaty of Amsterdam, offers new opportunities for Community action to tackle discrimination. Discrimination against people on the grounds of specific characteristics is not only unfair and an infringement of the general principles of human rights, but it also has an economic and social cost. Discrimination is also a distorting factor in the common market, preventing an efficient matching of workers and jobs and distorting the incentives to undertake education and training. It is therefore up to both the Member States and the European Union to help eliminate discrimination as far as possible, and Article 13 offers new possibilities for doing so.

Before the Amsterdam review, the Community had no powers to tackle discrimination based on religion or belief. Article 13 provided the European Union with a legal basis to take action to combat discrimination on grounds of racial or ethnic origin, religion or belief, disability, age or sexual orientation. The general principles of Article 13 are not themselves legally binding. To give effect to Article 13, the Council of Ministers have so far approved two Directives proposing minimum standards of legal protection against discrimination throughout the European Union, and an Action Programme to support practical efforts in the Member States to combat discrimination. We have discussed the Racial Equality Directive above, and here we concentrate upon the Framework Directive outlawing discrimination in employment on the grounds of religion or belief, disability, age or sexual orientation (Council Directive 2000/78/EC of 27 November 2000 establishing a general framework for equal treatment in employment and occupation).

Sexual orientation continues to be an EU-wide legal issue. In *Grant* (C-249/96 [1998] ECR I-621), the ECJ rejected the inclusion of the term 'sex' in the notion of sexual orientation and accordingly it determined the scope of Article 141 only by having regard to its wording and purpose, its place in the scheme of the Treaty, and its legal context. It concluded that Community law did not cover discrimination based on sexual orientation. Article 13 of the Amsterdam Treaty is the first time that discrimination on the grounds of sexual orientation has been mentioned in the EU Treaties. Article 13 however has no direct effect, but only provides the legal basis for the EU to take appropriate action to combat discrimination. The Parliamentary Assembly of the Council of Europe voted in January 2000 to support a recommendation that sexual orientation be included in the list of prohibited grounds in the new draft Protocol No. 12 to the Convention. It took the view that explicit reference should be made to grounds of discrimination that were 'especially odious', and that sexual orientation discrimination was amongst these. Finally, on 28 November 2000, the Council adopted the Framework Directive on equal treatment in employment and occupation, which forbids discrimination in employment on the grounds of religion or belief, age, disability or sexual orientation.

In the field of equality law, the ECJ has followed a broad approach to the term 'sex', including transsexuality. In *P* v. *S* (C-13/94), the ECJ held that the term 'sex' included sex change in the context of the Equal Treatment Directive. Therefore a male to female transsexual dismissed on the grounds of her sex change had a remedy in EC law. Specifically it stated that in view of the purpose and the nature of the rights which it sought to safeguard, the scope of the Directive applied to discrimination arising from the gender reassignment of the person concerned, since 'such discrimination is based, essentially if not exclusively, on the sex of the person concerned'. It has to be noted that the comparator selected in this case was a person of the sex to which the applicant was deemed to have belonged prior to the gender reassignment.

The definition of disability varies considerably from one European country to another, and in part reflects the diversity of social and cultural approaches to the issue. A society open and accessible to all is the goal of the European Union Disability Strategy and barriers to this goal need to be identified and removed. The European Union Disability Strategy has three main focuses: co-operation between the Commission and the Member States, full participation of people with disabilities and mainstreaming disability in policy formulations. The EU Charter of Fundamental Rights in Article 26 stipulates that, 'The Union recognises and respects the right of persons with disabilities to benefit from measures designed to ensure their independence, social and occupational integration and participation in the life of the community'. The Commission is committed to involving the social partners in efforts to integrate people with disabilities into the labour market. The social partners adopted a joint declaration on the employment of people with disabilities at a meeting of the Social Dialogue Committee on 19 May 1999. Specifically, they recommended that employers envisage developing equal opportunity policies for people with disabilities and make these policies known to all management and employees, with particular emphasis on raising the awareness of recruitment and human resources staff. Secondly, trade unions endeavour to examine disability issues with their members and develop equal opportunity policies in this area. Finally, they recommended that the Equal Treatment Directive's general framework include disability. Disabled persons represent a population of 38 million in the EU15; 46 per cent of these reporting a moderate disability and 24 per cent reporting a severe disability are in work. The EU launched a European Year of the Disabled in 2003, to publicise the difficulties faced by disabled persons in accessing or remaining in the labour market and to take decisive steps to better exploit their employment potential.

6.5.3 Discrimination in Occupational Social Security

Occupational social security is provided by an individual employer's scheme, a group of employers or a sector-wide scheme. It aims to supplement or replace the benefits provided by statutory social security schemes. The schemes can be compulsory or optional. According to Directive 86/378 (as amended by Directive 96/97) the principle of equal treatment in occupational social security implies that there shall be no discrimination based on sex, in particular in respect of the scope of the occupational social security schemes and the conditions of access to them; the obligation to pay contributions and the calculation of the contributions; the calculation of benefits; and the conditions governing the duration and retention of entitlement to benefits. Workers have the right to equal benefits when they are provided for by an occupational social scheme for the same risks as those covered by statutory schemes. Thus discrimination on the basis of sex is prohibited in occupational social security schemes, including pensionable age and survivors' benefits. Occupational social security schemes must treat men and women equally, especially as regards the scope of the schemes and the conditions of access to them, including age; the obligation to contribute and the calculation of the contributions; the calculation of the benefits due in respect of a spouse or dependants; and the conditions governing the duration and retention of entitlement to benefits. The right to equal occupational social security does not apply to individual employment contracts for self-employed workers or, in the case of salaried workers, to insurance schemes to which the employer is not party, and to schemes in which benefits are financed by contributions paid by workers on a voluntary basis.

Statutory social security is set up by national legislation. It covers, for instance, protection in case of sickness, invalidity, old age, industrial accidents and occupational diseases, and unemployment. Examples of such benefits are retirement or invalidity pensions or unemployment benefits. In this field, Directive 79/7 on equal treatment in State social security is intended to complement the two sex-equality Directives. In addition Regulation 1408/71, which aims at encouraging the co-ordination of national security schemes to ensure that those wishing to exercise their rights of free movement do not suffer detriment in terms of their social security benefits, stipulates the principle of equality of treatment or non-discrimination on the grounds of nationality in Article 3(1). Men and women doing the same type of work are in principle entitled to the same type and amount of statutory social security and equal access thereto, and must contribute in the same way to social security systems. Furthermore the benefits shall be calculated in the same way, including additional payments due to a spouse or dependants. The conditions determining duration of entitlement to these social security benefits shall also be the same for men and women doing the same work or work of equal value.

Different treatment under statutory schemes is permitted in several fields. For example the Member States may maintain unequal retirement ages and conditions for entitlement to a survivor's pension. In some Member States women may receive a retirement pension earlier than men, and sometimes widows' pensions are available and widowers' pensions are not. As this section has shown, policy within the EU context continues to develop into new areas, whilst also dealing with continuing problems relating to the social security provisions. Historically the original Community encountered difficulties in relation to discriminatory social security, as was evidenced before the ECJ. However in an enlarged EU it seems that these issues continue to recur, demonstrating the need for strong policies in the social security area to eliminate arbitrary practices based on age, gender and nationality discrimination.

6.5.4 Why Does Gender Discrimination Persist?

In 2002 the Commission called for a strong initiative to reduce disparities in both public and private sectors as part of its policy to increase labour force participation in accordance with the Lisbon Strategy. In doing so it was effectively acknowledging the at least partial failure of 30 years of equal pay and opportunities legislation. Despite the consistent growth of female employment since the 1990s, we have seen that occupational and sectoral segmentation remains strong and the gender pay gap has proven remarkably resilient. If we are to understand the reasons for this partial failure of sex discrimination measures then we need to re-examine the causes for the continuing 16 per cent gender pay gap in the EU.

The EU Commission's own research into this pay gap (2002a) utilised data from the European Community Household Panel (1994–98) and the 2001 European Community Labour Force Survey. It identified gender segregation by sector and occupation and found that female-dominated sectors and occupations paid lower wages. These two factors were the biggest contributors to the current gender pay gap in Europe. Cross-country differences in these determinants and in wage structure and female participation led to differences in the composition of the pay gap between Member States. In general more centrally determined wage systems were found likely to generate smaller gender wage differentials. Overall the study concluded that to reduce the pay gap further policy had to tackle 'differences in activity and employment rates; differences in the wage structure; differences in the workforce composition and differences in remuneration between men and women' (p. 42).

More specifically, the study identified horizontal and vertical segregation and the concentration of women in low-paying sectors and occupations as a key issue. This raises the question as to the extent to which this segregation may itself reflect discriminatory behaviour (OECD, 2002b). That is, social norms regarding women's educational and occupational choices may interact with discriminatory recruitment and promotion behaviour of employers, and incentives and disincentives created by existing wage structures and employment, family and taxation policies. A second central issue concerns the reasons for the differences in the returns to the same characteristics between men and women. In particular, why a higher female share of employment in an occupation or sector is associated with lower earnings, especially for women. The relatively low pay in female-dominated occupations suggests a prevailing low valuation of such jobs, whilst the relatively low pay of women within these occupations indicates the persistence of unequal treatment of women as regards remuneration and promotion.

Understanding these reasons for continuing gender gaps in employment helps us to explain some of the reasons for the partial failure of legislation. Whilst overt pay and hiring discrimination has been largely eliminated, horizontal and vertical segregation and the low valuation of employment in female-intensive occupations and sectors still persist. Hence the need to combine hard and soft legal instruments to target social norms and preferences which sustain gender differences in outcomes. This latter objective may not cause significant distortions to wage structures. Typically, female-intensive sectors such as caring, health and education face severe problems in measuring labour productivity. If society wishes therefore to attach a higher premium on such employment, then there need not be significant resource misallocation issues.

6.6 CONCLUSIONS

In this chapter we have traced the development of a multidimensional equality legal framework in the EU. Until recently equal opportunities policy targeted just females' and non-nationals' employment rights in the Community. Schiek (2002) argues that in practice we now have a hierarchy of equalities in which racial, ethnic, sex and gender discrimination have been given greater prominence in EC Law. She also points to the differences in exceptions and special provisions between the individual legislative instruments tackling discrimination and the failure to provide a coherent rationale for these differences. This may cause particular problems in tackling issues involving interrelations between different types of discrimination. Thus for example the interrelation between gender and religious discrimination in the case of women barred from employment for wearing an Islamic headscarf.

Together with this broadening of equal opportunities legislation, there has been what Bell (2002) terms 'a Europeanisation of enforcement strategies'. Previous to the Racial Equality Directive the remedies for breaches in European labour law had been largely a matter for individual Member States to determine. In this Directive there are explicit measures to improve enforcement, and compensation to the victim must be 'effective, proportionate and dissuasive'. In Chapter 8 we will meet exactly the same wording in the context of the Directive on informing and consulting employees. This new trend is particularly surprising given the recent emphasis on the principle of subsidiarity in Council decision-making.

Our discussion of the economic theory of regulation in Chapter 3 introduced the possibility that regulation could produce dysfunctional effects. The history of equal opportunities legislation is testament to the importance of these effects. Simple 'equal pay for equal work' policies worsen occupational segregation as employers practice circumventive innovation to limit their liability. Similarly parental leave policies that encourage the lower-paid parent to take up the leave, create both supply- and demand-side responses that worsen mothers' employment opportunities. Finally, consider policies that marketise caring activities and replace non-paid labour with paid employment. If society places a low valuation on such occupations then gender employment gaps may diminish whilst those for pay increase. Hence equal opportunities is a key example of the need for a coherent package of soft and hard law measures, with the former targeting the elimination of the dysfunctional effects of the hard law.

7. Restructuring enterprises in Europe

7.1 INTRODUCTION

We have argued previously that a range of factors, both internal and external to the Union, have increased the degree of competition in product and service markets in recent years. In combination with technological and organisational change and long-term structural changes these factors have increased the speed of business restructuring in Europe. More flexible employment has thus become less secure employment for many European workers as the threat of redundancy and business transfer increases. It was worker rights in these areas that formed the initial phase of EU social policy legislation. In this chapter we trace their legislative birth and explore the continuing policy dilemma of competing economic and social rights at work, focusing on the Collective Redundancies (CRD) and Acquired Rights (ARD) Directives. In drawing conclusions, this chapter will directly address the implications of our analysis for the modernisation of Social Europe.

This chapter commences with a discussion of the legal framework covering redundancies and business transfers in Europe which developed from the 1974 Social Action Programme. The adoption of this Social Action Programme reflected the acceptance by Member States that stimulating economic growth through closer European integration required the support of European social policy. This chapter considers what can be learned from over three decades of experience of case law under these Directives. In section 7.2.1 we address redundancy situations, outlining the 1975 Collective Redundancies Directive and its later amendment. The following section, 7.2.2, considers business transfers and the 1977 Acquired Rights Directive that sought to provide protection for workers whose contracts of employment were being transferred to another employer. These rights extend to consultation and protection of their terms and conditions of employment, with pension rights being an exception. Any non-compliance or unilateral changes to these terms and conditions made by the former or new employer makes them liable to claims for unfair dismissal.

In section 7.3 we examine the potential conflict between efficiency and equity considerations when determining the optimal level of workers' rights in the face of economic restructuring. We review theoretical arguments based on the analysis presented in Chapter 3, and the empirical evidence concerning the impact of mandatory employment protection on labour market behaviour and outcomes. Section 7.4 contains our evaluation of the development of EU job-security legislation. This evaluation reflects our focus on the legal instruments of employee protection. It concentrates upon the issues of contracting-out and consultation. Section 7.5 records how the European Court of Justice (ECJ) has failed to provide consistent rulings on the applicability and implications of these Directives. The following section contains our conclusions which identify the limitations of the current regulatory framework.

7.2 REDUNDANCIES AND BUSINESS TRANSFERS IN EUROPE

The Collective Redundancies (CRD) and Acquired Rights (ARD) Directives formed the first element of EU social policy. Both were based on the principle of employment protection, and they paradoxically also have a synergy with dismissal. That is, the outcome could be the opposite to job security, resulting in termination of employment. Below we assess the impact of these first generation social rights in Europe. As will be argued, these Directives indicate how even modest policy agendas can produce significant social and economic progress.

7.2.1 Redundancy Situations

The Collective Redundancies Directive emerged as the rapid post-war industrialisation across Europe had begun to face major global shocks, in particular the first OPEC crisis, resulting in a wave of business collapses and closures. Article 2(1) of the 1975 Collective Redundancies Directive (75/129) (CRD) provides that 'where an employer is contemplating collective redundancies, he shall begin consultations with the workers' representatives in good time with a view to reaching an agreement'.

These rights are discussed in Chapter 8 in detail. Such consultations with the workers' representatives serve only to consider ways of avoiding such collective dismissals and mitigating towards alternatives to such dismissals. The latter is derived from the Germanic concept of the 'social plan', which includes the retraining of the redundant worker. In any event, the emphasis of this Directive was placed on consultation rather than information; it sought to allow the workers' representatives to make constructive proposals to the employer about any alternatives to dismissal. As Kohler and Kittner (2000) explain, often regulatory schemes place obstacles in the path of an employer's ability to dissolve the employment relationship. The overall social aim of the CRD prevails to ensure that workers are protected against exploitation on business closure. However the definition of redundancy requires objectivity concerning the scale of the redundancies, but subjectivity over the reasons for such redundancies. The 1992 amending Directive (92/56) sought to ensure that the worker representatives being consulted about the pending redundancies be informed of 'the criteria proposed for the selection of workers to be made redundant in so far as national legislation and/or practice confers this power on the employer'. Whilst the scope of the 1975 Collective Redundancies Directive was at least ten redundancies with 20–100 workers or at least 10 per cent of the workforce where over 100 workers are employed, Directive 92/56 lowered the threshold to at least five redundancies. The ECJ sought to help clarify these inconsistencies. For example, in the *Rockfon* case (C-449/93), involving collective redundancies, the ECJ defined an 'establishment', since the Directive did not provide a definition, as synonymous to 'undertaking', 'work centre', 'local unit' or 'place of work'. The ECJ noted that a broader interpretation of the term 'establishment' would allow companies belonging to the same group to try to make it more difficult for the Directive to apply to them. As a result they would attempt to evade the 1975 Collective Redundancies Directive (75/129). Consequently the ECJ defined the central term 'establishment' to be 'the unit to which the workers made redundant were assigned to carry out their duties'.

Later the ECJ in *Commission* v. *UK* (C-383/92) ruled that the British definition of 'redundancy' (that is, the cessation of a business, or cessation or diminution in the requirements of a business to carry out work of a particular kind) was too narrow because it failed to cover situations where UK employees were dismissed as a consequence of new working arrangements unconnected to the levels of business. Again the ECJ vowed to protect workers. However a redundancy does not occur, according to Community law, where it arises from the expiry of a fixed-term or specific-task contract, or applies to crews of seagoing vessels or workers employed in public law establishments (see *Nielsen*, C-284/83). This latter decision demonstrates how the ECJ can also conservatively retreat to uphold economic rights enshrined in Community law.

Notably, Article 2(1) was to ensure that 'where an employer is contemplating collective redundancies, he shall begin consultations with the workers' representatives in good time with a view to reaching an agreement'. Such consultations with the workers' representatives serve only to consider ways of avoiding such collective dismissals and mitigating towards alternatives to such dismissals. However the key components of such information and consultation are: 'in good time', 'with a view to reaching agreement' and how workers' representatives are chosen. 'In good time' commences when the employer contemplates such collective dismissals: no less than 30 days prior to them taking effect if less than 100 in number, 90 days if more. 'With a view to reaching agreement' requires consultation, that is a discussion of reason(s) and alternatives, and as a minimum must consider avoiding and mitigating the redundancies. 'Worker representatives' are those as defined by national law. The ECJ in the *Commission* v. *UK* case (C-383/92) sought to ensure the election of workers' representatives in the absence of recognised trade unions, in order to avoid an employer-biased selection and appointment of representatives. As Bourn (1993) explains, it was not until 1992 that the amending Directive (92/56) added the requirement for the employer to inform the worker representatives of the method for calculating any redundancy payments other than those arising out of national legislation and/or practice.

7.2.2 Business Transfers

The 1974 Acquired Rights Directive (ARD) (OJ C104, September 1974) covered workers subject to a business transfer but excluded share transfers. The EU Commission's 1977 proposal to make such an extension was deleted from the text by Council. The overwhelming political pressure from EU Member States which resulted in the exclusion of share transfers in 1977 has caused much of the complexity surrounding the term 'transfer of undertaking', ordinarily referred to as a 'business transfer'. Some EU Member States, such as France for instance, chose to include share transfers when transposing the ARD into domestic law. In an EU context, both the Third and Sixth Council Directives (78/855, OJ L 295 and 82/981, OJ L378) concerning public limited liability companies state that the ARD applies to mergers and divisions. Mergers, as defined under the Third Council Directive, refer to situations where one or more companies are transferred to another company by share acquisition. Normally the members of the acquired company or companies receive shares in the other joined company or companies, with or without an additional cash payment. As a result, following the transfer of the assets and other liabilities, the acquired company or companies ceases, as a general rule, to exist. The European Court of Justice (ECJ) in the *Perrier* case (T-96/92, [1995] IRLR 381 ECJ) reaffirmed that workers affected by a takeover by means of a share transfer are excluded from protection of the ARD. Hence the continuing distinction between sales of businesses externally by changes in the ownership of assets, and the movement of shares internally.

The 1977 Acquired Rights Directive (77/187) (ARD), as amended (98/50) and consolidated (01/23), seeks to safeguard employees' rights where they are subjected to transfers of undertakings. As Elias (1982) observed, the original Directive was a modest measure. Articles 1 and 2 of the original 1977 ARD concern its scope and definitions. Article 1 applies to the transfer of an undertaking, or part of an undertaking, as a result of a legal transfer within the territorial scope of the EU. Article 2 provides the necessary working definitions of the central terms 'transferor', meaning the person who ceases to be the employer; and 'transferee', meaning the person who becomes the employer. Article 3 sets out the aims of the Directive. An undertaking includes 'any trade or business', as well as commercial and non-commercial ventures, following *Redmond* v. *Bartol* (C-29/91). It can also be 'part of an undertaking', as decreed by the ECJ in *Botzen* (C-186/83).

The integral purpose of the ARD is that the transferor's rights, obligations and liabilities arising from the contract of employment existing on the date of the business transfer are transferred to the transferee, and that the transferee shall continue to observe those terms and conditions, collective agreements and any pre-existing trade union recognition. The only exception to the rule is contained in Article 3(3) which stipulates that such provisions shall not cover old-age, invalidity or survivor's benefits or any other pensions.

Central to this secondary legislation are Articles 4 to 6 that seek to safeguard employees' rights. Article 4 declares that a business transfer cannot result in dismissal or redundancy, except where such dismissals are for economic, technical or organisational (ETO) reasons. Where an employee is dismissed or made redundant prior to a business transfer, then the 'new' employer, the transferee, shall be regarded as having been responsible for termination of the contract. Article 5 asserts the primary aim of the ARD is to preserve the employees' rights post-transfer. In terms of consultation, Article 6 requires the parties to the business transfer, the transferor and transferee, to inform and consult their employees or their recognised unions, giving the reasons for the business transfer, and explaining the legal, economic and social implications of the business transfer, as well as the envisaged effects on employees. This consultation is to be undertaken 'in good time' prior to the transfer, and 'with a view to seeking agreement'. These obligations may be restricted to either trade unions only, or alternatively to individual employees only. Articles 7 to 10 involve the enforcement and implementation of the Directive.

In terms of business transfers, the 1977 ARD originally excluded insolvent businesses from its regulation. The 1998 amending Directive effects the most significant changes in relation to transfers by insolvent transferors (Painter and Hardy, 1996; Hunt, 1999), whilst the original Directive was silent on the question of its applicability in insolvency situations and so it was left to the jurisprudence of the ECJ to set out the parameters. The ECJ has ruled that the ARD does not apply to transfers in the context of liquidation proceedings, but that it does apply to proceedings short of liquidation aimed at ensuring the continuance of the business. As Bourn (1999) explains, the amending Directive permits EU Member States to exclude the application of the Directive in cases where the undertaking, business or part of the business being transferred 'is the subject of bankruptcy proceedings or any analogous insolvency proceedings which have been instituted with a view to the liquidation of the assets of the transferor and are under the supervision of a competent public authority'. The Insolvency Directive (80/987) itself confers protection on employees subject to insolvency proceedings. The protection granted extends to guarantee payments, social security and old-age benefits.

Evidently the ARD's long and controversial history highlights how legislation designed to promote greater social protection can potentially be undermined by economic policies. The provision that economic, technical or organisational reasons can be used to override the rights of transferred workers to protection under the ARD, seems to result in the supremacy of efficiency over equity criteria. As Barnard (2000) further argues, the absence of any EU regulation on dismissal law *per se* results in national law and practice prevailing in any event where EU redundancy and transfer laws are evaded. In the next section we analyse the economic rationale for employment protection against which we can assess the appropriateness of the Collective Redundancies and Acquired Rights Directives.

7.3 THE ECONOMIC DEBATE ON MANDATORY EMPLOYMENT PROTECTION

As we have noted in the previous chapters, particularly in our assessment of recent labour market trends in Chapter 4, a key concern of analysts and policy-makers has been the extent to which the perceived poor performance of European labour markets has been due to a policy-induced inflexibility. More specifically it has commonly been argued that rapid technological change and globalisation have necessitated faster structural changes in industrialised countries and that the more pervasive labour market regulation has restricted such adjustments in Europe. The consequence is that European companies have lost international competitiveness, resulting in a declining market share in the most technologically-intensive sectors of world trade, and high rates of job losses coupled with low rates of job creation (Pissarides, 2001). In particular, employment protection provisions in the EU have been identified as a key cause of this 'eurosclerosis' (OECD, 1994). De Michelis (2004) argues that given the faster rate of product market integration in Europe, high firing costs have an especially negative effect on aggregate employment. At the same time, the very same trends in technological change and globalisation have increased the risks of involuntary job loss in Europe (Givord and Maurin, 2003) and increased the demand for employment protection. The much larger negative impact of mergers and acquisitions on employment in Europe when compared to the US (Gugler and Yurtoglu, 2004) reflects the more rigid labour markets and further raises this demand for employment protection in the EU.

The term 'employment protection' is not used consistently in the literature; here we use it in a narrow manner to encompass any restrictions on the ability of employers to fire labour at will. It includes any requirement to provide advance notice of redundancies, minimum periods of notice and entitlement to severance pay, to continue existing contractual obligations in the event of a business transfer, and provide compensation in the case of 'unfair dismissal'. As we outlined in Chapter 3, the standard competitive model considers any such restrictions on the freedom of contract as reducing the efficiency of labour markets. This follows since the costs of adjusting employment increases, favouring longer working hours and leading to fewer lay-offs in periods of declining demand and fewer hires when demand is rising (Addison and Teixeira, 2001). Overall if wages do not fully adjust, then overall employment falls, though Bertola (1992) argues that the effect upon employment is ambiguous theoretically and dependent upon the specific form of the labour demand function, the discount rate and labour turnover. However given that employment protection slows down the transfer of labour from declining to new industries, and since employers' property rights are restricted, then in the long run net job creation is likely to fall.

More recent perspectives on labour market behaviour view employment protection as increasing the bargaining power of employed 'insiders'. This greater bargaining power results in increased wage pressure with a bias against job creation reflecting insiders' own preferences. In addition since such regulations make firing more expensive for employers, they make shirking more likely. Since workers face less risk of dismissal they are more likely to exploit incomplete contracts and costly monitoring by expending less effort. This lowers productivity, raises unit labour costs and is likely to result in lower levels of output, employment and real wages.

The above efficiency arguments against mandatory employment protection are largely discounted by those who view such protection as an effective response to the presence of serious market failures in the labour market. In simple terms, since greater stability of employment encourages greater investments in firm-specific training and less search, then productivity benefits. Hence the nature of this trade-off between the speed of labour market adjustment and productivity determines the optimal degree of employment protection (Belot et al., 2002).

There are several explanations for the presence of such market failures. The unequal bargaining power of employers was identified in Chapter 3 as a potential market failure. This may reflect that individual workers' threatening to quit generates insufficient power to either influence the terms of the employment contract or enforce them. Alternatively it may reflect that a lack of transferability of workers' skills creates an element of monopsony power for most employers. A further source of opportunistic behaviour by employers arises in contracts with deferred payments. As we explained in Chapter 3, in order to reduce turnover costs firms often offer contracts where initially wages are less than productivity, with wages rising faster than productivity as the duration of employment increases. With such Lazear contracts, as discussed in the previous chapter, firms face an incentive to fire workers with long tenure. Whilst reputation effects offset this incentive, Beck (1999) points out that effectively redistributing the property rights to a job through employment protection can also counter such opportunistic behaviour by employers.

Additional explanations for market failure have been based upon externalities and information asymmetries introduced in Chapter 3. The former argues that in the case of a possible plant closure the costs to the local community are unlikely to be taken into account by decision-makers. Here regulation such as early notification can internalise some of these costs and assist the adjustment process. With information asymmetries, given that workers have inferior information about future job security they may be unwilling to invest in firm-specific skills unless provided with employment protection. In addition, since employers are unable to identify the quality of applicants until they actually employ them, those firms that offer contracts with strong job-security provisions will be particularly attractive to workers who have a high propensity to shirk. This adverse selection problem causes all firms to provide too little employment protection and provides a further justification for regulation.

Pissarides (2001) provides a rationale for employment protection based upon insurance of workers against income risk. Given the absence of full unemployment insurance, workers want employment protection and firms do not resist this since their unit labour costs will be reduced through either higher productivity or lower real wages. More specifically, severance payments can provide workers with insurance against the uncertainty of duration of a job, whilst dismissal delays and advance notification reduce the mean time that workers spend unemployed and allow the closing of the gap between income in and out of work. Because employers have an incentive to renege on agreements, legislation can provide a cheap means of enforcing mutually beneficial contracts that specify such employment protection provisions.

In contrast to the conventional analysis of the economic costs and benefits of employment protection outlined above, Saint-Paul (2002) adopts a political economy approach to analyse the forces that generate and sustain such policies in a democracy. Employed insiders vote for such regulations because the benefits in terms of longer duration of their jobs and the associated rents they receive exceeds the slower growth of living standards resulting from the constrained expansion of high-productivity sectors. Hence such regulations are more likely where workers have more bargaining power and face lower growth rates. The difference in these factors between Europe and the US can explain their different employment protection legislation. Moreover since greater employment protection generates a higher proportion of older workers, and these form a higher proportion of voters, this generates political pressures that favour the retention of high levels of regulation. Given this inertia it may be appropriate to examine how the costs to the economy of providing employment protection can be reduced. Blanchard and Tirole (2003) point out that rather than relying upon payroll taxes to fund unemployment insurance, a lay-off tax would be more efficient and also enable a reduced role for the judicial system in the lay-off process.

Given the opposing theoretical arguments outlined above, it is clear that identifying the optimal level of employment protection can only be resolved by empirical studies which allow the costs and benefits to be compared. The general conclusion reached by the large number of empirical studies is that differing degrees of employment protection do not appear to generate significant differences in labour market performance. The OECD's (1999) review of the evidence concluded that stricter employment protection did not influence average unemployment rates or the overall employment rate. There is some evidence that stronger employment protection measures cause labour turnover decreases, with duration of both jobs and unemployment increasing, and that prime-age males benefit at the expense of entrants, re-entrants or older men. Addison and Teixeira (2001) in a more recent survey reach broadly similar conclusions, though they found that there is a negative overall effect on employment and a positive effect on self-employment. As expected, stricter employment protection encourages hours of working rather than employment adjustment, and is associated with lower overall job flows (Messina et al., 2004). Cazes and Nespora (2003) reach similar conclusions in their study of Central and Eastern Europe. In most European countries the strictness of employment protection varies across firm size, with small firms often being subject to less regulation. In Italy (Garibaldi et al., 2003) there is evidence that this results in small firms close to the threshold being less likely to expand employment. For the same country, Ichino and Riphahn (2003) find evidence that absenteeism increases once workers gain employment protection.

A final finding of the empirical literature, and one which we emphasised ourselves in Chapter 3, is the need to consider how different national policy mixes effect the impact of employment protection policies. Pissarides (2001) points out that unemployment insurance and employment protection systems interact, and their operation needs to be co-ordinated. For example in some Southern Member States poor unemployment insurance is compensated for by strict employment protection. Reform of unemployment insurance systems in these countries would facilitate the reform of employment protection and create a more dynamic labour market. Similarly as we noted in Chapter 5, in Spain strong employment protection has since 1984 been combined with the use of fixed-term contracts covering 30 per cent of the workforce by the early 1990s, with a large proportion of entrants being excluded from permanent employment. Reforms in 1997 to reduce both payroll taxes and dismissal costs appear to have increased labour market efficiency (Kugler et al., 2002).

If we now consider the context of the EU, there are additional political economy dimensions to the development of employment protection measures at this level. As Hardy and Adnett (1999) record: 'The consolidated version of the Treaty of Rome affirms that the essential objective of the Community is to constantly improve living and working conditions whilst recognising the need to remove barriers to balanced trade and fair competition' (p. 128). These two goals were recognised to differing extents in the first four social Directives: the Equal Pay Directive, the Equal Treatment Directive, the Collective Redundancies Directive and the Acquired Rights Directive. The competing economic and social goals debate arises from the two distinct approaches underlying the emergence of EU employment regulation: the first is based on the need to dissuade 'social dumping'; the second seeks to encourage the raising of labour standards. These approaches, be they races to the top or to the bottom, identify the dilemma faced in business transfers regulation: which race prevails depends largely upon the emphasis being placed either on the social or on the economic outcomes.

7.4 EVALUATING EU JOB SECURITY

Given the legal and economic discussion above in sections 7.2 and 7.3, three key issues have been identified which affect the future development of EU labour law and social policy in terms of the restructuring of EU enterprises: contracting-out, consultation and growing ECJ activism in this area. This unholy trinity prevails, since the ECJ's case law has mushroomed in this policy area, particularly on consultation and contracting-out issues. This section will assess the impact of each of these key factors in affecting the effectiveness of the current EU legal regime on restructuring EU businesses.

Firstly, contracting-out. The public sector throughout the EU is currently subject to a regime of contracting-out and market testing of various functions to external service providers. Contracting-out seeks to increase the effectiveness of market forces, in bringing about improved quality and cost-effectiveness by means of creating direct and indirect competition within the public sector. In practical terms in these reforms two categories of transfer can arise: ordinary or contracting-out. Contracting-out (or contracting-in) arises in three situations: an organisation contracts out a contract for goods or services for the first time (first generation); or the first contractor is replaced by a second, third, fourth and so on contractor (second generation); or the client takes the contracted-out activities back in-house (contracting-in). All other situations are ordinary sales of businesses (hence ordinary business transfers). Note that it is only under contracting scenarios that the ARD can frustrate the vendor or seller and purchaser's commercial intentions. As such it can be argued and legally supported that the ARD will not apply if the contract is won on a contracting-out basis by an in-house team because there is no change of employer.

Article 4(1) of the ARD expressly limits its application on dismissals subject to economic, technical and organisational (ETO) reasons provided by the employer. The nature and extent of these ETO defences have been examined in the European Court of Justice in two rulings. Advocate-General Darmon in *Bork* (C-101/87) suggested that the ETO defences were restricted where: 'the undertaking's resumption of business was envisaged'. Following this declaration, the ECJ has narrowly applied the ETO defences and most certainly made them inapplicable should the business continue post-transfer. Following this advice, the ECJ held that Article 4(1) of the ARD shall not in itself constitute grounds for dismissal and that the employees transferred were to be treated as still employed, albeit now by the transferee. Relying upon Darmon's comments in *Bork*, Advocate-General Van Gerven some three years later in *D'Urso* (C-362/89), restated more vociferously that the ARD:

> expressly prohibits dismissals when they are the result of the transfer of the undertaking. Only dismissals which would have been made in any case, for instance if the decision was taken before there was any question of transferring the undertaking, fall within the exclusion. Article 4 cannot therefore be relied upon as a support for an argument for dismissing some of the employees because the undertaking has been transferred.

Van Gerven therefore concluded that the ETO defences cannot be relied upon as a justification for dismissals. However the ECJ in *D'Urso* (1989) whilst generally approving of the Advocate-General's advice, stated that although Article 4(1) of the ARD forbade: 'the use of the transfer itself as a reason for dismissal ... on the other hand, the Directive shall not stand in the way of dismissals which may take place for economic, technical or organisational reasons'. Such reasoning, it can be argued, opens the floodgates for the next wave of contracting-out business transfers litigation. The contradictory nature of the ECJ's approach to the ETO defences perhaps explains the ECJ's passivity on these ETO defences. This provides further evidence, as introduced in Chapter 2, of the important role of the ECJ in developing an enlarged social Europe. For an enlarged EU, the central issue here is what constitutes an 'ETO' defence. Although it is now clear when they should apply, when they are appropriate not only depends upon the facts, but on their definition. The ARD fails to define them, and recently EU legislators sought not to define them in their amendment of the ARD. The ECJ up to now has also not clearly ruled on this issue.

Secondly, the extent of consultation rights in the transfer process has preoccupied much of the ECJ's caseload on the ARD. Worker participation is the touchstone to the social protection principles enshrined in both the CRD and the ARD. The 1992 amendments to the 1975 CRD (under Directive 92/56) provided for the consultation of workers' representatives 'irrespective of whether the decision regarding collective redundancies is being taken by the employer or by an undertaking controlling the employer' (Article 2(4)). Such an amendment ensured that transnational redundancy situations were accommodated under the Directive. An EU employer therefore cannot claim that the parent company did not provide the necessary information and this was consequently why they did not consult the workforce affected 'in good time', if at all. The problem of extra-territoriality is avoided by this amendment, unlike the provisions of the European Works Council Directive (94/45), to be discussed in Chapter 8, which allows for central decision-making by management. However in terms of redundancies the transnational nature of decision-making is addressed and the redundant workers receive the requisite payments.

The ECJ's 1994 ruling in *Commission* v. *UK* (C-383/92) requiring the UK to implement its obligations under the ARD 77/187 and Collective Redundancies Directive 75/129 into national law raised further important questions about information, consultation and representation in relation to business transfers. The ARD requires that any collective agreement made between the transferor and a trade union shall have effect as if it had been made with the transferee, and provides that any trade union which was recognised by the transferor shall be deemed to be recognised by the transferee. More importantly Articles 9 and 10 oblige the transferor and transferee to consult with recognised trade unions or elected representatives (in the absence of a recognised trade union) for the purposes of collective consultation. Employee representatives are defined as elected representatives. Once elected, the employer must provide facilities and assistance. For example good access must be given to the relevant employees or workforce(s). Elected representatives also have the right to paid time off during the working day to execute their duties as a representative or undergo training. Note also that any dismissals of elected representatives will be treated as automatically unfair if the reason is that the employee was an elected representative (or standing as a nominee in an elected representatives ballot). No such elected representatives should suffer any detriment whilst undertaking their duties or function as an elected representative.

The ECJ's rulings have insisted upon 'reasonable time' being given to the consultation process. Information about the transfer must also be given to the representatives 'long before the transfer to enable consultation to take place'. Whilst the ARD does not set out a clear timescale, it is clear that transferors should be careful not to rush the process, unlike redundancy consultation where timescales are set, since the ARD implicitly requires 'meaningful dialogue' about the economic, social and legal implications. 'Good time' may be 30 days or more (following the redundancy model) allowed for consultation 'with a view to reaching agreement' on the key issues. The transferor should provide the elected representatives with information on the facts of the transfer (date and reasons); the 'legal, social and economic' implications (as perceived by the transferee) for the affected employees; what measures are envisaged, post-transfer; and any other information provided or measures envisaged by the transferee. The ARD requires the transferee to notify the transferor of any information appropriate to be given to the elected representatives. What often troubles those involved in transfers in practice is not the openness, but the technical terms 'measures' and 'envisaged'.

Consultation should be conducted 'with a view to seeking the [elected] representatives' agreement to measures to be taken'. To that end, consultation only commences following information which leads to the transferor and transferee envisaging taking measures in connection with the transfer (that is, redundancies, changes to contracts, changes to working conditions or practices, union de-recognition or recognition, or any changes whatsoever). Once consultation commences the ARD implies that all proposed measures should be discussed in good faith and every effort is made to accommodate views and differences and reach agreement where possible. Effectively this establishes a collective bargaining model. Any breach of consultation rights provides grounds for a complaint to a national court on the grounds of failure to comply (that is, electoral defects; no or lack of information; no, limited or lack of consultation; lack of trade union recognition; or any other case affecting employees). Where a national court upholds the complaint, a Declaration is given and a penalty imposed under national law.

Changes to the regulation of consultation will impact upon future restructuring exercises in Europe. For example normally management reach a strategic decision before informing the respective workforce. Management decision-making was therefore, pre-Social Europe, often in practice unaffected by worker participation. However the 1975 Collective Redundancies Directive (75/129) was one of the first social Directives to change this practice, by requiring management once they have reached a decision affecting the workforce to consult with the workers' representatives. The term 'management (or managerial) prerogative' refers to 'the will of the employer'. It was recognised first by the ECJ in the *Nielsen* case (C-284/83) with regard to collective redundancies, when the Court argued that 'the [1975] Directive did not affect the employer's freedom to effect ... collective dismissals'.

Management prerogative, under Community law, is controlled by subjecting both the employers and workers to procedures for information and consultation, enforced by effective remedies. This requires a dialogue between employers and workers, or their representatives, by way of active processes of consultation, so as to control the employer's overall managerial prerogative. In the following chapter we discuss how this initial foray into consultation in EU employment law has since been strengthened through the European Works Council and the Information and Consultation Directives.

The third and final issue is that of the growing activism of the ECJ in this area. As Hunt (1998) points out the ECJ has become a key policy-driver and -setter of the social agenda, especially through its use of the ARD as its platform for social change. In the next section we re-examine the role of the ECJ and its growing activism in this area.

7.5 THE EUROPEAN COURT OF JUSTICE AND BUSINESS TRANSFERS

Our previous analysis in this chapter has shown that uncertainty for European employers and workers alike has arisen in respect of rights and responsibilities in the workplace. This uncertainty has often been due to the shortcomings of the EU legislators, whether in an attempt to marry social and economic rights or to appease various EU Member States. Consequently the ECJ, as observed earlier in Chapter 2, has frequently been pivotal in the development of EU social policy. Sciarra (2000) furthers this thesis by arguing that the ECJ becomes the voice of the national courts. To that end, the ECJ seeks overall to preserve the aims of Directives, though arguably an exception to this rule has been the area of business restructuring. The ARD has been the subject of a number of preliminary rulings, more than any other social Directive enacted by the EU, the purpose of these ECJ rulings being in principle to assist EU Member States with their interpretation of the obligations arising under the ARD. However in practice the Court has sometimes provided a morass of complexity and confusion regarding these obligations and/or demonstrated the robust and conservative natures of the metamorphic legal institution of the EU.

The ECJ ruled in *Schmidt* (C-392/92) that the contracting-out of a single cleaner came within the scope of the ARD and so the worker could be transferred. In particular the absence of tangible assets and the fact that it is an ancillary activity and performed by a single employee are not decisive factors for the purpose of establishing a transfer. The significance of *Schmidt* is the ECJ's conclusion that the retention of its identity is the decisive criterion for establishing whether a business transfer has occurred. In support of this is Advocate-General Van Gerven's question: 'whether the cessation of a specific operation within an undertaking and the consequent transfer of that operation to an outside undertaking is to be regarded as a transfer of a part of the undertaking within the meaning of the Directive?' An answer to this question is given by the ECJ in *Schmidt*, in holding contracting-out to be clearly within the scope of the ARD.

Previously in *Rask* (C-209/91), a case concerning the tendering-out of the operational running of a canteen service, ECJ had reaffirmed the 'retention of identity' test and categorically included contracting-out within the ARD. The ECJ's growing jurisprudence has been active in seeking to clarify the ARD. In particular the ECJ's ruling in *Spijkers* (C-24/85), which established the criteria for identifying 'a legal transfer', played a significant role in the development of the law relating to business transfers. The ECJ's rulings in *Redmond* (C-29/91) included public and private undertakings under the ambit of the ARD, whilst in *Katsikas* (C-253/96), granting employees with a right to resign should they disagree with the business transfer, highlights the growing important influence of the ECJ in enforcing social laws actually in the EU workplace.

Subsequently the *Schmidt* judgment met with strong criticism from many EU governments. Fuelling the controversy surrounding the scope of the ARD was the ECJ's later ruling in the *Rygaard* (C-48/94) case, concerning a firm of carpenters who were contracted to construct a canteen. In Rygaard, following the bankruptcy of the main contractor the carpenters, who had been made redundant as a consequence, were transferred to the subcontractor to complete the work. Ole Rygaard, one of the carpenters affected, sought damages for wrongful dismissal. Considering all the facts and applying the ECJ's previous ruling in *Spijkers*, the ECJ, disagreeing with the Advocate-General, held that there was no transfer where one undertaking merely made available to another certain workers and materials for carrying out particular works. The ECJ reasoned that the making available of workers and materials did not constitute a stable economic activity as no assets had been transferred. Thus such a failure meant that certain activities formerly undertaken by the transferor could not be transferred.

It can be contended that the ECJ's ruling in *Rygaard* marks a retreat towards a more conservative approach when compared with its other rulings since 1985 on business transfers. The ECJ in *Merckx* however confined the *Rygaard* ruling to the facts of its particular case, by finding that a change of workplace and name did not prevent the ARD from applying. Thus a business transfer occurs where a stable economic entity exists, irrespective of the contractual relationship. Until recently the ECJ, it could have been argued, had regained its enthusiasm for business transfers by reviving its 'robust' stance in *Merckx*. In *Henke* and *Suzen*, the ECJ returns to its conservative reservations about compulsory competitive tendering as witnessed in *Rygaard*. *Henke* (C-298/94) concerned the reorganisation of a municipal administration. The ECJ held that legal secretaries and other administrative staff working for local authorities in Germany could be dismissed or have their terms and conditions changed as a consequence of a business transfer between a former local authority and a contractor. The terse ruling by the ECJ, on Mrs Henke's dismissal as a mayor's secretary when the municipal administration was transferred to the regional authority, could now open the floodgates and allow many contracting-out exercises involving administrative staff to avoid the ARD. The ECJ's reasoning was based on the failure of these administrative workers to hold a stable economic entity, as service providers, to constitute a business transfer. Such a ruling has wide-ranging implications for many of the contracting-out scenarios, unless the decision in Henke is narrowly read to be applicable only to those activities that are administrative and not wholly economic in nature.

A similar ruling was made by the ECJ in *Suzen* (C-13/95) where a contract to clean a church-run secondary school in Bonn was terminated with one contractor and awarded to another, giving rise to eight dismissals on the grounds of redundancy. The ECJ held that the fact that the service provided by the old and new contractor was similar was not sufficient by itself to support the conclusion that a business transfer had taken place. In his Opinion Advocate-General La Pergola went further and contended that the transfer of a bare service contract from an outgoing to an incoming contractor, where no tangible or intangible assets were passing, did not constitute a business transfer within the scope of the ARD. The ECJ held in *Suzen* that a transfer of activities was insufficient to amount to a transfer of an undertaking. Rejecting the Advocate-General's opinion, the ECJ reaffirmed the orthodox 'economic entity' test which had been developed in *Spijkers* and later refined in *Schmidt* and *Merckx*. Thus no relationship need exist between the transferor and transferee prior to the transfer for the ARD to apply, but the passing of tangible assets or the taking-over of a workforce remain as prerequisites for meeting the *Spijkers* test. Had the ECJ followed the Advocate-General's advice, the *Suzen* decision would have impacted on all contracted labour-only services, further narrowing the scope of the ARD. In any event it can be contended that the *Schmidt* ruling marks the high-water mark on the ARD's application. Since that case, except for *Henke*, *Suzen* and *Rygaard* which it could be argued are rulings confined to their facts, the ECJ's jurisprudence since 1985 has been one which has emphasised their concern about defending the ARD's primary purpose: to protect employees subject to business transfers.

More confusion was created on 25 January 2001, when the ECJ in *Oy Liikenne Ab* v. *Liskojärvi and Juntunen* (C-172/99) (2001), a transfer involving the contracting-out of Finnish buses, concluded that because no buses had been transferred no transfer could have occurred. Despite transferring 33 of the 45 employees, none of the 26 buses nor other assets were transferred and the ECJ as a result ruled that whilst labour-intensive operations might be subjected to a transfer, other factors had to be considered where the undertaking depended on the use of substantial assets. To that end, the ECJ took the view that a bus service operation needed buses, and therefore the provision of such a service could not be viewed as a service based on labour alone. In this case, a contracting-out transfer was excluded from the Directive's remit. Clearly, as Sargeant (2002) argues, reform of the ARD since 1998 has had little affect on the ECJ's jurisprudential approach, thus affirming our view that the ECJ's growing activism in the EU policy area of restructuring has proved to be both helpful and problematical.

7.6 CONCLUSIONS: FUTURE REGULATION

As we argued in Chapter 4, much of the current debate about the future of EU social policy and modernisation of the ESM concerns the issue of the EU's 'global competitiveness'. The advent of the European Community with its internal market and its free movement of capital and labour in the 1950s presented many opportunities and threats for the workplace. Core social rights supported by effective worker representation were envisaged as the means of resolving such threats and exploiting the opportunities. This is particularly evident in the areas discussed here in relation to business restructuring. Both the 1975 CRD and the 1977 ARD entailed providing the individual worker with a minimum protection through representation. Such minimalistic protection was later challenged by the ECJ and amended by further Directives. Meanwhile the ECJ filled some of the legislative gaps, enabling more effective protection. Upholding basic social rights and advancing others, the ECJ has maintained its mantle as the 'Guardian of the Treaty', though it has been presented with a hard task when seeking to reconcile competing social and economic rights. This survey of the existing European case law records how the political debate surrounding the battle between social and economic rights has entered the legal ambit. Consequently the EU's legal processes have allowed the ECJ to effectively modify the ARD, but not the CRD, in line with the changing economic situation from the 1980s. Throughout this chapter we have seen evidence of the dilemma surrounding the economic and social paradox within EU social policy. The central question in connection with the achievement of the EU's social and economic goals in the workplace continues to be: how do we link economic flexibility and social justice? Applying the case study of enterprise restructuring to this question, it emerges that both legally and in economic theory, business reorganisations can be made compatible with economic and social rights. But the question remains, what happens when they conflict? Such an important question will be addressed in Chapter 9. The discussion above suggests two key conclusions relevant to the future modernisation of the ESM. Firstly, as identified by Hardy and Adnett (1999a), the lack of a binding precedent in the ECJ increases the importance of the precise drafting of Directives. Whether or not specific social rights can be reconciled with the perceived needs of economic efficiency, it is clear that imprecisely drafted Directives seeking to establish modern sophisticated social rights create confusion and uncertainty. This uncertainty distorts decision-making and reallocates resources away from welfare-enhancing production into welfare-redistributing litigation. The process which permits individual European Member States to transpose Directives into their national statutes places a further burden on the ECJ, contributing to additional legal uncertainties based upon unresolved conflicts between national and ECJ rulings.

Secondly, when the EU finally assesses the existing social rights established in the Charter on Fundamental Rights (ratified 2002) in terms of their impact upon economic flexibility, then it is important that policy-makers specify appropriate measures of such efficiency. In specifying an appropriate measure, a modernised Social Europe will have to reflect its new objectives of promoting high levels of both employment and social protection. As Hardy (2001) argues, the key to future labour law regulation of business restructuring will remain the provision of genuine clarity. Clearly this is the case with the ARD and CRD. To remedy the situation the 'minimum floor of rights' needs to be clearly reconstructed in order to promote both social justice and economic flexibility. In the absence of such measures, EU legislators now need to utilise the 'command and control' model and redraft the legislative framework which underpins enterprise restructuring on a directly legally enforceable legal base, similar to that provided for mergers across the EU under the 1986 Merger Regulations. These Regulations being directly enforceable overcomes any potential mismanagement of national transposition of these laws. Alternatively should such a model prove unattractive to policy-makers, then as a minimum response the ETO defences in the ARD should be formally defined in order to remove the current confusion. A clear definition would ensure that transparent labour standards and social rights are established, and that economic flexibility can only take precedence in prescribed circumstances. Above all, evidence from EU business reorganisations since 1974 has shown that it is a European-wide case of competing economic and social goals in the regulation of such restructuring, be it redundancies or business transfers. Finally, this chapter highlights that it may be premature to rely solely on the ECJ to trade-off social and economic rights in the workplace.

8. Consultation, participation and industrial democracy in Europe

8.1 INTRODUCTION

The social dialogue and the quality of industrial relations are at the centre of the European Social Model. In our opening chapters we have noted how the promotion of social dialogue became a key driving force behind the post-Lisbon economic and social reforms. So far we have concentrated our discussion on social dialogue at the European level; in this chapter we address a range of policies which target consultation and participation at the workplace level. In particular we are concerned with legislation which affect employers' decision-making processes, what Bercusson (2002) has called the evolution of EU policy on labour in the enterprise. In a simple 'right-to-manage' model it is assumed that efficient market economies require employers to have sole responsibility for decision-making. Collective bargaining allows interest representation but does not fundamentally question this managerial right to manage. Managers' search for maximum profits will ensure that they take into account in their decision-making process employee and customer interests. As we noted in Chapter 3, employment contracts are often incomplete by design, because the employer cannot fully specify in advance the particular tasks that it will require its employees to perform. As Collins (2002) points out, the contract by specifying the obligation of obedience to management, grants employers the right to direct workers as they see fit. However this traditional contract provides little incentive for workers to actively co-operate with employers.

As we discussed in Chapter 3, given the presence of asymmetric information, externalities and long-term relationships between workers and employers, allowing employers unrestricted decision-making powers may not produce socially optimal outcomes. Whilst most of the other chapters in this book address regulations which constrain employers' discretion, in this chapter we consider a range of measures which seek to encourage greater employee involvement in this decision-making. Whilst in part a rationale for such policies is potential efficiency gains, and the replacement of adversarial industrial relations with a more co-operative form of interaction, there are also equity considerations which have driven the evolution of limited property rights of workers to their jobs. In reality the reconciliation of these diverse considerations has led to a wide range of current practices between and within Member States.

As we noted in Chapter 4, recent changes in labour market behaviour have meant increasing labour market flexibility and uncertainty and this has coincided with a decline in trade union membership and influence. In addition globalisation has increased competitive pressures and presented new challenges to Europe's social legislation and systems of protection. These pressures have led to reforms of collective bargaining institutions and practices. In Britain and the USA these pressures together with associated changes in corporate governance revised expectations regarding the role and responsibilities of corporate management. The initial outcome was a greater emphasis on responsibilities to shareholders. Proponents of stakeholder voice pointed out that such an emphasis would be counter-productive if the ability of management to commit credibly to long-run relationships with other stakeholders was thereby weakened. The information and consultation provisions of European Community Directives now provide a countervailing force to shareholder primacy by favouring more stakeholder-orientated strategies (Armour et al., 2003).

Even prior to this legislation a new balance emerged in some Member States (European Commission, 2002a), 'co-ordinated decentralisation'. This was based upon multilevel framework bargaining and improved monitoring, allowing negotiated flexibility rather than a choice between standard solutions and deregulation. In addition, economic and monetary union shifted economic policy-making to the European level and increased the importance of co-ordinated wage bargaining and industrial relations at that level. At the same time technological change and the emergence of the knowledge economy have increased pressures to decentralise decision-making and speed up the dissemination of best practice and new ideas. Together these pressures have encouraged employers to seek a more flexible and better-educated workforce, whilst employees have sought more participation and information from their employers, and greater choice and flexibility in the organisation of their working life.

Collectively these changes have encouraged increased interest in extending worker participation (Mizrahi, 2002). They suggest the possible advantages of contracts which recognise that both parties act simultaneously not only as principals in their own right but also as agents for the other. This symbiotic contract model recognises not only that the employee is the agent of the employer in carrying out their work, but also that the employer is acting partly as the agent of the employee in creating the work being undertaken and enhancing the employee's employability (Collins, 2002). Such contracts, by effectively sharing profits, encourage management and workers to co-operate to maximise net returns. Though a conflict of interest remains, symbiotic contracts cause the pursuit of self-interest to lead to both employers and workers seeking to co-operate. If as we explain below there are mechanisms that prevent such contracts evolving, then a role for employment law is to stimulate the adoption of partnership arrangements.

Our discussion in this chapter is organised as follows. In the following section we identify and classify the various forms of information, consultation and co-determination mechanisms found within European labour markets. Building upon our examination of European industrial relations in Chapter 4, we again stress the diversity of practices both between and within Member States. In section 8.3 we examine the development of European legislation from the early consultation requirements contained in the Acquired Rights and Collective Redundancies Directives to the Amsterdam Treaty. After a review of the development of national legislation in section 8.3.3 we provide a more detailed analysis of the European Works Council Directive, examining the impact of this first attempt to develop the European Social Model to regulate multinational companies' labour market behaviour. Section 8.4 contains our analysis of the economic rationale for regulating information, consultation and co-determination practices. We examine arguments that suggest that market failures may prevent the emergence of efficient practices in the absence of regulation, and consider whether these provide a rationale for European-level legislation. This section also contains a review of the presently rather unsatisfactory situation regarding the empirical analysis of the impact of regulation on firm performance and employee welfare. In section 8.5 we analyse the two latest additions to EU legislation in this area: the National Consultation and Information Directive and the European Company Statute, and the related Directive on employee involvement. This is followed by a review of current issues and future challenges in section 8.6, containing some concluding thoughts on the future of EU workplace democracy.

8.2 THE DIVERSITY OF EMPLOYEE INVOLVEMENT IN THE EU

There are no universally agreed definitions for the terms 'workplace democracy' and 'partnership'. Here we use these terms to refer to any structures or institutional mechanisms that enable employees and/or their representatives to take part in the decision-making processes within their organisations. A basic distinction is between direct and indirect representation. The former occurs where the individual or groups of workers are directly involved in decision-making, and the latter where there is some body, say a trade union or works council, which represents and expresses workers' voice.

Indirect representation can be inclusive or merely act on behalf of certain groups of workers, such as trade union members (exclusive representation). The structures and mechanisms which enable workers to take part in the decision-making process can vary from producer co-operatives to mandatory or voluntary works councils and shop floor programmes addressing quality issues (Poole et al., 2001). A further distinction is between single and multi-channel representation. In the former, collective bargaining is favoured to the exclusion of joint consultation; until recently the British situation, with unions being wary of joint consultation and hostile to non-union channels of representation (Gospel and Willman, 2003). With multi-channel representation, as in Germany, collective bargaining outside the firm co-exists with joint consultation in the workplace at firm level and even representation on the supervisory board of companies.

Guest and Peccei (2001) identify three broad intellectual traditions and theoretical perspectives underlying most approaches to partnership and workplace democracy. First is the pluralist approach that acknowledges conflicts of interest between capital and labour and views consultation and co-determination legislation as a means of ensuring employees' interests are not ignored in intra-organizational decision-making. The key emphasis in the pluralist approach is on indirect participation through representatives of employees, trade union or not, to establish an independent employee voice within the organisation. Second is the unitarist approach that seeks to maximise employee commitment to the organisation through partnership, financial incentives and direct employee involvement in decision-making. The latter is largely limited to decisions related to employees' specific tasks, rather than employment issues in general. In its most recent American form this involves the utilisation of a range of high-performance human resources practices in recruitment, training and motivation which seek to generate commitment and loyalty amongst the workforce. Third is what Guest and Peccei term the hybrid approach, that incorporates elements of the previous two approaches. Here there are mutual gains to be generated from partnership, though formal representative mechanisms are thought likely to be needed to prevent opportunistic behaviour. Each of these approaches assumes that the social relations or political culture within an organisation shapes employees' and employers' perceptions, goals and bargaining strategies, and influences the outcomes of their actions (Frege, 2002).

We examined in Chapters 1 and 4 the emergence and persistence of different models of social policy and industrial relations in the individual Member States of the European Union. Perhaps nowhere are these differences greater than in the area of consultation and industrial democracy. Whilst many Member States have evolved multi-channel processes of representation, in Britain trade union and employer resistance to such processes has resisted a demarcation between wage determination and other aspects of the employment relation. Employee representation in managerial decision-making is equally diverse. At plant level different forms of work councils or workplace committees exist, with either directly elected or union-delegated employee representation. Member States' provisions on employees' board-level involvement differ even more widely, reflecting national differences in systems of corporate governance. In the dualistic systems (Austria, Denmark, Germany, Greece, Netherlands and Portugal) the management board is subject to monitoring and control by a supervisory board. In monistic systems (Ireland, Italy, Luxembourg, Spain, Sweden and the UK) the board of directors has independence of decision-making. Although as we explore below, European legislation harmonises statutory minima, there are few signs of common practice regarding disclosure and participation emerging across the EU.

8.3 THE DEVELOPMENT OF NATIONAL AND EUROPEAN LEGISLATION

The initial elements of EU labour legislation, such as the Acquired Rights Directive (77/187, 98/50 and 23/01) and Collective Redundancies Directive (Directive 75/129), as recounted in Chapter 7, included requirements for mandatory consultation between employers and employees. As such, they largely reflected the dominant European pluralist tradition towards workplace democracy, and tacit agreement that the 'German model' represented the best prospect of eliminating adversarial industrial relations. In essence this initial legislation created a reactive or event-driven, indirect form of workplace democracy. That is, after management unilaterally reached a decision to either transfer or close a business, then workers' representatives were informed of this decision and the consequences jointly considered. As Member States lost their enthusiasm for convergence on the 'German model', harmonisation of national systems through a transfer of legislative authority to Brussels lost its political support (Streeck and Vitols, 1995). However in the 1980s the EU Commission under the auspices of the Health and Safety Framework Directive (Directive 89/391) set out to provide for limited proactive workplace democracy in the form of worker safety representatives instigating discussion with their employers on relevant issues.

In the 1990s both the formalising of social dialogue within EU policy-making and the European Works Council Directive reflected the re-emergence of policy-making based upon the pluralist approach. This approach has been further encouraged by the repeated and increasing emphasis on the need for social partner involvement in the design and implementation of Member

States' National Action Plans under the European Employment Strategy. Indeed since 2001 the Annual Guidelines have included a specific horizontal objective requiring the full involvement of the social partners at all levels in the implementation and monitoring of the EES.

Fundamental changes in the organisation of work, as noted above, have now encouraged further legislative measures related to employee involvement. As the European Commission's Green Paper, 'Partnership for a New Organisation of Work', notes:

> The concepts of workplace, firm, factory, and, in particular, the notion of employer is undergoing the process of diversification, leading to an erosion of traditional employment relationships. Downsizing, outsourcing, subcontracting, tele-working, networking and joint ventures bring new dimensions to the world of work for which traditional labour provisions do not appear to have adequate answers.

In 2001 the Commission argued that the effective management of industrial change in this new environment requires an improvement in the framework of rules on workers' rights to be informed and consulted. The Directives on collective redundancies, transfers of undertaking and European works councils were felt to no longer provide an adequate framework. Accordingly a Directive accompanied the adoption of a Regulation on the statute for a European company covering the involvement of employees in such companies (October 2001), followed by the Directive on informing and consulting employees in March 2002. Taken together this present EU policy package appears to lack a common underlying rationale, and for Member States like Britain without a tradition of mandatory workplace representation it represents a radical new departure for employment law (Bercusson, 2002).

8.3.1 Europeanised Freedom of Association and National Employment Relations Models

The right to freedom of association, broadly derived from many international legal instruments on human rights, is defined as the rights and freedoms associated with the membership of employers' and workers' associations. Article 11 of the 1989 Social Charter provides that:

> employers and workers of the EU shall have the right of freedom of association in order to constitute professional associations or trade unions of their choice for the defence of their economic and social interests. Every employer and employee shall have the freedom to join or not to join such organisations without any personal or occupational damage being thereby suffered by him.

The right to freedom of association can also be found in many other international legal instruments, such as ILO Conventions Nos 87 and 98, the

UN Declaration of Human Rights and Article 11 of the 1950 European Convention on Human Rights (ECHR). The 1961 European Social Charter replicated the ECHR's Article 11.

Article 11 of the 1989 Charter recognises the right to establish trade unions and the right of workers to join unions. The 1989 Charter also expressly recognises the negative freedom, the right of the worker not to join a trade union. Consequently a closed shop might contravene a worker's fundamental right. Notably Article 137 expressly excludes freedom of association from the EU's legal competence, although in a staff case the ECJ has accepted the right to freedom of association (see *Kortner*, C-175/73). Advocate-General Jacobs confirmed the precedent set by *Kortner* in the *Albany* case (C-67/96). The *Bosman* case (C-415/93) further recognised the general right to freedom of association in Community law and *Maurissen* (C-193 and 194/87) recognised the role of trade unions in Community law under the banner of freedom of association. Articles 27 and 28 of the Charter of Fundamental Rights of the 'Solidarity' chapter indirectly encourage the right to freedom of association.

In a modernised European context, the term 'social dialogue' is applied to refer to the discussions that occur between management and labour either voluntarily or by national regulation. It was the Agreement on Social Policy (1989) which first promoted the consultation of management and labour (Article 3(1)), though the first Social Action Programme of 1974 had called for 'the progressive involvement of workers or their representatives in the life of undertakings'. In fact the 1952 Treaty of Paris advocated the idea of social participation in decision-making at Community level. Consequently management and labour may initiate social dialogue that may lead to contractual relations including agreements between them. 'Autonomous social dialogue' is the term often used now to distinguish it from the formal social dialogue created under the Treaty. Collectively bargained labour standards were first proposed in the Proof on Employment Directive (91/533) 1991 (COM(90) 563 Final), that includes collective agreements as part of the contractual relationship. More recently Article 27 of the Charter of Fundamental Rights states that workers or their representatives are 'guaranteed' the right to information and consultation 'in good time'. Article 28 guarantees collective bargaining in that process. These future provisions will be considered in Chapter 9. In any event, Directive 2002/14 on establishing a general framework for informing and consulting employees seeks to guarantee these mandatory standards across the board.

The usage of collective agreements as minimum standards was also promoted in the Posting of Workers Directive, discussed in Chapters 1 and 5. This Directive aims at prescribing the working conditions applicable to workers from another State performing work in the host country. However in a case predating the Directive, *Rush Portuguesa* (C-113/89) the ECJ ruled that

'Community law does not preclude Member States from extending their legislation, or collective agreements entered into by both sides of industry ... within their territory'. The Directive, by giving an entitlement to posted workers to collectively agree standards, sets a minimum standard, since the ruling presumes that posted workers should be no better off than the host-country workers.

The evolution of European economic and monetary union provided incentives for further developments. The 'Doorn group' (which takes its name from the Dutch town where in 1998 the unions concerned adopted a joint declaration) expressed a need for close cross-border co-ordination of collective bargaining within EMU. The Doorn declaration represented the first time that unions from different European countries had determined a set of joint bargaining guidelines. In order to prevent possible downward competition in wages and working conditions, the unions involved agreed 'to achieve collective bargaining settlements that correspond to the sum total of the evolution of prices and the increase in labour productivity'; 'to achieve both the strengthening of mass purchasing power and employment creating measures (e.g. shorter work times)'; and regularly to 'inform and consult each other on developments in bargaining policy'. The Doorn group has since attempted to improve its co-operation on non-wage aspects of collective bargaining policy, concentrating on the issues of working time and continuing training.

Although social dialogue has been promoted (see Section 1.4.3 above) since Val Duchesse in 1985, it was Article 3(1) of the Agreement on Social Policy 1989 that formalised social dialogue as a means of consultation between management and labour. Consequently management and labour may initiate social dialogue which may lead to contractual relations including agreements between them. The participation of the social partners, CEEP, ETUC and UNICE, was first described as 'bargaining in the shadow of the law'. Yet from these humble beginnings, the later Amsterdam and Nice Treaties have pushed the social partners, and social dialogue, centre stage under Article 138 of the Amsterdam Treaty. The success of such an initiative was seen in the Parental Leave Directive (96/34), which was instigated and agreed between the social partners and became a framework agreement for Europe. Chapter IV on solidarity of the Charter of Fundamental Rights seeks to encourage further social dialogue. National trade union movements are a fundamental part of most industrial-relations and labour-law systems. Various models of trade unions exist in Europe, including occupational, white-collar, craft, industrial, general, sectoral and enterprise unions. The challenge faced by supranational legality as a vehicle to harmonise the levels of economic decision-making and set fixed working conditions requires unions to construct representation at the supranational level (not only in the EU) without abandoning their local and national role. This initial basis of representation required by the European works councils stands as a first step in this process. It promotes the relationship among worker representatives from different countries and places on the table the contradictions resulting from country-based representation.

The European Trade Union Confederation (ETUC) has achieved a greater level of protagonism in the so-called negotiated directives with European employer associations. These negotiated Directives have led to the implementation of such communitary legislation as parental leave, and protections for temporary and part-time workers. However in the design of these EU laws, which have been called guideline Directives, the Member States hold a determinant role in the development of the transfer of the principle of legal subsidiarity to the terrain of collective bargaining, which is obliged to continue to work out its negotiating objectives within national contexts. Collective bargaining, which precedes negotiated legislation, is absorbed within the legislation that seems as a result to legitimise the negotiated outcome. In this sense negotiated legislation seems to follow more the model of legislative process than that of autonomous mechanisms for the social partners to fix working conditions.

During the preparations for the Amsterdam Summit of June 1997, transnational trade union rights were discussed. Consequently when the Treaty was revised, one change was that it included a reference to the fundamental trade union rights contained in the 1961 European Social Charter and the 1989 Community Charter of Fundamental Social Rights of Workers. These minor amendments however did not solve the complicated problems the EU is facing in this area. The provision of information and consultation rights at transnational level through the European Works Councils Directive constitutes the exception to this lack of EU initiative in the field of transnational trade union rights. As will be discussed in Chapter 9, the EU Charter of Fundamental Rights makes no reference to the transnational level in relation to the right of association in Article 12, and the rights of collective bargaining and collective action in Article 28.

We have noted in Chapters 2 and 4 the disparate development of employment relations across Member States. For example the French Revolution and the consequential codification of law by Napoleon, encapsulating the Code du Travail, has enshrined in French law both a role and a mandatory functional purpose for the five nationally recognised trade unions in France. Since 1916, where a French business has more than 11 workers a *delegation syndicaux* (worker representative) must be elected. Moreover where 50 or more French workers exist, then a *comité des enterprises* (a works council) must be formed, comprising elected union and worker representatives. Under German law since 1972, where five or more workers exist and petition for representation, a works council is constituted. Similarly, works councils are present in Spain (a *sociedad anomina/empressa*) and Italy (*rappretanza*). Such mandatory mechanisms do not exist in Eire and the UK, where voluntary trade union recognition applies, unless statutory recognition is litigated for. Elsewhere in Europe, for example Belgium, the Netherlands, Denmark and Sweden, sectoral bargaining or national collective bargaining takes place between employer and employee groups. From this comparative evidence three common paradigms emerge in relation to EU employment relations systems: the works council, collective bargaining and individual bargaining models. Consequently various EU Member States' national employment relations systems can be allocated to one of the three categories illustrated. These categories represent varying levels of commitment to worker participation, consultation and information processes. In sum, the distinctive national models of the Member States of the EU demonstrate the diversity of the current legal implementation of EU ideals on representation and consultation in the EU workplace.

8.3.2 The Origins of European Legislation on Industrial Democracy

It was the 1974–76 Social Action Programme that first addressed worker participation at the supranational level. Such embryonic ideals resulted in worker representatives being involved in industrial reorganisation as well as such issues as redundancies and business transfers. Historically at EU level collective bargaining has developed at three levels: supranational negotiations, multinationals' cross-border enterprise agreements and social dialogue. However whilst these forms cover bargaining, in terms of negotiation rights EC labour law has become more focused on establishing consultation, information and participation rights. For instance the Collective Redundancies Directive, discussed in Chapter 7, embraces the need for workers to be informed of future job losses. Whereas the Acquired Rights Directive, also discussed in the previous chapter, provides a similar framework of information and consultation for workers affected by business transfers.

As Gospel et al. (2000) explain, prior to these Directives in some Member States such as the UK, provisions were based upon disclosure for collective bargaining rather than for consultation. This tension between the pluralist and unitarist approaches led to persistent criticism in the 1980s and 1990s that the UK had not fully implemented the consultation requirements contained in these initial social policy directives. This culminated in the EU Commission taking infringement proceedings against the UK Government for failing to ensure effective sanctions for non-compliance by employers; not requiring employers to consult 'with a view to reaching agreement'; narrowly defining redundancy dismissals; and failing to ensure the supply of the information required under the Directive. The resulting European Court of Justice (ECJ) ruling imposed an absolute obligation on British employers to consult with worker representatives. However the 1995 Collective Redundancies and Transfer of Undertakings (Protection of Employment) (Amendment) Regulations, the result of another ECJ ruling against the British Government once again highlighted the failure of the British Government to extend the right of consultation to employee representatives where a trade union was not recognised. These Regulations were short-lived, since in 1999 they were amended again to allow for election of employee representatives where no recognised trade unions existed for the purposes of consultation on redundancy and business transfers. Similar problems are rare elsewhere in the EU: for example in France trade union representation is guaranteed, and in Germany the extensive system of works councils provides the vehicle for consultation.

8.3.3 The European Works Council Directive

It was not until the 1994 European Works Council (EWC) Directive (Directive 94/45/EC, as amended by 97/74/EC) that issues concerned directly with workplace democracy reappeared in European-level legislation. This was the first Directive to be approved under the Social Policy Agreement procedure from which Britain had initially opted-out. The Directive applies to those undertakings with more than 1000 employees in a Member State and at least 150 employees in another two Member States (the three other countries of the European Economic Area, Iceland, Liechtenstein and Norway, are considered as Member States for the purposes of this Directive). These thresholds are applied on the basis of the average number of employees, including part-time workers, over a two-year period according to national legislation or practice. The Directive aimed to establish a body, termed a European Works Council (EWC), representing the interests of all workers for bargaining purposes by ensuring that management and worker representatives were elected to a supervisory board of the company. The central precondition of the Directive relies on both the employer and the employees requesting that a works council be established. In 2002 it was estimated that about 1865 firms fall within the scope of the Directive, though according to the European Trade Union Institute (ETUI) at that time only 639 had European Works Councils, 46 of these being established before the Directive was adopted (Kerckhofs, 2002). In total these cover directly around 11 million employees.

Generally EWCs seek to improve the right to information and consultation insofar as they establish a consistent system of worker participation in all transnational EU enterprises. EWCs set up before 15 December 1999 were exempt from this Directive, the effect of which was, as Bercusson (1996) noted, to encourage 'bargaining in the shadow of the law'. Furthermore as Barnard (2000) explains, Article 13 of the Directive allows the retention of voluntary agreements existing prior to the coming into force of the Directive. Consequently only EU employers who negotiate an agreement after this date must cover the matters contained in the Directive. Moreover EU employers must set up a body to negotiate an EWC agreement if there is a written request from at least 100 employees in at least two Member States. It was left to Member States to determine the specific method of election of the members of this special negotiating body to establish the EWC, and the default requirements in the case of failure to reach an agreement. The default had to meet minimum requirements such as meeting at least annually, and the provision of certain information on the operation and future plans of the organisation.

Article 2(1) of the EWC Directive defines consultation as 'the exchange of views and establishment of dialogue between employees' representatives and central management'. This distinction, between information being unilateral and consultation bilateral, clarifies the national differences in approaches to workplace democracy. However employers were concerned about the costs of operating EWCs, their relevance to increasingly decentralised corporations, and the dangers of rent-seeking behaviour by employees. Fears of the Europeanisation of collective bargaining were also present, and together these arguments initially encouraged the British Government to resist this legislation. As we have noted above, the UK has generally resisted participation and seeks minimalist consultation arrangements, whilst the French framework of *comites d'entreprises* and the Italian *rappresentanza sindicale unitaria* both embrace proactive consultation. As explained above, it took legal action by the Commission to change the UK's laws, as Davies, quoted in Hall (1996), noted: 'This is the first time the Court has required a Member State to amend collective representation structures in order to bring them in line with Community norms' (p. 16). The UK belatedly abandoned institutional nationalism with the introduction of the EWC Directive on 15 January 2000 in its Transnational Information and Consultation of Employees Regulations (1999). This reversal of the UK's opt-out from the EWC Directive added over 200 multinationals within the UK to the Directive's remit. As Carley and Hall (2000) suggest: 'The EWC Directive is widely seen as one of the most significant developments ever in the regulation of transnational employment relations' (p. 103).

Initial research is now available on the impact of the European Works Councils Directive. There appears to have been a rush to negotiate voluntary EWCs, with nearly 500 companies completing agreements before the deadline. Gilman and Marginson (2002) find evidence of a 'bargaining under the shadow of the law' effect in that the details of the negotiated voluntary agreements were constrained by the Directive, though they also find that the presence of sector and countrywide influences on the provisions of these agreements indicate that employers and employee representatives have made use of the flexibility of the Directive to maintain existing specific industrial relations structures. The presence of both national and sector influences on the provisions of agreements is consistent with a more general process of 'converging divergences' (Gilman and Marginson, 2002). This process is one in which growing divergences in industrial relations arrangements and practices within national systems are evolving, whilst practices are converging within individual sectors.

The rush to negotiate voluntary agreements before the deadline has been interpreted as indicating opportunistic behaviour by management, trying to capture the EWC for a managerially sponsored agenda. Addison and Belfield's (2002) study of early British, and therefore voluntary, adopters of EWC finds no evidence of managerial opportunism, though they do find that these companies had a pre-existing tendency towards internationalising their human resource policies. They also found some indications that workers covered by EWCs had a more favourable attitude to their employers, though there was no association between the establishment of EWCs and labour productivity. Whilst there are some caveats concerning the inevitable self-selection of their sample, their generally neutral findings suggest that this first explicit extension of the European Social Model to multinationals' labour market behaviour has been relatively inexpensive. Whether there have been any significant advantages in terms of reduced opportunistic exploitation of asymmetric information, and greater job security and mutual trust, remains to be addressed in forthcoming research.

Gilman and Marginson (2002) find some evidence that there is a learning effect with best practice evolving through the periodic review and renegotiation of agreements. One particular issue that has concerned trade unions and the European Parliament is the absence in the Directive of the need for information and consultation to be 'in good time'. Only a small minority of agreements specifically cover the issue of the timing of information and consultation. Previous Directives requiring consultation between employers and employees share this weakness, and it is only in its latest legislation that the EU has seriously addressed this issue. Other concerns cover the absence of health and safety, training and equal opportunities from the issues covered by information and consultation.

The Commission initiated formal consultations in April 2004 as part of its review of the EWC Directive. Its consultation document claims that the Directive has had 'very substantial success' in meeting its objectives, though it points out the criticisms that the Councils have not always been effective in restructuring situations. It also notes the absence of EWC agreements in about

60 per cent of the relevant organisations. Interestingly, the consultation document contains no specific proposals, suggesting that the Commission is seeking to maximise the chances of the social partners reaching agreement on required revisions.

8.3.4 Moving the Boundaries: The Amsterdam Treaty

As we have noted previously, the Amsterdam Treaty established social dialogue as a legislative mode at EU level. This can be seen as an attempt to devolve responsibility for resolving the trading-off of economic and social rights directly to the social partners. According to Szyszczak (2000), under the Treaty, Article 137 'information and consultation of workers [is brought] within the remit of agreements between the social partners' (p. 31). Articles 138 and 139 of the Treaty also provide for consultative and negotiation dimensions to EU collective bargaining. Wedderburn (1997) argues that their previous limited remit reflects a perennial weakness in the development of EU collective labour law. Yet EC collective labour law has sought to provide for the rights of information, consultation and participation, for instance Articles 17–18 of the 1989 Community Charter of Fundamental Social Rights of Workers as reinforced at the Nice Summit in December 2000. As Hall (1996) argues, the EWC Directive moves EU law on from its consultation origins in business transfers and redundancies towards a 'broader consultative remit' (p. 26).

However even before the 2002 National Consultation and Information Directive (2002/14), and apart from concerns regarding its impact upon employers' costs and profitability (Weber et al., 2000), it was clear that the move towards a more proactive workplace democracy raised fundamental questions concerning the rationale for such regulations.

8.4 EXAMINING THE ECONOMIC RATIONALE FOR WORKPLACE DEMOCRACY

Increased workplace democracy may promote political democracy and social cohesion, and provide employees with a greater voice in decision-making, but in the context of the Lisbon Strategy EU legislators have been increasingly concerned with its potential impact upon economic efficiency. In general, increased worker participation changes the institutional framework within which the principal–agent relationship is determined. As such, increased employee involvement may influence efficiency through changes in the objectives of an organisation and the extent of trust and flows of information between its employees and employers. Increased trust and improved flows of information impact upon the motivation and level of effort of the workforce, and the ability of both the organisation to implement change and of the social partners to bargain efficiently.

The current reorganisation of working life appears to have increased the potential benefits from increased co-operation within organisations, whilst increasing the costs associated with centralised collective bargaining (Lindbeck and Snower, 2001). As explained for example in the Report of the High Level Group on Industrial Relations and Change in the European Union (European Commission, 2002a), the replacement of standardised tasks and hierarchical 'tayloristic' organisations by multitasking and flatter structures has promoted greater decentralisation of decision-making. Since information is now more dispersed within an organisation, the latter can benefit from encouraging the sharing of accurate information. More information creates a better-informed decision-making process and promotes better problem-solving. Moreover given the existence of communal working conditions that are common to all workers, there is likely to be a public goods problem of preference revelation as discussed in Chapter 4. Increased consultation and information exchange enables the preferences of all workers to be collected and could lead to more efficient combinations of wages and working conditions being introduced.

For organisations to decentralise decision-making in an environment where the asymmetry of information is increasing, mutual trust is necessary. Employers must trust their workers not to misuse their increased discretion and employees must believe that their employers will not behave opportunistically. As Rogers and Streeck (1994) explain, the formal institutionalisation of worker participation can contribute to the growth of trust, increased information-sharing and an emphasis upon long-term productivity growth. As workers gain greater voice in the decision-making process then their need to exit diminishes. Hence we expect that hiring and training costs would be reduced in organisations with greater consultation and partnership. However increased employee participation may slow down the decision-making process and increase insider power to the detriment of employment growth (Addison et al., 1997). Employees will be particularly concerned to sustain the existing level of employment, and use their influence to slow down the adjustment to shocks and structural changes. They will also use any increase in their bargaining power as a result of increased consultation or partnership to redistribute profits towards existing workers in the form of additional wages and fringe benefits, and away from shareholders and potential employees. Existing workers will also favour increased investment in human capital as the preferred means of enhancing productivity, hence encouraging organisations to reposition in higher-quality markets. Overall then there is a trade-off between increased employee involvement that can provide greater information and innovation, and the costs of delay and lower profits and short-term employment growth that may accompany that increase.

As Addison et al. (2003) point out, the currently popular collective voice argument outlined above was originally developed in the context of assessing the contribution of trade unions to labour market behaviour. The outcomes of any extension of consultation and co-determination therefore depend upon the motivations of both management and unions, and whether the changes in workplace organisation consolidate or fragment worker solidarity.

Whether increased employee involvement raises overall efficiency in any organisation, sector or economy is thus an empirical issue. Research in this area faces severe problems, not just related to the diversity of the institutional frameworks and the economic, social and technological environments, but also in specifying the appropriate dependent variable and in establishing causation in any empirical relationships (Cappelli and Neumark, 2001; Delbridge and Whitfield, 2001). It is thus hardly surprising that the vast literature on this topic (see for example Levine and Tyson, 1990; Rogers and Streeck, 1995; Freeman et al., 2000; Frege, 2002; Addison et al., 2004b) has failed to reach a finite conclusion on this question. Peccei et al. (2003) find that the effects of information disclosure on organisational performance is more complex than commonly assumed. Systematic sharing of information on performance targets appears to help worker commitment and therefore productivity, whilst performance feedback and the disclosure of general information by management have differing effects depending upon the level of worker commitment. In general the positive effects of disclosure were strongest in non- or weakly unionised organisations. Askildsen et al. (2002) find that works councils may help to internalise externalities. Their study of German panel data found a strong relationship between investments in improving local environment quality and council activities. They also found that establishments with works councils that were employee-led or jointly led were likely to make higher environmental investments.

Even if we accept that in certain environments greater employee involvement increases the joint-surplus of the firm–worker relationship, a rationale for mandatory participation at EU level is still absent. Why cannot we rely upon European firms and their workforces to instigate the level of employee involvement that maximises social welfare? Indeed given also the globalisation of production and political changes that have advanced the neo-liberalist agenda and increased managerial prerogative, it is tempting to conclude that any 'rights-based' approach to partnership has no place in the modernisation of the European social policy. However Levine and Tyson (1990) suggested that the market system might be systematically biased against participatory workplaces. Unstable aggregate demand, low firing costs and short-termism in financial markets together effectively subsidise non-participatory firms. Non-participatory organisations can use the threat of unemployment to prevent shirking, whilst participatory firms have to invest in costly screening and monitoring to counter adverse selection problems amongst their employees. Where non-participation is the dominant strategy, and since the resulting social costs of high unemployment are not internalised, then a suboptimal level of participation can prevail. Within the EU these arguments indicate that short-term competitive advantages may prevent the emergence of high-productivity, high-participation equilibria, and necessitate supranational regulation. Moreover as Rogers and Streeck (1995) argue, mandatory works councils are likely to reduce opportunistic behaviour. Since employers know that they cannot abolish the works council they will target their efforts on generating co-operative behaviour; similarly workers will be less defensive given the security provided by legislation. Hence mandatory co-determination may help to moderate employee and employer demands in difficult periods and promote longer-term decision-making.

Freeman and Lazear (1995) provide an alternative explanation for the possible persistence of suboptimal levels of employee involvement. They argue that employee involvement affects the distribution as well as the amount of the joint surplus. The focus of trade unions on wage bargaining deters management from granting significant powers to workers since they fear that workers will indulge in rent-seeking activities. The greater the participation of employees, the greater will be their share of the economic rent. If increased participation raises employees' share at a faster rate than the increase in total rent, then employers will oppose further productivity-enhancing increases in participation. So where local unions are strong, management may choose to offer a level of employee involvement well below the socially optimal level. Freeman and Lazear also showed that socially optimal levels of involvement may be prevented by unforeseen economic changes that shorten time horizons, or by the existence of high fixed costs borne by employers in extending involvement, say in establishing works councils.

Equivalently, where workers have the (trade union) power to enforce their preferred level of employee involvement they will choose a level in excess of that which maximises the joint surplus. Since employers and employees cannot be relied upon to negotiate optimal levels of employee involvement there are potential benefits from mandatory employee involvement. However the Freeman–Lazear argument suggests that some limit has to be placed on the power of the works council. As Addison et al. (2001) point out, this is why German works councils have been so much researched. Their provisions for information, consultation and co-determination rights, together with centralised wage-setting and the pre-emption of industrial action correspond to the type of system championed by Freeman and Lazear. Thus the dual German system potentially separates the factors which determine the size of the surplus from those that determine its distribution, though Addison et al. (2003) question the extent of this separation in practice.

Given the potential for multinational companies to play off one national government or workforce against another, there may be a rationale for this legislation being adopted at the EU level. However since the socially optimal level of participation is firm-specific, subsidiarity requires that EU policy merely establishes broad principles. Addison et al. (2000) test Freeman and Lazear's predictions and their results are generally favourable to that model. They conclude that distributive bargaining can prejudice the positive productive benefits of employee involvement, and that mandated employee involvement can be beneficial. More specifically they suggest that, contrary to the analysis of Freeman and Lazear, mandated employee involvement may be most effective in environments with strong trade unions and decentralised bargaining. As explained above, Germany presents a particularly important case study. In contrast to the usually negative findings of earlier studies, Addison et al. (2001) find that works councils are associated with reduced employment fluctuations and higher productivity (in larger organisations). However they are also associated with lower profits and higher wages. More recently Addison et al. (2003) find no works council effects on productivity on average for 1997–2000, but a positive effect on plant closings (Addison et al., 2004a). As noted above, there are severe methodological problems in trying to quantify the economic impact of German works councils. Given these problems and the lack of a current consensus it remains important to remember, as Frege (2002) points out, that works councils were introduced to enhance the democratic rights of employees, not to further efficient production.

Mizrahi (2002) provides additional arguments against too prescriptive legislation. He argues that both parties need to recognise the mutual advantages of increased participation if bargaining over participatory rules is to replace bargaining over wages and working conditions. Where employers are forced to establish say works councils, they will seek to retain the key decision-making area under their control, and the resulting councils fail to deliver effective co-operation. More recently the rush to negotiate voluntary European works councils prior to implementation of the 1994 Directive has been seen as capturing the EWC for a managerially sponsored agenda (Addison and Belfield, 2002).

Economic analysis thus provides a rationale for mandatory employee involvement regulations at EU and national levels. However it suggests that to be most effective, regulation needs to limit the power of both management and workers. Regulation also needs to reflect the broader features of the specific national and sectoral bargaining and employment environments.

8.5 RECENT LEGISLATION AND CURRENT ISSUES

Following recent US and EU financial scandals, such as Enron and Paramalat, proposals to reform corporate governance to include greater stakeholder, including worker, involvement abound. In the EU, plans to enhance worker involvement in the 'planning of the day to day activities of the entity' have been debated for some time. In the following sections we analyse two radical new Directives.

8.5.1 The National Information and Consultation Directive

At the EU Council of Ministers meeting on 17 December 2001, after three years of detailed negotiation, the latest EU law on workplace democracy was finally agreed under the EU's co-decision procedure. This co-decision procedure allows for conciliation when the EU Council of Ministers are not prepared to accept all of the European Parliament's amendments. Consequently this new law transitionally comes into force from 2005, with the UK and Ireland being allowed to defer until 2007. The National Consultation and Information (NIC) Directive (2002/14) is based upon the social partnership or hybrid approach to partnership. That is, workers should have the basic right to consultation, but a mechanism for bargaining should be agreed between the parties and utilised accordingly. Although the Directive requires no major changes to existing law and practice in a majority of Member States, its origins lie in the abrupt closure of a Renault factory in Vilvoorde, Belgium without the 3000 employees being consulted (European Commission, 2002b). Despite prompting, the European organisation of employers (UNICE) had twice explicitly failed to enter into social dialogue with the unions, aimed at reaching a framework agreement. Hence in November 1998 the European Commission published their proposal for a new Council Directive; three years later the NIC emerged.

This new law sets out 'minimum' requirements for employees' rights to information and consultation in Member States. It requires companies with 50 or more employees to regularly inform on the enterprise's economic situation and to consult with workers on key decisions regarding the organisation's future. These include situations where jobs are threatened and where any anticipatory measures, such as training, skill development and other measures increasing the adaptability of employees, are planned. Consultation is also compulsory for decisions that are likely to lead to substantial changes in work organisation or in contractual relations. National governments will enact their own implementing measures, with sanctions for breaches, and are free to extend further these minimal information and consultation rights. From 2005 this law will apply to those organisations with 150 or more workers, from

2007 for those businesses with over 100 workers and from 2008 for those with more than 50 workers.

As Bercusson (2002) points out, the new Directive was subject to two familiar pressures. First, those Member States with existing systems of representation and consultation were eager to maintain discretion in the implementation of the Directive. Thus the German Government perhaps surprisingly objected, fearing that it might have to dismantle the existing German system of works councils, which has existed since 1972 under its Works Constitution Act. This was amended in 2001 to extend the authority of works councils and clarify their legally regulated composition (Addison et al., 2004b). Second, pressure from the social partners for flexibility in adapting the Directive by derogation through collective bargaining. In addition, the UK Government opposed the NIC Directive on the grounds of subsidiarity, insofar as it believed it to be an unnecessary measure. Notwithstanding the change of government in 1997 and the market failure arguments advanced above, the British unitarist or voluntarist approach remained intact. The Danish Government also disliked the social market approach underlying this new Directive, and the Irish Government considered that it duplicated existing EWC provisions. The ensuing Directive can be seen as the result of these competing pressures, and suspicion that these three Member States would exploit discretion and social partner flexibility to evade the obligations contained in the Directive. Weaknesses are apparent in the approved Directive regarding the need for information and consultation prior to a decision being made, and the extent of sanction when employers violate this requirement to inform and consult. As a consequence the ECJ will again be required to resolve these weaknesses.

Under the new NIC Directive, consultation is required where an employer proposes to dismiss 20 or more workers as redundant at one establishment within 90 days or less. Where 100 or more redundancies are proposed, consultation must commence at least 90 days before the first dismissal. However these rules duplicate existing legal arrangements required under the Collective Redundancies Directive, discussed previously. The information that must be disclosed is a statement of the proposed dismissals and reasons for such; the numbers affected; and the proposed method of selection and what payments are available.

The three controversial elements of this new Directive concern issues related to early information and consultation, commercial confidentiality and remedies. This Directive seeks to encourage ‘early consultation’; this contrasts with the 1970s Directives on business transfers and collective redundancies, where consultation was merely required to be ‘in good time’. These previous provisions were ambiguous, since what ‘in good time’ actually means was not specified, and consequently the EU Commission has resorted to mandatory schedules. In terms of confidentiality, the new Directive sets out an objective test of whether the disclosure of information would damage the business, in which case it need not be disclosed. It remains ambiguous though whether other rules such as those set out by national regulatory bodies, such as the UK's Financial Services Authority (FSA) would apply. For instance the FSA's rules require commercially sensitive information to remain confidential and be exempt from consultation in order to preserve fair trading on the stock markets. Finally, sanctions are to be 'effective, dissuasive and proportionate'; such might not only include fines and/or compensation to those not consulted as at present, but could extend to injunctions and other remedial orders. Under UK law, failure to consult results in 13 weeks' pay being awarded to those who are not consulted, whereas under German law the process is redone with consultation, and French law makes consultation compulsory and therefore failure could result in imprisonment.

We have argued above that given informational asymmetry and employer reluctance to disclose, there is a role for law. Prior to the NIC, there was a range of legal approaches to information disclosure reflecting the diversity of industrial relations and corporate governance systems in Member States. In Germany, as Gospel and Willman (2004) explain, given the emphasis upon the promotion of co-operative relations within an insider system of governance, information disclosure was essential for the creation of trust and the maintenance of co-operation. In France, employers' reluctance to disclose to trade unions reflected the lack of mutual trust. Government attempts to require disclosure had often been ineffective and created unintended effects. In the UK, the emphasis upon adversarial collective bargaining in a market system of governance within a voluntaristic setting had led to much more limited legislation. Initially the UK system was one of process-driven disclosure based exclusively on collective bargaining. Following the earlier EU Directives, event-driven disclosure and consultation were introduced. With the EWC and NIC Directives there is a return to process-driven disclosure, but based on consultation (Gospel and Willman, 2004). The overall coherence of these new systems remains to be seen, though the process of transposition of EU Directives into national law ensures that major national differences will remain even with the guarantee of a floor of information and disclosure rights.

8.5.2 Regulation for a Company Statute and Directive on Employee Involvement

After a record 31 years of EU negotiation, on 8 October 2001 the EU's Employment and Social Policy Council adopted a Regulation for a European Company Statute (Regulation 2157/2001) and a related Directive on Employee Involvement (Directive 2001/86). Both these legal instruments took effect from 2004. The basic rationale of the Statute is to allow European enterprises operating in several Member States to unify their organisational structures and fully adapt to the transnational nature of their activities. In other words, they can operate within a single legal framework. The adoption of the Statute arose after many years of controversy surrounding both the Fifth Directive on Company Law, which proposed worker representatives on company boards, and the failed Vredling Directive which proposed compulsory worker representatives in multinationals. As Keller (2002) explains, resistance to the earlier drafts came both from those Member States with highly developed national systems (Germany and the Netherlands) and from those with weak or no statutory rights in this area (Ireland and the UK). The former feared that individual companies might exploit the Statute to circumvent stricter national requirement (the 'Delaware' effect) whilst the latter countries feared that they would effectively import further binding regulations into their largely 'voluntaristic' systems.

The Regulation provides for companies located in the EU and operating in more than one Member State to register as a Societas Europea (SE) (a so-called 'European company') and to adopt one set of national rules and a single management reporting system as a means of governance. More importantly, this Regulation permits trading within the EEA without having to register in each Member State in which they operate, on condition that the SE has a minimum capital of 120 000 euros. The Directive also provides further regulation of information and consultation on matters concerning the SE itself and allows for employee participation in the supervisory or administrative body of the SE. The purpose of this Directive is to ensure that when a SE is established no reduction in employee involvement occurs. These additional workplace democracy provisions are modelled on those contained in the EWC Directive. They again include a 'default' set of rules whereby if no agreement on employee involvement can be reached then a consequential works council is established consisting of between 3 and 30 employees.

The EWC Directive and the European Company Statute (ECS), in both seeking to promote indirect representation, have some strong similarities in their requirements for employee involvement. They both make a priority of encouraging voluntary negotiation between social partners rather than relying solely on binding legislation. Where such voluntary negotiations fail, binding fall-back provisions are specified. However as Keller (2002) points out, a more detailed examination of the two measures reveals important differences in three areas: the special negotiating body, the standard rules and scope. He argues that the procedural principles of the ECS have benefited from the experience gained from the initial experience of the EWC Directive. According to the ECS, management now have responsibility for launching the negotiating process and both the role of trade union officers and external experts are explicitly recognised in that process. Interestingly, although the negotiations are likely to be more complicated in the SE case, the duration has been explicitly fixed at a maximum of six months. Since employee involvement has to be resolved before the establishment of a SE, this has the effect of preventing management from delaying agreement.

The 'standard rules for information and consultation', the statutory fall-back provisions specified in the Annex to the ECS, are similar to the 'subsidiarity requirements' of the EWC Directive. Similar rights for the representative body, such as access to the papers of board and shareholder meetings, are identified. However the standard rules for the SE are explicitly defined and more wide-ranging. Unlike the specific size requirements applicable to the EWC Directive, the scope of the ECS covers all SEs, independent of size, though the number of companies who will find it attractive to convert to a SE are not yet clear. However if a SE also fulfils the specified criteria for an EWC, then the ECS takes precedence, which in the long run may reduce the scope of application of the EWC Directive.

At the European level, employee involvement even after the EWC Directive and the ECS will remain modest in relation to the national regulations which have existed in many Member States for many years. It is possible that many SEs, for example as a result of a merger between British, Irish, Portuguese or Spanish companies, would be established without any employees' representation on their board and with only a separate representative body. In others there may be employees' representatives on boards but their negotiated rights on information and consultation may be weak. In sum, managerial prerogative is unlikely to be seriously threatened by these attempts to renew the European Social Model (ESM).

8.6 CONCLUSIONS: TOWARDS THE EUROPEANISATION OF INDUSTRIAL RELATIONS?

The passing of the European Company Statute Regulation, as well as the Employee Involvement and NIC Directives, with their potential impact to establish EU-wide frameworks for workplace democracy, are highly significant for the future development of a fully participative European social partnership model. However the actual take-up rate of these new initiatives is uncertain, since Marginson and Sisson's (1998), Weber et al.'s (2000) and Kerckhofs's (2002) research suggests an EU-wide employer reluctance to establish supranational bargaining units under the EWC Directive. If such reluctance applies to EU-wide national bargaining, then it is clear that the NIC Directive is also doomed to fail. The significance of these Directives on future workplace democracy is potentially immense, particularly in terms of information being readily available on the company's activities and economic and financial situation at both EU and national levels, as well as decisions likely to lead to changes in work organisation or contractual relations.

The discussion in this chapter has once again shown the changing nature of EU social policy. A modernised ESM sought to revitalise a transnational approach under the NIC Directive, yet on the basis of a derogated model (that is, each Member State will decide). This approach underlines the newly enlarged EU's desire to make hard law work under soft law methods. In part this represents an acceptance of the diversity of industrial relations systems in the EU25 and their disparate measures of worker involvement which presently exist and are already deeply embodied. Whilst enlargement of the ESM further increased this diversity, it coincided with a challenge to the orthodoxy of long-established EU law-making based upon hard law approaches. Increasingly the EU is challenging Member States to grasp the policy dilemma nettle and utilise soft law mechanisms to resolve the social and economic paradox on a case-by-case basis. In the following final chapter, we further examine this dilemma as well as returning to our key theme of whether modernisation of the European Social Model threatens its historical role of promoting a balance between those economic and social rights.

9. The future of the European Social Model: modernisation or evolution?

9.1 INTRODUCTION

In this closing chapter we assess the future of the European Social Model (ESM). The Lisbon Strategy, the consolidation of EMU and the recent enlargement together pose major challenges for Social Europe. Extending or even sustaining social protection seems especially problematic within the context of ambitious EU economic objectives, tightening fiscal policy and the challenges and opportunities posed by enlargement. At the same time the new emphasis upon policy-making through social dialogue and the developing role of soft law through the Open Method of Co-ordination (OMC) are changing EU social policy towards a bottom-up approach.

Our concluding arguments are structured as follows. In section 9.2 we reassess the current state of European social policy. We summarise the current status of the Charter of Fundamental Rights and the new Constitution, and identify the main challenges and opportunities. A modernised social model will have to embrace more variant legal traditions and systems as well as increasingly competitive, insecure and flexible labour markets. Having set out the challenges and opportunities for the EU25 in terms of future social and economic goals, section 9.3 re-examines whether greater diversity will threaten to reinvent a more aggressive form of social dumping. Addressing the social and economic paradox, section 9.4 provides a resolution of the hard law versus soft law debate, whilst section 9.5 emphasises how the OMC has emerged as the new face of soft law. This prevalence of soft law establishes a third way of governance in the ESM examined in section 9.6. The continuing key role of the ECJ in resolving disputes when social and economic rights conflict is analysed in the following section. Our thesis concludes in section 9.8. Overall we suggest that enlargement has made soft law more significant in its standing, and allowed OMC to prevail, establishing a bottom-up approach for the ESM, although under the EU's new Constitution the ECJ will remain the key to resolving conflict, ensuring that its pre-federal device remains intact in the newly enlarged EU25. In summary, this chapter evaluates the overall book's theme of the development of the ESM, arguing in favour of a rights-based approach. We conclude that a strengthened role for social rights is possible, if the soft law approach proves to provide a more effective mechanism – legally, politically and economically – in the enlarged post-Lisbon EU. If so, then we may conclude that the ESM has been modernised.

9.2 MODERNISING THE EUROPEAN SOCIAL MODEL IN AN ENLARGED EU

It was the Greek Presidency in the first part of 2003 whose agenda sought to revitalise the EU's modernisation of the European Social Model (ESM). This naturally followed on from the Summit at Nice in 2000, where the Charter of Fundamental Rights was drafted. In principle the Charter, as argued in Chapter 1, provides a more solid foundation for the furtherance across the EU of social citizenship. In 3 parts, 6 chapters and over 50 rights, nearly a draft European Social Constitution itself, the Charter provides an opportunity for the consolidation of social rights. Moreover the Charter establishes a minimum 'floor of rights' from which the employment relationship can evolve.

Until the new Constitution, agreed in June 2004, incorporating these rights is formally agreed by Member States, the Charter is non-binding. Once the Charter is incorporated, the ECJ will be able to enforce these basic rights. At present the ECJ can only utilise the Charter as an interpretative tool where EU Member States' laws are ambiguous. In any event the Charter itself in its current form provides both challenges and opportunities which we now examine.

9.2.1 Challenges to the Enlarged ESM

The current Treaty base for social protection has served the EU well in terms of developing principles, rights and freedoms. However as we have repeatedly discovered in the previous chapters, this Treaty or hard law approach often results in variations amongst the Member States which may invoke a long drawn-out litigation process. For example the Working Time Directive's implementation epitomises such a process, as noted in Chapter 5. More importantly, hard law results within a perennial market freedom versus social protection dilemma, as argued in Chapters 2 and 3, which the ECJ is continually being required to resolve. Therefore a major challenge, post-enlargement, is that the threat of enforcing 25 national variations could restrict the further development of the ESM.

9.2.2 Opportunities to Modernise in the Enlarged ESM

The consolidation of social rights in a single Constitution ensures a minimum floor of social rights, by enacting basic labour standards throughout the EU. More significantly perhaps, consolidation generates an opportunity to confirm the importance of soft law approaches in the modernisation of the ESM.

At the Nice Summit (December 2000) EU leaders paved the way for enlargement of the EU by agreeing to the necessary institutional changes prior to enlargement. Recognising the temporary nature of these reforms, the leaders called for 'a deeper and wider debate about the future of the EU'. In an annex to the Nice Treaty entitled 'Declaration on the future of the Union', the Swedish and Belgian Presidencies were encouraged to launch wide-ranging discussions with all interested parties: representatives of national Parliaments and all those reflecting public opinion (such as representatives of civil society). The Laeken Declaration was the result of the European Council of 14–15 December 2001, at the conclusion of the Belgian Presidency of the European Union. It provided for the establishment of a Convention to draw up proposals for the reform of the European Union. This represented an entirely new political process in the history of European integration. The Laeken Declaration included three parts. Part I was entitled 'Europe at a Crossroads', which provided a short analysis of the state of the EU at that moment. It identified the challenges facing the EU and attempted to summarise 'the expectations of Europe's citizens'. Part II was much more important. This focused on 'Challenges and Reforms in a Renewed Union', and formulated the objectives and aims of the Convention. It presented a list of questions which the Convention was to answer, which are grouped into four topics: competencies, 'simplification of the Union's instruments', 'more democracy, transparency and efficiency in the EU', and 'towards a Constitution for European citizens'. The Convention produced its draft new Constitution in September 2003, but it was rejected at the special Brussels Summit in December 2003, delaying its conclusion until 2004. According to Alesina and Perotti (2004), the Constitution represents a potential solution to the two problems hindering the development of European integration. The first of these is an emphasis upon 'institutional balance', in which a complex web of institutions have overlapping jurisdictions.

The second problem results from a conflict between *dirigiste* and a more *laissez-faire* approach to government. The consequence of the first problem, as Alesina and Perotti point out, is confusion regarding the distribution of powers between national governments and European institutions resulting in a lack of transparency and accountability. The second problem results in grandiose policy announcements which lack a clear underlying policy framework.

9.3 DIVERSITY AND SOCIAL DUMPING

Our discussion in the previous chapters has recorded how the perceived threat of social dumping has periodically acted as a catalyst for the further development of Social Europe. In recent years there has been a recurrence of concern with the potential for such a process: for example the abandonment in 2004 by German workers of 35-hour-week contracts at Siemens and DaimlerChrysler under the threat of jobs moving to Hungary and South Africa respectively. The new emphasis on social dialogue has provided the trade unions with a platform to publicise their particular aversion to this process. We have previously recounted the forces that have given rise to this concern. The acceleration of globalisation during the 1990s, in particular the increasing geographical mobility of production, has limited the capacity of traditional domestic labour law to promote social protection by increasing the ability of transnational producers to escape from the jurisdiction of less business-friendly regimes. In part this has itself generated pressures for global, rather than just pan-European, labour standards as championed by the International Labour Organisation (ILO). Efforts to move such issues to the multilateral level through the World Trade Organisation have so far been unsuccessful.

The budgetary constraints on EMU Member States, resulting from the Growth and Stability Pact, have been a further cause for concern. Together with the budgetary pressures arising from ageing identified in Chapters 4 and 6, governments have been facing increased pressures to reform social protection systems to reduce demands upon public funding (Terwey, 2004). This combination of a reduced willingness of governments to fund social protection, together with a reduced ability to levy employers discussed above, has led to funding being switched to workers and/or reductions in the level of protection. Whilst the area of state retirement and disability pensions have been the most fiercely debated, other areas of social protection face similar pressures.

The recent enlargement of the EU has to be analysed in the context of these pressures. As recorded in Chapter 4, most of the new Member States have much lower wage costs than those found in the EU15, and much lower levels of social protection. As such they have become desirable locations for Western European organisations seeking to outsource or relocate their labour-intensive stages of production. From the perspective of the new Member States of Central and Eastern Europe this process, and that of the related migration of some of their workers to the old Member States, are the means by which convergence on Western European levels of productivity and per capita income are achieved. However for those workers in the then EU15 affected by such outsourcing and relocation, and who face increased competition for those available jobs in their domestic economy, the process appears to be one of social dumping. In previous enlargements the extent of the intra-Community mobility of jobs and workers has been much lower than initially forecast. Most commentators (for example Boeri and Brucker, 2001) again expect the recent enlargement to have only minor effects on wages and employment. In summary, further reductions of unemployment in the Big Four Continental Member States will be much more dependent on their achievement of faster economic growth and further reforms of their unemployment and disability benefit systems. Whilst the fear of social dumping remains a powerful instrument for motivating a rise in the European floor of social rights, its practical importance remains in question.

9.4 HARD LAW VERSUS SOFT LAW

A further theme in our analysis of individual policy areas has been the relative attractions of soft law as compared to hard law in delivering the social policy agendas. Soft law refers to informal instruments targeted at attaining a certain policy goal, for example the Social Charter and the later Charter of Fundamental Rights. So-called 'hard laws', the 'Community Method', are formed from the Treaty base or Directives and create uniform rules which Member States must adopt, or suffer sanctions. Soft laws often arise in order to fill legislative gaps, though soft laws can bring about integration in just the same way as hard laws. The central distinguishing feature is that hard laws are by the nature of their legal source legally binding. In the past, when the Commission had a wide-ranging social agenda to achieve, then its main elements were implemented through Directives and Regulations, and soft law was used to manage those outstanding issues and concerns not achieved. For example in 1984 the Commission adopted a Recommendation on the promotion of positive action for women and in 1999 a Code of Practice on sexual harassment. Both these issues are controversial and transnational, as well as important for the social progress of the EU, but the EU Commission had resigned itself to adopt soft law approaches to seek to influence the regulation of these social areas by way of prompting action at each EU Member State's national level. Although clearly not a satisfactory substitute for binding legislative action, overall soft law was viewed as a legitimising and supporting governance process.

Throughout this book we have observed and critiqued the development of 'soft' *acquis*. In contrast to the avalanche of hard law since 1974 under the first SAP and onwards, as Bercusson (2002) and Kenner (2003) chart, the 1990s saw the evolution of the OMC, albeit in another name – social dialogue. This allowed for an era of alternative approaches and the rescuing of social policy from suffocation, because it made its modernisation workable – socially (that is, legally), economically, politically and normatively. Articles 138–9 of the Treaty have ensured that social dialogue has become an integral part of EU policy, as well as its legal competence. The Charter itself furthers this. For instance Chapter IV of the Charter on solidarity encourages social dialogue, whilst Articles 27 and 28 provide the right to information and consultation, as well as collective bargaining. Such Charter provisions reignite social dialogue as an active mechanism. However as we argue in the following section, it is the Open Method of Co-ordination (OMC) that now heralds a more important role for soft *acquis*.

9.5 THE OPEN METHOD OF CO-ORDINATION: AN ASSESSMENT

As noted in Chapter 1, the Open Method of Co-ordination (OMC) was implemented post-Lisbon to further 'coherent and systematic approaches' to policy- and law-making. Primarily, OMC is designed to assist Member States in developing their own policies, whilst encouraging some element of co-ordination through peer pressure. Member States agree common objectives, prepare national action plans, and examine each other's performance as a means of learning from their successes and failures. Part of the OMC model is to instigate a 'high-level forum' which would bring together the EU institutions, the social partners and other bodies to consider progress of policies to date. In supporting the principle of subsidiarity insofar as it encourages activities at regional and local levels (Gore, 2004), as well as at national and social partner levels, the OMC creates a horizontal method of EU governance. Overall the OMC is claimed to provide flexible, but structured, co-operation. Alesina and Perotti (2004) question the analytical and political relevance of the OMC in the context of the European Employment Strategy. They point out that national governments rarely take the Guidelines as a significant constraint on domestic employment policy and National Action Plans have generally failed to drive policy decisions. For these authors, this is a classic example of their '*dirigiste* rhetoric' where some EU institution knows the magic formula to resolve unemployment and social problems, if only Member States would implement those policies. Symptomatic of this problem for them is the adoption of numerical targets, such as employment rates, undifferentiated among Member States. Similarly, the adoption of self-evident 'goods' that lack an evidence base, such as the championing of the extension of training programmes, where evaluations have generally been unable to show their cost-effectiveness.

The Open Method of Co-ordination has indeed been associated with the extension of target-setting, evaluation and benchmarking. Since the mid-

1980s, there has been the importation of performance management strategies from modern management practice in the private sector into the public sector and eventually to EU level (Sisson et al., 2003). At Lisbon over 60 targets were set for Member States, the first time that a European Council had specified explicit goals. At Lisbon the OMC was confirmed as the EU's system for benchmarking of framework conditions, coupled with an explicit monitoring system and sponsorship of an evaluation culture. While in part, as we have argued above, the OMC was adopted as a result of the perceived limitations of the legislative approach and the anticipated challenges of enlargement, it was also championed by employers anxious to avoid further social regulation (Sisson et al., 2003). Indeed it is this latter rationale which generates a key concern with the OMC. For several key actors – employers, some Member States and elements in the Commission – the OMC is viewed as a means of avoiding debates about modernisation or the relative importance of competing economic and social objectives. In practice, without more uniform implementation and proper enforcement, including fines, the OMC just becomes a way of sidetracking these issues. However such strengthening of the OMC would in reality be turning it into a quasi-hard law process. Hence the arguments for hybrid combinations of hard and soft law measures reflecting the relative capabilities and exploiting complementarities of these two modes (Trubek and Trubek, 2003).

9.6 NEW GOVERNANCE: THE EU'S THIRD WAY

The Convention on the Future of Europe has had a major impact on the institutional framework and governance mechanisms of the EU. Issues of legitimacy and political authority are at the core of the reforming process. As Dashwood (2001) noted, the Convention was charged with four main tasks to propose:

- Division of competences: clarify when and where competence lies, whether at the Community level, national or sub-national level.
- Institutional reform: resolve whether the EU should have a 'federal' structure with the European Commission acting as Government and the European Parliament as legislature, or remain a Europe of nation States with a stronger role for the Council.
- Simplification of the Treaties: at present the legal basis of the EU rests on four Treaties and assorted other Constitutional acts. These should be integrated into a single text in a manner which makes them accessible to EU citizens.
- Democratisation: throughout Europe national Parliaments are losing

power to their Governments; for those in EU countries this effect is greater due to the increasingly important role of the European Parliament as co-legislator.

The resulting process of change may provide, as Barnard and Deakin argue (Hepple, 2002), a new form of EU governance based on democratic legitimacy. Such a basis might make the ESM more acceptable and therefore more effectively implemented, resolving the problems of transnational law-making presented by Ball (2001).

In response to these tasks the Convention pointed out that no Member State had a Charter of Rights which goes significantly beyond the basic civil and political rights. The limited additions deal with discrimination, rights to freedom of association and some 'directive principles' to inform policy-making in the socio-economic field. The European Union Charter of Fundamental Rights sought in a single text, for the first time in the European Union's history, to establish a whole range of civil, political, economic and social rights in relation to European citizens and all persons resident in the EU. These rights are divided into six sections: dignity, freedoms, equality, solidarity, citizens' rights and justice. Social rights as provided for in the European Social Charter are the following: rights concerning labour protection, trade unions' rights and labour conditions; rights of teenagers, children, mothers, families, handicapped individuals, working immigrants and their families, the elderly; rights concerning health and access to the medical and social services. The categories of persons protected by the European Social Charter are children, women, workers, working immigrants and their families, the elderly, handicapped and disabled people and their families.

These rights are intended to fill the gaps identified within this book. For example EU25's new Charter of Fundamental Rights, now incorporated into the new EU Constitution (2004) stipulates that economic and social rights corresponding to provisions of labour law on one hand – such as the union's right to strike, the right to a minimum level of wages, the right to professional training, the right to professional integration for individuals with specific needs; and to provisions of social law on the other hand – such as social protection and the right to health care. The principle of the indivisibility of human rights is a keystone of EU policy. This means, as argued constantly throughout this book, that economic, social and cultural rights should be accorded as much importance as civil and political rights. This principle not only reflects the doctrine embodied in both the Universal Declaration of Human Rights and the Council of Europe's human rights regime, but also the consensus on the importance of the European Social Model.

There were three options relating to the incorporation of the Charter. First, insert the text of the Charter articles at the beginning of the Constitutional

Treaty in a title or chapter of the Treaty. Second, insert a reference to the Charter and annex it to the Treaty as a Protocol, or thirdly, insert an indirect reference to the Charter, making it potentially justiciable without giving it Constitutional status. There was very strong support in the Convention in favour of the first option. Eventually this approach won the day, and such incorporation will no doubt give rise to complex legal questions, such as the possible scope of the Charter's application. This is where the so-called horizontal clauses in the Charter Articles 51–2 come into play, as they act to identify clearly its scope and application. Changes have been made in the 'horizontal articles' which concern the field of application of those rights. Incorporation of the Charter does not modify the competences of the Union and Member States. However as Craig (2001) describes it, the EU's new Constitution is based on simplification of key principles. These key principles include the Community method, reiterating the roles of the institutions, making EU administration more effective, and rationalising the legal instruments available. Firstly, in order to simplify the general use of the Community method, qualified majority voting and co-decision procedures are extended. Secondly, the new Constitution refocuses each institution on its core function (rather than its powers) in order to underscore the fact that the Council and Parliament perform the legislative function, and the Commission the executive function (indeed this is its own function), whilst the Council retains 'autonomous' decision-making power. These changes ensure that the Council only has the residual decision making executive power; there is no reason to opt for a Union Presidency as an institution. Similarly the new Constitutional framework ensures that the administration of the Union is the Commission's preserve. Lastly, laws replacing Regulations, Directives and framework decisions are the prime instruments of secondary legislation. A distinction is drawn between institutional laws (that is, those governing the organisation of the institutions and the workings of the Union) and ordinary laws, an approach that fosters further hard law approaches to EU law-making. Yet with such a mixture of soft and hard law approaches, how will such a new blend of social and economic rights affect social citizenship and labour law? In the next section, we begin to answer this question.

9.7 THE ECJ'S NEW PRE-FEDERAL ROLE

We have seen in the foregoing sections that the new enlarged EU is seeking to blend soft and hard law approaches. Such a combination, as this book has testified throughout, can only lead to additional pressure on the ECJ when resolution is required. As Sciarra (2001, 2002) explains, the cases for and against a 'judge-made social Europe' are compelling, but only as pre-federal devices. Now that a federal EU is beginning to emerge in EU25, it is time to readdress the Sciarra conundrum and decide whether the ECJ should uphold economic over social rights, or vice versa.

Both ECJ case law and the Treaty are inspired to uphold fundamental human rights by two other sources: the 1950 European Convention on Human Rights and the long-established Constitutional traditions of the EU Member States. In *Nold KG* (C/4/73), the ECJ stressed that 'in safeguarding fundamental rights, the Court is bound to draw inspiration from constitutional traditions common to the EU Member States, and it cannot therefore uphold measures which are incompatible with fundamental rights recognised and protected by the Constitutions of those States'. On April 1977, a joint declaration of the Parliament, the Commission and the Council stressed the prime importance that the latter institutions attach to the protection of fundamental rights, as derived in particular from the Constitutions of the Member States and the European Convention for the Protection of Human Rights and Fundamental Freedoms (ECHR, 1950). This confirmed the willingness of the EU institutions to respect these rights in the exercise of their powers. In *Internationale Handelsgesellschaft mbH* (Case 11/70), the Court stated that:

> respect for fundamental rights forms an integral part of the general principles of law protected by the Court of Justice. The protection of such rights, whilst inspired by the constitutional traditions common to the Member States, must be ensured within the framework of the structure and objectives of the Community.

The notion of 'labour standards' has two distinct meanings. The first refers to the actual terms of employment, quality of work and well-being of workers at a particular location and point in time. The second meaning is a normative one: thus standards specify rights, such as the right to form associations of workers and employers, and the right to bargain collectively; they stipulate normative rules such as minimum wages, or maximum work per week, or rules of conduct and dispute resolution. The ILO has recognised as core labour standards the following: freedom of association and protection of the right to organise; right to organise and collective bargaining; abolition of forced labour; an end to discrimination in the workplace; equal remuneration; and the elimination of child labour.

Arguably the most important set of rights enshrined in these core standards is the freedom of association, which gives workers the right to join trade unions and to free collective bargaining. The Discrimination Convention of the ILO bans discrimination on any basis (whether on race, sex, religion, disability or sexual orientation) and also includes equal pay for equal work for equal value for men and women. The final set of rights that is covered by these core standards is the elimination of child labour, covered in three Conventions.

There are a range of other issues that are addressed by Conventions that are not considered part of the core standards, which are arguably of equal importance: the need for a minimum wage, working hours, working conditions and so on. All EU Member States have ratified all eight of the core ILO Conventions.

The EU's Charter of Fundamental Rights was ratified in late 2002. The underlying idea of the Charter is to mould the embryonic EU citizenship into social citizenship, though the final Charter still excludes the latter. The Preamble reasserts the EU's proclamation of 'an ever closer union' with fundamental rights. The rights themselves are headed under six titles: dignity, freedoms, equality, solidarity, citizens' rights and justice. The 'Solidarity' chapter covers EU employment and social law. Chapter IV confers employment rights and social entitlements, including:

- Article 27: information and consultation
- Article 28: collective bargaining and action
- Article 30: protection from unfair dismissal
- Article 31: fair and just working conditions
- Article 32: prohibition of child labour and protection of young people
- Article 33: family and professional life
- Article 34: social security and assistance.

Although this chapter does not provide an exhaustive list of comprehensive fundamental social rights, this cursory catalogue does provide a higher profile for social citizenship. Yet the rights to work, remuneration and housing remain omitted. Again this Charter provides evidence of the emerging soft law approach to EU labour law and social policy.

In contrast, the 1961 European Social Charter and its 1988 additional Protocol guaranteed a series of fundamental rights, which can be divided into two categories: those that concern employment conditions and those pertaining to social cohesion. Rights relating to employment include the right to work, the right to vocational guidance and training, non-discrimination in employment, prohibition of forced labour, trade union rights, the right to bargain collectively and the right of women and men to equal pay for work of equal value. Social protection rights include the right to health protection and to social security. An additional Protocol to the European Social Charter providing for a system of collective complaints was adopted in 1995, and allowed certain workers' and employers' organisations and non-governmental organisations to lodge complaints with the European Committee of Social Rights if there is an alleged violation. Clearly progress has been made under the new Constitution, with revisions being made primarily to bring it up to date and to extend its scope to new categories of rights. These rights include in particular protection against poverty and social exclusion, the right to decent housing and the right to protection in cases of termination of employment.

However as Hepple (2002) warns, the hierarchy of norms within the EU is typical of a non-unitary system. The higher law of the Community is of course the Treaty itself. Neither Community organs nor the Member States may violate the Treaty in their legislative and administrative actions. In addition, Member States may not violate Community Regulations, Directives and decisions. As we have noted in this book, such violations may be either noticeable and therefore subject to enforcement action by the EU Commission, or more likely, part of the implementation process where Directives are concerned and largely unnoticeable, presenting the further possibility of a two-speed Europe, those Member States who do and those who do not comply. In the context of our discussion of the closure of Member States' attempts to disregard those obligations they dislike, the effectiveness of enforcement is weak. More effective enforcement, including sanctions, remains an important issue omitted from the enlarged EU's Constitution. Instead, as explained throughout this text, in principle the EU is committed to respecting fundamental rights and therefore only requires Member States to comply with the minimum standards (Deakin, 1997) which the rights lay down when they are implementing Community law (cf. Article 10 (5) of the EC Treaty; cf. *Kremzow* v *Austrian Republic*, judgment of 29 May 1997, ECR I-2629 at 15 et seq, 19). It is this approach which we argue potentially undermines the ESM and will further restrict social progress within the enlarged EU. It will continue to rely constantly upon the ECJ to rectify the mistakes of the 'minimum standards' approach to EU social law-making. The authors of this book would conclude that such reliance is deeply questionable. In the last section, we draw our conclusions and suggest reforms.

9.8 CONCLUSIONS

If it is to preserve balance between economic, social, cultural and environmental objectives whilst maintaining the commitment of its people to the European project, EU25 must consolidate and develop the integration of Europe. To preserve this balance, the Commission has pinpointed three fundamental tasks for an enlarged Union: consolidating the European model of economic and social development with a view to guaranteeing its people prosperity and solidarity; developing a European area of freedom, security and justice, to give full meaning to the concept of European citizenship; and enabling EU25 to exercise the responsibilities of a world power (COM(2002) 728 final).

The elaboration of a Constitutional Treaty for the enlarged EU constituted the main objective of the European Convention in 2004. The Convention was composed of the representatives of the Governments and Parliaments of the EU Member States and of the candidate countries, as well as by the representatives of the European Parliament and of the European Commission. It was therefore, as Chapter 2 observed, a more democratic organ in relation to the classic model of the Intergovernmental Conference for the conclusion of a new Constitutional Treaty for the European Union. The birth of the new Constitution in June 2004, as a result of such a legitimately democratic process, enhances the values and principles upon which the enlarged EU25 is based. If it is eventually ratified by each Member State, it will delimitate the powers, functions and competences of the Union, especially in relation to the nation state. We have shown how the current EU social policy is the result of a long historical process that commenced with the Treaty of Rome. The Treaty of Rome established in its Articles 117–18 that the pursuit of economic objectives would carry as an automatic consequence an improvement in the quality of life and of work for workers. Thus reaching the intended economic objectives was assumed to bring better conditions for workers. In the initial phase, the European Union only sought to develop worker rights that either proved decisive for the freedom of circulation or involved distortions to competition. In practice therefore it was clear that social objectives were at this time subservient to the economic objective of creating an integrated European economy. This initial lack of interest in developing a model of social rights corresponds to the requirement for Member State unanimity in approving laws bearing on social rights. Unanimity as a procedural requirement was simply one manifestation of the reigning values shaped by a Union more interested in achieving economic objectives than in configuring a Europe with legal forms recognising social rights. Legislation on social rights was therefore quite limited in the EU's formative period; when rights were developed they were rarely achieved through juridical forms of direct effect, that is, Council Regulations.

It was in the second half of the 1970s that the EU decided it had to intervene more widely in the regulation of social rights. Specifically, guaranteeing some rights for workers involved in business restructuring, establishing the right to equal treatment for women and men, and articulating a social security system for migrant workers, as discussed in Chapters 5, 6 and 7. This extension of Social Europe reflected both the need to maintain popular support for European integration and a belief in the complementarity of the social and economic objectives. It was during this period that the ECJ, through its jurisprudence, began to emerge as the great artifice of Community social law, this emergence reflecting the limitations of both the political process formulating EU Directives and Regulations, and the legal process which transposed them into national law.

The importance of jurisprudence of the ECJ, as examined throughout this book, which began to emerge clearly in this phase was consolidated with time and today it can be said that this is one of the defining characteristics of the Community social model. The European Social Model now covers a wide range of both living and working issues, such as social protection, health, education and environmental issues, public services, as well as all aspects of employment rights, social dialogue, direct participation, training and non-discrimination issues. Central to the European Social Model is the achievement of social inclusion in all aspects of life, increasingly being sought through promoting a culture of partnership between local, regional and national governments, the social partners and voluntary organisations. The contents of the European Social Model are based on common European values and rights set out and formally agreed in the Charter of Fundamental Social Rights: justice, freedom, equity, dignity, democratic participation, quality of work and employment, social protection and inclusion, quality of working and living conditions.

A key challenge faced by the enlarged EU post-Lisbon concerns whether these social rights can be sustained as economic and employment objectives predominate. The loss of confidence in the ability of the European Social Model to support the ambitious Lisbon economic targets was behind the call for its modernisation, whilst the adoption of the Open Method of Co-ordination and the formalisation of the role of the social partners could be seen as a recognition of the political inability to make the perceived necessary reforms of hard law.

Social dialogue has resulted in negotiated Directives covering such areas as parental leave and protections for temporary and part-time workers. However in the design of these EU laws, which have been called guideline Directives, the Member States continue to hold a determinant role in the development of the transfer of the principle of legal subsidiarity to the terrain of collective bargaining, which is obliged to continue to work out its negotiating objectives within national contexts. Collective bargaining, which precedes negotiated legislation, is absorbed within the legislation that seems as a result to legitimise the negotiated outcome. In this sense, negotiated legislation seems to follow more the model of legislative process than that of autonomous mechanisms for the social partners to fix working conditions.

Consequently it can be argued that if the EU25 has a strong collective bargaining and effective information and consultation framework, then the modernisation of other employment protection rights and social entitlements should follow. Recent hard law measures, under the auspices of the Worker Information and Consultation Directive and employee involvement under the

European Company Statute will reinforce, and in some EU Member States reconstruct, national social dialogue. Whilst being sceptical about the effect of such national measures, in contrast to fully incorporated social rights under the Charter, such collective bargaining supported by active social partners, at both national and EU levels, may assist in modernising the ESM, though the need for consolidated social rights to enhance the role of the social partners and social dialogue will be a prerequisite. Two weaknesses arise with such a soft law approach. One relates to the new EU Member States with little experience of collective bargaining. The other concerns the 'representativeness' and democratic legitimacy of the existing social partners at the EU level.

In conclusion, the displacement of hard law represents a shift from binding law towards a more flexible implementation to meet local needs, and provides a pragmatic answer to a rather complex social-economic dilemma. The Charter sets out common social values which form the foundation for an integrated approach to rebuilding Social Europe. An incorporated Charter would create legally binding social citizenship, enforced and monitored by the social partners. This new incorporated social citizenship must, in our view, provide a 'minimum floor of rights' approach. The Charter must be activated by an extended role for the social partners at both EU and national levels, with social dialogue enforcing the Charter's rights within the framework of the Open Method of Co-ordination. However this will not remove the need for the Council to confront the social-economic dilemma. Perhaps Habermas (2001 and 2004) was right when he concluded that the Member States could no longer guarantee social solidarity, though whether, as Sciarra (2002) argues, social partners at national, sectoral or workplace levels can regulate social rights more effectively remains to be seen. Above we have provided a rationale for the current reliance upon soft *acquis* in the enlarged EU. We await with interest to see whether it can deliver a modernised Social Europe in which the social objectives of the EU25 are recognised as legitimate constraints upon the achievement of its economic objectives.

Bibliography

Acemoglu, D. (2003), 'Cross country inequality trends', *Economic Journal*, **113**: F121–F149.

Addison, J., C. Barrett and W. Siebert (1997), 'The economics of labour market regulation', in J. Addison and W. Siebert (eds), *Labour Markets in Europe: Issues of Harmonization and Regulation*, London: Dryden Press, pp. 62–104.

Addison, J. and C. Belfield (2002), 'What do we know about the new European works councils? Some preliminary evidence from Britain', *Scottish Journal of Political Economy*, **49**(4): 418–44.

Addison, J., L. Bellman and A. Kölling (2004a), 'Works councils and plant closings in Germany', *British Journal of Industrial Relations*, **42**(1): 125–48.

Addison, J., L. Bellman, C. Schnabel and J. Wagner (2004b), 'The reform of the German Works Constitution Act: a critical note', *British Journal of Industrial Relations*, **43**(2): 392–420.

Addison, J., T. Schank, C. Schnabel and J. Wagner (2003), 'German works councils in the production process', IZA (Bonn) Discussion Paper No. 812.

Addison, J., C. Schnabel and J. Wagner (2001), 'Works Councils in Germany: their effects on establishment performance', *Oxford Economic Papers*, 53: 659–94.

Addison, J., W. Siebert, J. Wagner and X. Wei (2000), 'Worker participation and form performance: evidence from Germany and Britain', *British Journal of Industrial Relations*, **38**(1): 7–48.

Addison, J. and P. Teixeira (2001), 'The economics of employment protection', IZA (Bonn) Discussion Paper No. 381.

Adnett, N. (2001), 'Modernizing the European Social Model', *Journal of Common Market Studies*, **30**(2): 353–64.

Adnett, N. and A. Dawson (1998), 'The economic analysis of industrial accidents: a re-assessment', *International Review of Applied Economics*, **12**(2): 241–55.

Adnett, N. and S. Hardy (2001), 'Reviewing the Working Time Directive: rationale, implementation and case law', *Industrial Relations Journal*, **32**(2): 114–25.

Agell, J. (1999), 'On the benefits from rigid labour markets: norms, market failures and social insurance', *Economic Journal*, **109**(February): F143–64.

Agell, J. (2002), 'On the determinants of labour market institutions: rent seeking vs. social insurance, *German Economic Review*, **3**(2): 107–35.

Alesina, A. and G-M. Angelotos (2002), 'Fairness and redistribution: US versus Europe', Harvard Institute of Economic Research Working Paper No. 1983.

Alesina, A., E. Glaeser and B. Sacerdote (2001), 'Why doesn't the US have a European-style welfare state? Harvard Institute of Economic Research Working Paper No. 1933.

Alesina, A. and R. Perotti (2004), 'The European Union: a politically incorrect view', National Bureau of Economic Research Working Paper No. W10342.

Andersen, T. (2003), 'From excess to shortage: recent developments in the Danish labour market', CESifo Working Paper No. 933.

Andersen, T., N. Haldrup and J. Sørensen (2000), 'Labour market implications of EU product market integration', *Economic Policy*, **30**: 105–33.

Anker, R. (1998), *Gender and Job: Sex Segregation of Occupations in the World*, Geneva: IILO.

Argandoña, A. (2001), 'The social dimension of labour market institutions', paper originally prepared for the 6th IESE International Conference on Job Creation, Barcelona, 2000.

Armour, J., S. Deakin and S. Konzelmann (2003), 'Shareholder primacy and the trajectory of UK corporate governance', *British Journal of Industrial Relations*, **41**(3): 531–55.

Ashenfelter, O. and D. Card (2002), 'Did the elimination of mandatory retirement affect faculty retirement?' *American Economic Review*, **92**(4): 957–80.

Askildsen, J., U. Jirjahn and S. Smith (2002), 'Works councils and environmental investment: theory and evidence from German panel data', CESifo Working Paper Series, No. 785.

Auer, P. and S. Cazes (2003), *Employment Stability in an Age of Flexibility*, Geneva: ILO.

Ball, S. (2001), 'The European employment strategy: the will but not the way?', *Industrial Law Journal*, **30**(4): 353–74.

Barnard, C. (2000), *EC Employment Law*, 2nd edn, Oxford: Oxford University Press.

Barnard, C., S. Deakin and R. Hobbs (2003), 'Opting out of the 48 hour week: employer necessity or individual choice? An empirical study of the operation of Article 18(10(b) of the Working Time directive in the UK', *Industrial Law Journal*, **32**(4): 223–52.

Basu, K. (2002), 'Sexual harassment in the workplace: an economic analysis with implications for worker rights and labor standards policy', MIT Department of Economics Working Paper No. 02-11.

Bauer, T. and K. Zimmermann (1999), 'Overtime work and overtime compensation in Europe', *Scottish Journal of Political Economy*, **46**(4): 419–36.

Beck, M. (1999), 'The law and economics of dismissal regulation: a comparative analysis of the US and UK systems', in G. De Geest, J. Siegers and R. van den Bergh (eds), *Law and Economics and the Labour Market*, Cheltenham, UK and Northampton, MA: Edward Elgar Publishing, pp. 92–131.

Becker, G. (1957), *The Economics of Discrimination*, Chicago: University of Chicago Press.

Becker, G. (1968), 'Crime and punishment: an economic approach', *Journal of Political Economy*, **76**: 169–217.

Begg, D., J. Crémer, J.-P. Danthine, J. Edwards, V. Grilli, D. Neven, P. Seabright, H.-W. Sinn, A. Venables and C. Wyplosz (1995), 'Making sense of subsidiarity: how much centralization for Europe', *Monitoring European Integration* **4**, Annual Report, Centre for Economic Policy Research, London, p. 101.

Belke, A., M. Gocke and M. Hebler (2004), 'Institutional uncertainty and the European Social Union: impacts on job creation and destruction in CEECs', IZA (Bonn) Discussion Paper No. 1039.

Bell, D. and R. Hart (1999), 'Unpaid work', *Economica*, **66**: 271–90.

Bell, L. and R. Freeman (2001), 'The incentive for working hard: explaining hours worked differences in the US and Germany', *Labour Economics*, **8**(2): 181–202.

Bell. M. (2000), 'Equality and diversity: anti-discriminatory law after Amsterdam', in J. Shaw (ed.), *Social Law and Policy in an Evolving European Union*, Oxford: Hart Publishing, pp. 157–70.

Bell, M. (2002), 'Beyond European Labour Law? Reflections on the EU Racial Equality Directive', *European Law Journal*, **8**(3): 384–99.

Belman, D. and M. Belzer (1997), 'The regulation of labor markets: balancing the benefits and costs of competition', in B. Kaufman (ed.), *Government Regulation of the Employment Relationship*, Madison, WI: Industrial Relations Research Association, pp. 179–219.

Belot, M., J. Boone and J. Van Ours (2002), 'Welfare effects of employment protection', CEPR Discussion Paper No. 3396.

Bercusson, B. (1996), *European Labour Law*, London: Butterworths.

Bercusson, B. (2002), 'The European Social Model comes to Britain', *Industrial Law Journal*, **31**(3): 209–44.

Bernard, N. (2000), 'Legitimising EU law: is the Social Dialogue the way forward? Some reflections around the UEAPME case', in Josephine Shaw (ed.), *Social law and Policy in an Evolving EU*, Oxford: Hart, pp. 279–302.

Bertola, G. (1992), 'Labor turnover costs and average labor demand', *Journal of Labor Economics*, **10**: 389–411.

Bertola, G. (2000), 'Policy choices and interactions with existing instruments', *OECD Economic Studies*, **31**: 185–98.

Bhaskar, V., A. Manning and E. To (2002), 'Oligopsony and monopsonistic competition in labor markets', *Journal of Economic Perspectives*, **16**(2): 155–74.

Blainpain, R. and F. Hendrickx (eds) (2002), *European Labour Law and Social Security Law: CODEX*, Kluwer: Netherlands.

Blair, T. and G. Schröder (1999), *Europe: The Third Way – die Neue Mitte*, London: Labour Party and SPD.

Blanchard, O. (2004), 'The future of Europe', MIT Economics Working Paper No. 04-04.

Blanchard, O. and A. Landier (2002), 'The perverse effects of partial labour market reform: fixed duration contracts in France', *Economic Journal*, **112**(June): F214–37.

Blanchard, O. and J. Tirole (2003), 'Contours of employment protection reform', MIT Department of Economics Working Paper No. 03-35.

Blau, F. and L. Kahn (1999a), 'Institutions and Laws in the Labor Market', in O. Ashenfelter and D. Card (eds), *Handbook of Labor Economics*, Vol. 3A, Amsterdam: Elsevier Science, pp. 1399–1461.

Blau, F. and L. Kahn (1999b), 'Analyzing the gender pay gap', *Quarterly Review of Economics and Finance*, **39**: 625–46.

Blau, F. and L. Kahn (2002), *At Home and Abroad: US Labor-market Performance in International Perspective*, New York: Russell Sage Foundation.

Bluestone, B. and S. Rose (1998), 'The macroeconomics of work time', *Review of Social Economy*, **56**(4): 425–41.

Boeri, T. and H. Brucker (2001), 'Eastern enlargement and EU-labour markets: perceptions, challenges and opportunities', IZA (Bonn) Discussion Paper No. 256.

Boheim, R. and M. Taylor (2003), 'Option or obligation? The determinants of labour supply preferences in Britain', *Manchester School*, **71**: 113–31.

Booth, A., J. Dolado and J. Frank (2002a), 'Symposium on temporary work: introduction', *Economic Journal*, **112**(June): F181–8.

Booth, A., M. Francesconi and J. Frank (2002b), 'Temporary jobs: stepping stones or dead ends?', *Economic Journal*, **112**(June): F189–F213.

Bosch, G. and S. Lehndorff (2001), 'Working-time reduction and employment: experiences in Europe and economic policy recommendations', *Cambridge Journal of Economics*, **25**: 209–43.

Botero, J., S. Djankov, R. La Porta, F. Lopez-de-Silanes and A. Shleifer (2003), 'The regulation of labor', National Bureau of Economic Research Working Paper No. W9756.

Bourn, C. (1993), 'Amending the Collective Dismissals Directive: a case of rearranging the deck-chairs', *International Journal of Comparative Labour and Industrial Relations Law*, **9**: 227.

Bourn, C. (ed.) (1999), *The Transfer of Undertakings in the Public Sector*, Aldershot: Ashgate.

Bruning, G. and J. Plantenga (1999), 'Parental leave and equal opportunities experience in eight European countries', *Journal of European Social Policy*, **9**(3): 195–209.

Buchele, R. and J. Christiansen (2000), 'Workers rights and socio-economic performance in the OECD', paper presented at the 22nd International Working Party on Labour Market Segmentation, Manchester.

Buti, M., D. Franco and L. Pench (eds) (2002), *The Welfare State in Europe: Challenges and Reforms*, Cheltenham: Edward Elgar Publishing.

Cappelli, P. and D. Neumark (2001), 'Do "high-performance" work practices improve establishment-level outcomes?', *Industrial and Labor Relations*, **54**(4): 737–75.

Carley, M. and M. Hall (2000), 'The implementation of the EWC Directive', *Industrial Law Journal*, **29**: 103–24.

Carnoy, N. (1999), 'The family, flexible work and social cohesion at risk', *International Labour Review*, **138**(4): 411–29.

Cazes, S. and A. Nespora (2003), *Labour Markets in Transition : Balancing Flexibility and Security in Central and Eastern Europe*, London: ILO.

Chapon, S. and C. Euzéby (2002), 'Towards a convergence of European social models', *International Social Security Review*, **55**: 37–56.

Coase, R. (1960), 'The problem of social cost', *Journal of Law and Economics*, **3**: 1–44.

Collins, H. (2000), 'Regulating the employment relation for competitiveness', *Industrial Law Journal*, **30**(1): 17–48.

Collins, H. (2002), 'Is there a Third Way in labour law?', in J. Conaghan, R. Fischl and K. Klare (eds), *Labour Law in an Era of Globalization*, Oxford: Oxford University Press, pp. 449–70.

Conaghan, J., R. Fischl and K. Klare (eds) (2002), *Labour Law in an Era of Globalization: Transformative Practices and Possibilities*, Oxford: Oxford University Press.

Conde-Ruiz, J. and V. Galasso (2003), 'The macroeconomics of early retirement', CEPR Discussion Paper No. 3896.

Cornelisse, P. and K. Goudswaard (2001), 'On the convergence of social protection systems in the European Union', *International Social Security Review*, **55**: 3–17.

Craig, P. (2001), 'Constitutions, constitutionalism and the EU', *European Law Journal*, **7**: 125–35.

Crépon, B. and F. Kramarz (2000), 'Employed 40 hours or not employed 39: lessons from the 1982 mandatory reduction of the workweek', Centre for

Economic Policy Research Discussion Paper No. 2358.

Darity, W. and P. Mason (1998), 'Evidence on discrimination in employment: codes of color, codes of gender?', *Journal of Economic Perspectives*, **12**(2): 63–90.

Dashwood, A. (2001), 'The Constitution of the EU after Nice: law-making procedures', *European Law Review*, **26**: 215–38.

Davies, H., H. Joshi and R. Peronaci (2000), 'Foregone income and motherhood: what do recent British data tell us?', *Population Studies*, **54**: 293–305.

De Geest, G., J. Siegers and A.-S. Vandenberghe (2001), 'The expectation measure, labor contracts and the incentive to work hard', *International Review of Law and Economics*, **21**: 1–21.

De Grauwe, P. and M. Polan (2003), 'Globalisation and social spending', CESifo Working Paper No. 885.

De Michelis, A. (2004), 'Sand in the wheels of labor markets: the effect of firing costs on employment', FRB International Finance Discussion Paper No. 976.

Deakin, S. (1986), *Cambridge Law Journal of Economics*, **10**: 225.

Deakin, S. (1997), 'Integration through law? The legal and economic foundations of European social policy', in J.T. Addison and W.S. Siebert (eds), *Labour Markets in Europe: Issues of Harmonization and Regulation*, London: Dryden Press, pp. 118–51.

Deakin, S. (1999), 'Organisational change, labour flexibility and the contract of employment in Great Britain', in S. Deery and R. Mitchell (eds), *Employment Relations: Individualism and Union Exclusion: An International Study*, Annandale, NSW: Federation Press.

Deakin, S. and F. Wilkinson (1991), *The Economics of Employment Rights*, London: Institute of Employment Rights.

Deakin, S. and F. Wilkinson (1994), 'Rights vs Efficiency? The economic case for transnational labour standards', *Industrial Law Journal*, **23**: 289.

Deakin, S. and F. Wilkinson (1999), 'Labour law and economic theory: a re-appraisal', in G. De Geest, J. Siegers and R. Van den Bergh (eds), *Law and Economics and the Labour Market*, Cheltenham, UK and Northampton, MA: Edward Elgar Publishing, pp. 1–33.

Dehousse, R. (1992), 'Integration v regulation? On the dynamics of regulation in the EC', *Journal of Common Market Studies*, **30**(4): 383–402.

Delbridge, R. and K. Whitfield (2001), 'Employee perceptions of job influence and organizational participation', *Industrial Relations*, **40**(3): 472–89.

Desai, T., P. Gregg, J. Steer and J. Wadsworth (1999), 'Gender and the labour market', in P. Gregg and J. Wadsworth (eds), *The State of Working Britain*, Manchester: Manchester University Press, pp.168–84.

Dex, S. and F. Scheibl (2001), 'Flexible and family-friendly working arrangements in UK-based SMEs: business cases', *British Journal of Industrial Relations*, **39**(3): 411–31.

Dickens, R., P. Gregg and J. Wadsworth (2000), 'New Labour and the labour market', *Oxford Review of Economic Policy*, **16**(1): 95–113.

Disney, R. and S. Smith (2002), 'The labour supply effect of the abolition of the Earnings Rule for older workers in the United Kingdom', *Economic Journal*, **112**(March): C136–52.

Dolado, J., F. Felgueroso and J. Jimeno (2001), 'Female employment and occupational changes in the 1990s: how is the EU performing relative to the US?', *European Economic Review*, **45**(4–6): 875–89.

Dolado, J., F. Felgueroso and J. Jimeno (2002), 'Recent trends in occupational segregation by gender: a look across the Atlantic', CEPR Discussion Paper No. 3421.

Dolado, J., C. García-Serrano and J. Jimeno (2002), 'Drawing lessons from the boom of temporary jobs in Spain', *Economic Journal*, **112**(June): F270–95.

Dolado, J. and V. Llorens (2004), 'Gender wage gaps by education in Spain: glass floors versus glass ceilings', CEPR Discussion Paper No. 4203.

Donohue, J. (2001), 'Understanding the reasons for and impact of legislatively mandated benefits for selected workers', *Stanford Law Review*, **53**(April): 1–19.

Edin, P.-A. and K. Richardson (2002), 'Swimming with the tide: solidarity wage policy and the gender earnings gap', *Scandinavian Journal of Economics*, **104**(1): 49–67.

Eichengreen, B. and T. Iversen (1999), 'Institutions and economic performance: evidence from the labour market', *Oxford Review of Economic Policy*, **15**: 121–38.

Elias, P. (1982), 'The transfer of undertakings: a reluctantly acquired right', *Company Lawyer*, **3**: 147.

Esping-Andersen, G. (1990), *The Three Worlds of Welfare Capitalism*, Princeton, NJ: Princeton University Press.

European Commission (2001), *EU Employment and Social Policy 1999–2001: Jobs, Cohesion, Productivity*, Luxembourg: Office for Official Publications of the European Communities.

European Commission (2002a), *Employment in Europe – 2002*, Luxembourg: European Communities.

European Commission (2002b), *The Life of Women and Men in Europe: A Statistical Portrait Data 1980–2000*, Luxembourg: Eurostat.

European Commission (2002c), *The Social Situation in the European Union – 2002*, Luxembourg: European Communities.

European Commission (2002d), *Report of the High Level Group on Industrial*

Relations and Change in the European Union, Luxembourg: Office for Official Publications of the European Communities.

European Commission (Employment and Social Affairs) (2002e), *Social Agenda*, Issue No. 1, April.

European Commission (2003a), *Employment in Europe 2003*, Brussels: European Commission.

European Commission (2003b), *Communication on Immigration, Integration and Employment*, COM(2003) 336, Brussels: European Commission.

European Commission (2004a), *Delivering Lisbon: Reforms for the Enlarged Union*, COM(2004) 29 final/2, Brussels: European Commission.

European Commission (2004b), *Strengthening the Implementation of the European Employment Strategy: Guidelines and Recommendations for Member States' Employment Policies*, COM(2004), Brussels: European Commission.

European Industrial Relations Observatory (EIRO) (2000), 'Industrial relations and the ageing workforce: a review of measures to combat age discrimination in employment', *EIRO Observer*, 6/2000: i–iv.

European Industrial Relations Observatory (EIRO) (2002a), 'Economically dependent workers, employment law and industrial relations', *EIRO Observer*, 4/2002: i–viii.

European Industrial Relations Observatory (EIRO) (2002b), 'Gender pay equity in Europe', *EIRO Observer*, 3/2002: i–viii.

European Industrial Relations Observatory (EIRO) (2003), 'Breakthrough on new national agreement', *EIRO Observer*, 2/2003: 7–8.

European Industrial Relations Observatory (EIRO) (2004), 'Working time review', *EIRO Observer*, 2/2004: 2–3.

Eurostat (2000), *Central European Countries' Employment and Labour Market Review*, Luxembourg: Eurostat.

Eurostat (2001), 'Women and men in tertiary education', *Statistics in Focus Theme 3*, Luxembourg: Eurostat.

Euwals, R. and M. Hogerbrugge (2004), 'Explaining the growth of part-time employment: factors of supply and demand', IZA (Bonn) Discussion Paper No. 1124.

Evans, J. (2001), 'Firms' contribution to the reconciliation between work and family life', OECD Labour Market and Social Policy Occasional Papers No. 48.

Felstead, A., D. Ashton and F. Green (2000), 'Are Britain's workplace skills becoming more unequal?', *Cambridge Journal of Economics*, **24**(6): 709–28.

Fertig, M. (2002), 'The impact of economic integration on employment: an assessment in the context of EU enlargement', IZA Discussion Paper No. 919.

Figart, D. and E. Mutari (2000), 'Work time regimes in Europe: can flexibility and gender equity coexist?', *Journal of Economic Issues*, **34**(4): 847–71.

Fischl, R.M. and K. Klare (eds) (2002), *Labour Law in an Era of Globalization*, Oxford: Oxford University Press.

Fredman, S. (2002), *Discrimination Law*, Oxford: Clarendon Law Series.

Freeman, R. (1998), 'Work-sharing to full employment: serious option or populist fallacy?', in R. Freeman and P. Gottschalk (eds), *Generating Jobs: How to Increase Demand for Less-Skilled Workers*, New York: Russell Sage Foundation, pp. 195–222.

Freeman, R. (2000), 'The divergence in employment and income distribution in the EU and the US', in B. Marin, D. Meulders and D. Snower (eds), *Innovative Employment Initiatives*, Aldershot: Ashgate Publishing, pp. 115–42.

Freeman, R. (2002), 'Institutional differences and economic performance among OECD countries', London School of Economics, Centre for Economic Performance, Discussion Paper No. 557.

Freeman, R., M. Kleiner and C. Ostroff (2000), 'The anatomy of employee involvement and its effects on firms and workers', National Bureau of Economic Research Working Paper No. W8050.

Freeman, R. and E. Lazear (1995), 'An economic analysis of works councils', in J. Rogers and W. Streeck (eds), *Works Councils: Consultation, Representation, and Cooperation in Industrial Relations*, Chicago, IL: University of Chicago Press, pp. 27–50.

Freeman, R. and J. Rogers (1999), *What Workers Want*, New York: Cornell University Press.

Freeman, R. and R. Schettkat (2002), 'Marketization of production and the US–Europe employment gap', National Bureau of Economic Research Working Paper No. W8797.

Frege, C. (2002), 'A critical assessment of the theoretical and empirical research on German works councils', *British Journal of Industrial Relations*, **40**(2): 221–48.

Garibaldi, P. and P. Mauro (2002), 'Employment growth: accounting for the facts', *Economic Policy*, **17**(34): 67–113.

Garibaldi, P., L. Pacelli and A. Borgarello (2003), 'Employment protection legislation and the size of firms', IZA (Bonn) Discussion Paper No. 787.

Giddens, A. (2000), *The Third Way and its Critics*, Cambridge: Polity Press.

Gilman, M. and P. Marginson (2002), 'Negotiating European works councils: contours of constrained choice', *Industrial Relations Journal*, **33**(1): 36–51.

Givord, P. and E. Maurin (2003), 'Changes in job security and their causes: an empirical analysis for France 1982–2002', CEPR Discussion Paper No. 3830.

Glynn, A. (1998), 'Economic policy and social democracy', *Oxford Review of Economic Policy*, **14**: 1–18.

Goetschy, J. (1999), 'The European employment strategy: genesis and development', *European Journal of Industrial Relations*, **5**(2): 117–37.

Goldin, C. (2002), 'A pollution theory of discrimination: male and female differences in occupations and earnings', National Bureau of Economic Research, Working Paper No. W8985.

Gonzalez, J. (1995), 'The principle of subsidiarity', *European Law Review*, **20**(4): 355.

Gore, T. (2004), 'The open method of coordination and policy mainstreaming: the EES and regional conversion programmes in the UK', *European Planning Studies*, **12**(1): 123–41.

Gospel, H., G. Lockwood and P. Willman (2000), 'The right to know: disclosure of information for collective bargaining and joint consultation', London School of Economics and Political Science, Centre for Economic Performance, Discussion Paper No. 453.

Gospel, H. and P. Willman (2003), 'High performance workplaces: the role of employee involvement in a modern economy. Evidence on the EU Directive establishing a general framework for informing and consulting employees', London School of Economics, Centre for Economic Performance, Discussion Paper No. 562.

Gospel, H. and P. Willman (2004), 'Comparatively open: statutory information disclosure in Germany, France and the UK', London School of Economics, Centre for Economic Performance, Working Paper No. 615.

Green, F. and S. McIntosh (2001), 'The intensification of work in Europe', *Labour Economics*, **8**(2): 291–308.

Gregg, P. and J. Wadsworth (2002), 'Job tenure in Britain, 1975–2000: is a job for life or just for Christmas?, *Oxford Bulletin of Economics and Statistics*, **64**(2): 111–34.

Gual, J. (1998), 'The employment debate: employment performance and institutional change', in J. Gual (ed.), *Job Creation: The Role of Labour Market Institutions*, Cheltenham, UK: Edward Elgar, pp. 1–33.

Guest, D. and R. Peccei (2001), 'Partnership at work: mutuality and the balance of advantage', *British Journal of Industrial Relations*, **39**(2): 207–36.

Gugler, K. and B. Yurtoglu (2004), 'The effects of mergers on company employment in the USA and Europe', *International Journal of Industrial Organization*, **22**(4): 481–502.

Habermas, J. (2001), *The Post-national Constellation*, Cambridge: Polity Press.

Habermas, J. (2004), 'Why Europe needs a constitution', in E.O. Eriksen, J.E.

Fossum and A.J. Menéndez (eds), *Developing a Constitution for Europe*, London: Routledge.

Hall, M. (1996), 'Beyond recognition? Employee representation and EU law', *Industrial Law Journal*, **25**: 15–27.

Hardy, S. (2001), *Understanding TUPE: A Legal Guide*, Oxford: Chandos Publishing.

Hardy, S. and N. Adnett (1999a), 'Entrepreneurial freedom versus employee rights: the Acquired Rights Directive and EU social policy post-Amsterdam', JESP, **9**: 127.

Hardy, S. and N. Adnett (1999b), 'Flexible labour markets and employment rights in the EU: competitive tendering, business transfers and the revised acquired rights directive', in W. Meeusen (ed.), *Economic Policy in the European Union: Current Perspectives*, Cheltenham, UK and Northampton, MA: Edward Elgar Publishing, pp. 183–98.

Hardy, S. and N. Adnett (2002), 'The Parental Leave Directive: towards a "family-friendly" Social Europe?', *European Journal of Industrial Relations*, **8**(2): 157–72.

Harnay, S. and I. Vigouroux (2002), 'Judicial competition, legal innovation and European integration: an economic analysis', in A. Marciano and J.-M. Josselin (eds), *The Economics of Harmonizing European Law*, Cheltenham, UK and Northampton, MA: Edward Elgar Publishing, pp. 87–100.

Hashimoto, M. (1990), 'Employment and wage systems in Japan and their implications for productivity', in A. Blinder (ed.), *Paying for Productivity*, Washington, DC: Brookings Institution, pp. 245–94.

Hepple, B. (2002), *Social and Labour Rights in a Global Context: International and Comparative Perspectives*, Cambridge: Cambridge University Press.

Hepple, B. and G. Morris (2002), 'The Employment Act 2002 and the crisis of individual employment rights', *Industrial Law Journal*, **31**(3): 245–69.

Herbertsson, T. (2001), 'The economics of early retirement', *Journal of Pensions Management*, **6**(4): 326–35.

Herbertsson, T. and J. Orszag (2001), 'The cost of early retirement in the OECD', University of Iceland, Institute of Economics Studies, Working Paper No. W01:02.

House of Lords Select Committee on the European Union (2002), 'The future of Europe: "Social Europe"', HL Paper 79.

Hunt, J. (1998), 'The Court of Justice as a policy actor: the Acquired Rights Directive', *Legal Studies*, **18**: 336.

Hunt, J. (1999), 'Success at last? The amendment of the Acquired Rights Directive', *ELRev*, **24**: 215.

Hunt, J. (2002), 'The transition in East Germany: when is a ten-point fall in the gender wage gap bad news?', *Journal of Labor Economics*, **20**: 148–69.

Iankova, E. and L. Turner (2004), 'Building the New Europe: Western and Eastern roads to social partnership', *Industrial Relations Journal*, **35**(1): 76–92.

Ichino, A. and R. Riphahn (2003), 'The effect of employment protection on worker effort: a comparison of absenteeism before and after probation', CEPR Discussion Paper No. 3847.

Issacharoff, S. and E. Harris (1997), 'Is age discrimination really age discrimination? The ADEA's unnatural solution', *New York University Law Review*, **72**(4): 780–840.

Issing, O. (2000), 'Europe, common money – political union?, *Economic Affairs*, March: 33–9.

James, H. and D. Johnson (2001), 'Why are there explicit contracts of employment?', University of Missouri, Contracting and Organizations Research Initiative Working Paper No. 01-06.

Jensen, J. and S. Jacobzone (2000), 'Care allowances for the frail elderly and their impact on women care-givers', OECD Labour Market and Social Policy Occasional Papers No. 41.

Jolls, C. (1996), 'Hands-tying and the Age Discrimination in Employment Act', *Texas Law Review*, **74**: 1813–46.

Jolls, C. (2000), 'Accommodation mandates and antidiscrimination law', UC Berkeley Law and Economics Working Paper No. 2000-9.

Joshi, H., P. Paci and J. Waldfogel (1999), 'The wages of motherhood: better or worse?', *Cambridge Journal of Economics*, **23**(5): 543–64.

Keller, B. (2002), 'The European Company Statute: employee involvement – and beyond', *Industrial Relations Journal*, **33**(5): 424–45.

Kenner, J. (2003), *EU Employment Law: From Rome to Amsterdam and Beyond*, Oxford: Hart Publishing.

Kerckhofs, P. (2002), *European Works Councils: Facts and Figures*, Brussels: ETUI.

Kitson, M., R. Martin and F. Wilkinson (2000), 'Labour markets, social justice and economic efficiency', *Cambridge Journal of Economics*, **24**(6):631–44.

Kohler, T. and M. Kittner (2000), 'Conditioning expectations: the protection of the employment bond in Germany and American law', *Comparative Labor Law and Policy Journal*, **21**(Winter): 263–330.

Krueger, D. and K. Kumar (2003), 'US–Europe differences in technology-driven growth: quantifying the role of education', National Bureau of Economic Research Working Paper W10001.

Kugler, A., J. Jimeno-Serrano and V. Hernanz (2002), 'Employment consequences of restrictive permanent contracts: evidence from Spanish labor market reforms', IZA (Bonn) Discussion Paper No. 657.

Landers, R., J. Rebitzer and L. Taylor (1996), 'Rat race redux: adverse selection in the determination of work hours in law firms', *American Economic Review*, **86**(3): 329–48.

Landers, R., J. Rebitzer and L. Taylor (1997), 'Work norms and professional labor markets', in F. Blau and R. Ehrenberg (eds), *Gender and Family Issues in the Workplace*, New York: Russell Sage Foundation, pp. 166–99.

Lazear, E. (1979), 'Why is there mandatory retirement?', *Journal of Political Economy*, **87**: 1261–84.

Lazear, E. (2000), 'The future of personnel economics', *Economic Journal*, **110**: F611-39.

Levine, D. and L. Tyson (1990), 'Participation, productivity and the firm's environment', in A. Blinder (ed.), *Paying for Productivity*, Washington, DC: Brookings Institution, pp. 183–243.

Lewis, J. (2001), 'Social insurance and future work', in *Labour Law and Social Insurance in the New Economy: A Debate on the Supiot Report*, LSE, Centre for Economic Performance, Discussion Paper No. 500.

Lindbeck, A. and D. Snower (2000), 'Multitask learning and the reorganization of work: from Tayloristic to holistic organization', *Journal of Labor Economics*, **18**(3): 353–76.

Lindbeck, A. and D. Snower (2001), 'Centralized bargaining and reorganized work: are they compatible? *European Economic Review*, **45**(10): 1851–75.

Lindbeck, A. and D. Snower (2002), 'Insider versus outsiders', *Journal of Economic Perspectives*, **15**(1): 165–88.

Loewenstein, G. and N. Sicherman (1991), 'Do workers prefer increasing wage profiles?', *Journal of Labor Economics*, **9**: 67–84.

Lommerud, K. and S. Vagstad (2000), 'Mommy tracks and public policy: on self-fulfilling prophecies and gender gaps in promotion', CEPR Discussion Paper No. 2378.

Machin, S. and P. Puhani (2002), 'Subject of degree and the gender wage differential: evidence for the UK and Germany', IZA (Bonn) Discussion Paper No. 553.

Machin, S. and L. Rahman (2001), 'The economic effects of the introduction of the UK national minimum wage', Centre for Economic Performance, London School of Economics, mimeo.

Makepeace, G., H. Joshi and P. Dolton (2002), 'The fall and rise of unequal treatment: new evidence on the pay of men and women from the British Birth Cohort Studies', paper presented at the 2002 DfES Research Conference.

Malcomson, J. (1999), 'Individual employment rights', in O. Ashenfelter and D. Card (eds), *Handbook of Labor Economics*, Vol. 3B, Amsterdam: Elsevier Science, pp. 2291–372.

Marginson, P. and K. Sisson (1998), 'European collective bargaining: a virtual prospect?', *Journal of Common Market Studies*, **36**: 505–28.

Marsden, D. (1999), *A Theory of Employment Systems*, Oxford: Oxford University Press.

Marsden, D. (2004), 'The "Network Economy" and models of the employment contract: psychological, economic and legal', London School of Economics, Centre for Economic Performance, Working Paper.

Messina, J., G. Vallanti and R. Salvador (2004), 'Gross job flows and institutions in Europe', ECB Working Paper No. 318.

Michie, J. and M. Sheehan (2003), 'Labour market deregulation, "Flexibility" and innovation', *Cambridge Journal of Economics*, **27**: 123–43.

Mizrahi, S. (2002), 'Workers' participation in decision-making processes and firm stability', *British Journal of Industrial Relations*, **40**(4): 689–707.

More, G. (1995), 'The Acquired Rights Directive: frustrating or facilitating labour market flexibility', in J. Shaw and G. More (eds), *New Legal Dynamics of the European Union*, Oxford: Clarendon, pp. 129–46.

Muhl, C. (2001), 'The Employment-At-Will Doctrine: three major exceptions', *Monthly Labor Review*, **124**(1): 3–12.

Neumark, D. and W. Stock (1999), 'Age discrimination laws and labor market efficiency', *Journal of Political Economy*, **107**(5): 1081–1125.

Nickell, S. (1997), 'Unemployment and labor market rigidities: Europe versus North America', *Journal of Economic Perspectives*, **11**(3): 55–74.

Nickell, S. (2003a), 'Poverty and worklessness in Britain', Centre for Economic Performance Discussion Paper No. 579.

Nickell, S. (2003b), 'A picture of European unemployment: success and failure', Centre for Economic Performance Discussion Paper No. 577.

Nickell, S. and G. Quintini (2002), 'The recent performance of the UK labour market', *Oxford Review of Economic Policy*, **18**(2): 202–20.

North, D. (1990), *Institutions, Institutional Change, and Economic Performance*, Cambridge: Cambridge University Press.

OECD (1994), *The OECD Jobs Study: Evidence and Explanations*, Vols 1 and 2, Paris: OECD.

OECD (1998), *Employment Outlook*, Paris: OECD.

OECD (1999), 'Employment protection and labour market performance', *Employment Outlook*, Paris, OECD.

OECD (2001a), *OECD Employment Outlook 2001*, Paris: OECD.

OECD (2001b), 'Balancing work and family life: helping parents into paid employment', *Employment Outlook*, June: 129–66.

OECD (2002a), *Employment Outlook 2002*, Paris: OECD.

OECD (2002b), 'Women at work: who are they and how are they faring?', *Employment Outlook*, 61–125.

OECD (2002c), 'Increasing employment: the role of later retirement', *Economic Outlook*, **72**: 1–21.

OECD (2003), *OECD Employment Outlook 2003*, Paris: OECD.

Ogus, I. (1998), *Regulation*, Oxford: Oxford University Press.

O'Neill, J. (2003), 'The gender gap in wages, circa 2000', *American Economic Review*, **93**(2): 309–14.

Orchard, L. and H. Stretton (1997), 'Public choice: critical survey', *Cambridge Journal of Economics*, **21**: 409–30.

Painter, R. and S. Hardy (1996), 'Acquiring revised rights? Council proposal to revise the Acquired Rights Directive', *Maastricht Journal of European and Comparative Law*, **3**: 35.

Pannenberg, M. (2002), 'Long-term effects of unpaid overtime: evidence for West Germany', IZA (Bonn) Discussion Paper No. 614.

Parkinson, J. (2003), 'Models of the company and the employment relationship', *British Journal of Industrial Relations*, **41**(3): 481–509.

Peccei, R., H. Bewley, H. Gospel and P. Willman (2003), 'Is it good to talk? Information disclosure and organisational performance in the UK', London School of Economics, Centre for Economic Performance, Working Paper No. 602.

Peltzman, S. (1976), 'Towards a more general theory of regulation', *Journal of Law and Economics*, **20**: 211–40.

Pissarides, C. (2001), 'Employment protection', *Labour Economics*, **8**(2): 131–59.

Poole, M., R. Lansbury and N. Wailes (2001), 'A comparative analysis of developments in industrial democracy', *Industrial Relations*, **40**(3): 490–525.

Posner, R. (1995), *Aging and Old Age*, Chicago: Chicago University Press, pp. 319–51.

Puhani, P. (2003), 'Labour mobility: an adjustment mechanism in Euroland?', *German Economic Review*, **2**: 127–40.

Pylkkänen, E. and N. Smith (2003), 'Career interruptions due to parental leave – a comparative study of Denmark and Sweden', OECD Social Employ-ment and Migration Working Papers, DELSA/ELSA/WD/SEM(2003).

Rabin, M. (1998), 'Psychology and economics', *Journal of Economic Literature*, **36**(March): 11–46.

Rangelova, R. (2002), 'Gender relations and EU enlargement', *South East Europe Review*, 3/2002: S105–26.

Rodríguez-Ibeas, R. (2002), 'Regulatory enforcement with discretionary fining and litigation', *Bulletin of Economic Research*, **54**(2), 105–18.

Rogers, J. and W. Streeck (1994), 'Workplace representation overseas: the works council story', in R. Freeman (ed.), *Working Under Different Rules*, New York: NBER/Russell Sage Foundation, pp. 97–156.

Rogers, J. and W. Streeck (eds) (1995), *Works Councils: Consultation,*

Representation, and Cooperation in Industrial Relations, Chicago, IL: University of Chicago Press.

Rose-Ackerman, S. (1988), 'Progressive law and economics: and the new administrative law, 98', *Yale Law Journal*, **341**: 358–60.

Rubery, J., J. Humphries, C. Fagan, D. Grimshaw and M. Smith (2000), 'Equal opportunities as a productive factor', paper given at the 22nd International Working Party on Labour Market Segmentation, Manchester.

Ruhm, C. and J. Teague (1997), 'Parental leave policies in Europe and North America', in F. Blau and R. Ehrenberg (eds), *Gender and Family Issues in the Workplace*, New York: Russell Sage Foundation, pp. 133–56.

Ruiz, A., L. Gomez and M. Narvaez (2002), 'Gender inequalities, education and job mobility', mimeo.

Saint-Paul, G. (1997), 'Is labour rigidity harming Europe's competitiveness? The effect of job protection on the pattern of trade and welfare', *European Economic Review*, **41**: 499–506.

Saint-Paul, G. (2000), *The Political Economy of Labour Market Institutions*, Oxford: Oxford University Press.

Saint-Paul, G. (2002), 'The political economy of employment protection', *Journal of Political Economy*, **110**(3): 672–704.

Saint-Paul, G. (2004a), 'Why are European countries diverging in their unemployment experience?', IZA (Bonn) Discussion Paper No. 1066.

Saint-Paul, G. (2004b), 'Did European labour markets become more competitive in the 1990s? Evidence from estimated worker rents', IZA (Bonn) Discussion Paper No. 1067.

Sakellaropoulos, T. and J. Berghman (eds) (2004), 'Connecting welfare diversity within the European Social Model', *The Political Economy of Labour Market Institutions*, Social Europe Series 9, Intersentia: Antwerp.

Sargeant, M. (2002), 'New transfer regulations', *Industrial Law Journal*, **31**(1): 35–54.

Schmidt, M. (2001), 'The right to part-time work under German law: progress in or a boomerang for equal employment opportunities', *Industrial Law Journal*, **30**(4): 335–52.

Schöb, R. and D. Wildasin (2003), 'Economic integration and labor market institutions: worker mobility, earnings risk and contract structure', IZA (Bonn) Discussion Paper No. 945.

Schiek, D. (2002), 'A new framework on equal treatment of persons in EC law', *European Law Journal*, **8**(2): 290–314.

Sciarra, S. (2001) (ed.), *Labour Law in the Courts*, Oxford: Hart Publishing.

Sciarra, S. (2002), 'Market freedom and fundamental social rights', in B. Hepple (ed.), *Social and Labour Rights in a Global Context: International and Comparative Perspectives*, Cambridge: Cambridge University Press, pp. 95–121.

Shaw, J. (2000) (ed.), *Social Law and Policy in an Evolving EU*, Oxford: Hart Publishing.

Shaw, J. (2003), *A Strong Europe is a Social Europe*, Federal Trust: London.

Shaw, J. and G. More (1995) (eds), *New Legal Dynamics of the European Union*, Oxford: Oxford University Press.

Siebert, H. (1997), 'Labor market rigidities: at the root of unemployment in Europe', *Journal of Economic Perspectives*, **11**(3): 37–54.

Sinn, H.-W. (2001), 'The new systems competition', Center for Economic Studies and Ifo Institute for Economic Research, Munich (CESifo), Working Paper No. 623.

Sinn, H.-W. and W. Ochel (2003), 'Social union, convergence and migration', *Journal of Common Market Studies*, **41**: 869–96.

Sisson, K., J. Arrowsmith and P. Marginson (2003), 'All benchmarking now? Benchmarking and the "Europeanisation" of industrial relations', *Industrial Relations Journal*, **34**(1): 15–31.

Snower, D. (1993), 'The future of the welfare state', *Economic Journal*, **103**: 700–17.

Sosvilla-Rivero, S., J. Herce and J.-J. De Lucio (2003), 'Convergence in social protection across EU countries 1970–1999', Foundation for Applied Economic Research (FEDEA) Working Paper No. 2003-01.

Sousa-Poza, A. and F. Henneberger (2002), 'An empirical analysis of working-hours constraints in twenty-one countries', *Review of Social Economy*, **60**(2): 209–42.

Streeck, W. and S. Vitols (1995), 'The European Community: between mandatory consultation and voluntary information', in J. Rogers and W. Streeck (eds), *Works Councils: Consultation, Representation and Cooperation in Industrial Relations*, Chicago, IL: University of Chicago Press.

Stewart, M. (2004), 'The employment effects of the national minimum wage', *Economic Journal*, **114**(494): C110-16.

Stone, K. (2002), 'Knowledge at work: disputes over the ownership of human capital in the changing workplace', *Connecticut Law Review*, **34**: 721–63.

Stone, K. (2004), *From Widgets to Digits: Employment Regulation for the Changing Workplace*, Cambridge: Cambridge University Press.

Summers, L. (1989), 'Some simple economics of mandated benefits', *American Economic Review*, **79**(2): 177–83.

Sunstein, C. (2001), 'Human behaviour and the law of work', *Virginia Law Review*, **87**(2): 205–76.

Supiot, A. (1999), 'The transformation of work and the future of labour law in Europe: a multidisciplinary perspective', *International Labour Review*, **138**(1): 31–46.

Supiot, A. (2000), 'The dogmatic foundations of the market', *Industrial Law Journal*, **29**(4): 321–45.

Supiot, A. (2001), *Beyond Employment: Changes in Work and the Future of Labour Law in Europe*, Oxford: Oxford University Press.

Szyszczak, E. (2000), *EC Labour Law*, London: Longman.

Tanzi, V. (2002), 'Globalization and the future of social protection', *Scottish Journal of Political Economy*, **49**(1): 116–27.

Taqi, A. (2002), 'Older people, work and equal opportunity', *International Social Security Review*, **55**: 107–20.

Terwey, F. (2004), 'Trends in the development of a European Social Union', *International Social Security Review*, **57**(1): 105–17.

Thum, C. and S. Übelmasser (2001), 'Mobility and the role of education as a commitment device', Centre for Economic Studies and Ifo Institute for Economic Research, Munich (CESifo) Working Paper No. 450.

Trubek, D. and L. Trubek (2003), 'Hard and soft law in the construction of Social Europe', paper prepared for workshop on Opening the Open Method of Coordination, European University Institute, Florence, July.

Van den Bergh, R. (2002), 'Regulatory competition or harmonization of laws? Guidelines for the European regulator', in A. Marciano and J.-M. Josselin (eds), *The Economics of Harmonizing European Law*, Cheltenham, UK and Northampton, MA: Edward Elgar, pp. 27–49.

Van der Ploeg, F. (2003), 'Do social policies harm employment and growth?', CESifo Working Paper No. 886.

Vaughan-Whitehead, D. (2003), *EU Enlargement versus Social Europe: The Uncertain Future of the European Social Model*, Cheltenham, UK and Northampton, MA: Edward Elgar Publishing.

Velluti, S. (2004), 'Towards the constitutionalization of new forms of governance: a revised institutional framework for the EES', *Yearbook on European Law*, Cambridge: Cambridge University Press, pp. 353–405.

Vigneau, C. (2002), 'Information technology and workers' privacy: the French law', *Comparative Labor Law and Policy Journal*, **23**(4): 351–76.

Wasmer, E. (2002), 'Interpreting Europe and US labor market differences: the specificity of human capital investments', IZA Bonn Discussion Paper No. 549.

Watson, P. (1997), 'The role of the ECJ in the development of Community labour law', in K.D. Ewing, C.A. Gearty and B.A. Hepple (eds), *Essays for Paul O'Higgins*, Oxford: Oxford University Press, pp. 76–105.

Weber, T., P. Foster and K. Egriboz (2000), *Costs and Benefits of the European Works Council Directive*, Department of Trade and Industry, Employment Relations Research Series No. 9.

Wedderburn, B. (1997), 'Consultation and collective bargaining in Europe: success or ideology', *Industrial Law Journal*, **26**: 1–34.

Weichselbaumer, D. and R. Winter-Ebmer (2003), 'A meta-analysis of the international gender wage gap', IZA (Bonn) Discussion Paper No. 906.

Weil, D. (2003), 'Individual rights and collective agents: the role of old and new workplace institutions in the regulation of labor markets', National Bureau of Economic Research, Working Paper No. W9565.

Whiteford, E. (1993), 'The Hoover Affair and social dumping', *European Industrial Relations Review*, **230**: 14.

Wood, S. (1999), 'Family-friendly management: testing the various perspectives', *National Institute Economic Review*, **168**: 99–116.

Wright, F.B. (1999), *The Law of Health and Safety*, London: Sweet & Maxwell.

Yeandle, S. (1999), 'Gender contracts, welfare systems and non-standard working: diversity and change in Denmark, France, Germany, Italy and the UK', in A. Felstead and N. Jewson (eds), *Global Trends in Flexible Labour*, London: Macmillan, pp. 141–65.

Index